READERS' CO

The following are excerpts from some
from readers of the first edition of *The W*

Continued at the back ▶

The Way to Inner Peace

Buddhism, Science and Uncommon Sense for Daily Living:
- A Practical Guide -

~

Kingsley Rajapakse

~

Revised and Enlarged Second Edition
~
Serena Publications, Box 5255, Penetang, ON L9M 2G4, Canada

The Way to Inner Peace

Buddhism, Science and Uncommon Sense for Daily Living:
- A Practical Guide -

Kingsley Rajapakse

Published by: **Serena Publications**
For all inquiries visit: www.TheWayToInnerPeace.com

Disclaimer.

This book is an exploration, with some aspects being pioneering in nature, of the *relationship* between (a) Buddhism that is 2½ millennia old and (b) the new and emerging sciences, including in particular, health-related sciences. The latter is a continually changing field. The book is intended to provide informative material in the subject matter covered but is in no way intended as a substitute for medical/health counseling and treatment. It is sold with the understanding that the author and the publisher are not engaged in rendering professional services to the readers. Readers must consult their physician or other health professional in all matters concerning their health. The author and publisher disclaim any responsibility whatsoever for any liability, risk, or loss, personal or otherwise, incurred as a direct or indirect consequence of the use and application of the contents of this book.

National Library of Canada Cataloguing in Publication

Rajapakse, Kingsley, 1939-
 The way to inner peace : Buddhism, science and uncommon sense for daily living : a practical guide / by Kingsley Rajapakse. ~ Rev. and enl. 2nd ed.

Includes bibliographical references and index.
ISBN 0-9681692-1-X

 1. Self-actualization (Psychology)~Religious aspects~Buddhism.
I. Title.

BQ4022.R35 2003   294.3'44   C2003-901094-5

Preface to the First Edition

The seeds of this book were the essays I regularly contributed to *The Wheel* Newsletter of the West End Buddhist Center (Mississauga, Canada) over a period of two years. The book would not have been a reality if not for the encouragement I received from many readers, and later, suggestions from the monks at the Center as well as a number of readers, to put together a book based on the essays.

Fundamentals of Buddhism come to us often in heavily laden doctrinal descriptions couched in an unmanageable mix of words of Pali (the original language in which Buddhism was documented) and Sanskrit (ancient literary language of India). Admittedly, doctrinal writings are the guideposts that ensure we do not stray from the unchangeable essence of Buddha's teaching. However, to most of us, they do not seem to translate into practical guidelines for daily living.

Buddhism is a way of living that helps to bring out the potential best in us and is intended to be easily accessible to all, not a select few. If we are unable to meaningfully capture the wisdom of Buddhism, as a beacon for daily living, then all our preoccupation with dogma and rituals would have served no useful purpose, and we would have missed the primary objective of Buddhism. This book attempts to bridge that gap, to bring into the 'living room' of today's home, the healing essence of Buddha's teaching.

The focus of this presentation gradually shifts from an exploration of the key principles of Buddhism needed for effective practice to the actual practice itself. Where appropriate, the 'eye of science' has been used to enhance the presentation. I have tried to make both theory and practice easy to understand, yet not deviate from the primary intentions behind the doctrine or its essence.

The original essays, and now this book, are the products of notes I made for personal use and practical application as I waded through the information maze on Buddhism and other relevant subjects. I hope the reader will benefit from the book at least much as I did from the notes and thoughts that were generated from what turned out to be, for me, a fascinating exploration.

Kingsley Rajapakse

Mississauga, Canada (1997)

Preface to the Second Edition

It is more than six years since the first edition of *The Way to Inner Peace* was released. The comments received from readers worldwide far surpassed anything I expected when the first edition was released. The benefits realized by readers, as evidenced from their letters, ranged from simply feeling good to lives being saved. It certainly is gratifying to know that the Buddha's teaching, conveyed with simplicity in language and presentation, does make a significant (and often profound) difference in our lives.

In moving from the first edition to the second, those who have read the first edition will discover some significant differences:

1. The second edition has three parts.

    *   Part A: *The Seekers' Digest.* Because of the established beneficial role of the first edition, it is retained as Part A. Some minor changes have been made to suit the new structure of the book and improve clarity. This part serves as an introduction and covers key concepts of Buddhism with little attention paid to in-depth reasoning of principles.

    *   Part B: *Homo Sapiens Under Distress.* The material in this part was assembled on the premise that the inquiring mind of today's seeker assimilates and integrates a new insight better when the why and the how relating to the insight are explained. In other words, the seeker wants to know the rationale behind statements made. To that extent, this part explores the underlying mechanisms of the mind-body-world phenomenon from the point of view of both Buddhism and science. Thus, coming under scrutiny here are: perception and reality, stress/distress response mechanisms, brain wiring, impact of multiple conditions on our existence and the birth and growth of the notion of self. In view of the emphasis placed on science, we may view this second edition as an exploration of the relationship between (a) Buddhism, which is 2½ millennia old and (b) the new and emerging sciences, including in particular, health-related sciences.

- Part C: *Distress Relief*. This part examines how the concepts covered in Parts A and B can be applied to solve our problems in daily living.

2. Diagrams are used in parts B and C for better illustration ("A picture is worth a thousand words").

3. The principle of *no-self* (leitmotiv of the Buddha's teaching) is intentionally revisited again and again to view it from different angles, thus helping in its integration to our lives.

4. A new entry "Highlights and Insights" placed at the end of each chapter gives a summary of key points for the readers' benefit.

I would like to repeat here (from Chapter 2) the Buddha's admonition - a gem of advice - to the Kalamas[*] regarding teachers of, and teachings on, spiritual practice.

"Don't accept a thing merely because it is handed down by tradition, or because many people repeat it, or on the authority of the sage who teaches it, or because it is found in the so-called scriptures, or because probability is in its favor, or because you have imagined it, or that it is inspired by some supernormal agency.

"After examination, after testing it for yourself, if you find it reasonable and is in conformity with your wellbeing and the wellbeing of others as well, then accept it and follow it."

In practical terms, if a certain method or principle applied to one's life contributes to the wellbeing of oneself and others, then add it to the collection of one's 'recipes' for living; otherwise, let it go. Then move onto the next method or principle. If the need arises, revisit some principles earlier discarded, for a review perhaps from a new angle. Continue until one has a complete collection of recipes which, applied to one's daily living, contribute to and maintain, inner peace. The technique works.

That advice should apply equally well to this book, or for that matter, any book that a seeker holds in his/her hands for help in realizing inner peace.

---

[*] Abridged

In the practice of Buddhism, as common to all religions, there is a tendency to spend undue time debating terminology and "not see the forest for the trees". In using this book, I would urge the reader not to get hung up on terminology but to seek meaning in context and let the ensuing wellbeing of oneself and those around be the sole test.

In general, each chapter of the book depends on the prior chapters for a proper understanding. Hence it is essential that the chapters be read in the presented sequence.

Bon voyage on *The Way to Inner Peace.*

Kingsley Rajapakse

Penetang, Canada (2003)

Acknowledgements

1St Edition

For encouraging me to continue with my writings on the theme 'Buddhism for Daily Living', I thank:

- Ven. Bhikku Bodhi, President of the Buddhist Publication Society.

- Ven. Dhammawasa, Chief Thera, Toronto West End Buddhist Center and Venerable Muditha, Deputy Chief Thera.

- Ven. Punnaji, former Chief Thera, Toronto Maha Vihara.

For reading over and commenting on the final draft I thank:

- Dan Jinapriya, Vivian Macdonald, Janet McLellan and Aloy Perera

My very special thanks go to my wife for her patience, understanding and support without which I could not have devoted the major part of my waking hours in the recent past to complete the book.

2nd Edition

My gratitude and thanks are offered to:

- Marilyn Murray, Sylvia McLean, Ngan Van Nguyen, Adrian Senn and Shane Rajapakse for review of the draft.

- Dinali Alexander for a wonderful job at the word processor.

- Johann Raj of MindConcepts.com (Toronto, Ontario, Canada) for designing a cover that perfectly reflects the book's message of inner peace; also for designing a web site for the book. (www.TheWayToInnerPeace.com)

- Asoka and Malkanthi Jayasundera for assistance with the printing.

There is a way to end distress

- From the Four Noble Truths

PART A

THE SEEKER'S DIGEST

PART B

HOMO SAPIENS UNDER DISTRESS

PART C

DISTRESS RELIEF

~

The
Seeker's Digest

~

1

The Jackal and the Mange

A person's present thoughts build his/her life of tomorrow;
a person's life is the creation of his/her own mind[1].

The Buddha[2]

No other story from the life of the Buddha reveals the cardinal point of his teaching as profoundly as the following story[3] of the jackal[4] and the mange[5].

One day when they were in the forest, the attention of the Buddha and his disciples was drawn to a jackal that seemed restless. In silence they watched the animal. The jackal stood still for a moment. Then it ran under the bush. A moment later it ran out of the bush and stood still again. Then nervously it made a few circles and sat down. Not for long, though. With apparent discomfort and agitation it ran into a cave. Back again. It jumped up and then ran into the hollow of a large tree. For a while it continued to move from one thing to another. Then, it disappeared out of sight. At that point, the Buddha addressed his disciples thus:

---

[1] From *The Dhammapada Verse1*. In providing the English translations of extracts of Pali scriptures, our primary objective has been the delivery of the essential meaning of the extract in easily understandable language, to the modern day reader. Thus, existing scholastic translations are either not used, or not used verbatim, when they do not serve that practical objective.

Quotations from, and references to, various authoritative Buddhist writings are given throughout the book. The keen student of Buddhism may want to refer to these writings for further study.

[2] The use of 'the' before 'Buddha' may appear as a grammatical error if we regard 'Buddha' as a proper noun. However when we take the meaning of 'Buddha' as 'Awakened One' then 'The Awakened One', and therefore 'The Buddha', becomes meaningful.

[3] In this book, the reader will come across a number of stories from ancient scriptures. We will give our rendition of the stories as we remember, to convey a core message which may not necessarily be an exact narrative of the original story.

[4] A dog-like wild animal found in Africa and southern Asia, hence India – the country where the Buddha was born, lived and attained Full Enlightenment.

[5] An itchy skin disease of mammals caused by parasitic mites.

"Monks, you saw that jackal. Standing it suffered. Running it suffered. In the cave it suffered and so did it in the bush. For its distress it 'blamed' the standing, the sitting, the running, the cave, the bush, the tree hollow and so on. But the problem was not due to any of those. That jackal had mange. That was the root cause. *Until the mange is got rid of, the jackal will continue to suffer......*"

The Buddha then went on to show that when it comes to the effort to avoid discomfort, the human predicament is the same as that of the jackal. We focus on externals hoping to eliminate discomfort and find lasting comfort. But none of that helps, because the root cause of our problem is *wrong views*, or wrong thinking – that is 'our mange'. Until we change our views, we will continue to be unhappy like the jackal, no matter what else we do.

Keeping that important revelation from the Buddha in our mind let's travel forward about 2500 years in time to our familiar world of today. Then, we will try to understand the nature of 'our mange' and how we can get rid of it using Buddhism to create inner peace in our lives. Let's first take a look at a typical sampling of human existence in today's world.

Little Barny[6] is a bundle of joy as he plays in the park. Equally happy is his mother as she watches him. Later on, when mom says it's time to go home for lunch, Barny protests and continues to play in defiance. Eventually a crying Barny follows an angry mother home. One moment joy, another moment unhappiness.

Twenty-five years later, the adult Barny (whom we will now refer to by the unabridged name Barnaby) marries sweetheart Adeline. Within the first three years they are blessed with two lovely children. Life has never before been so joyous for both – dreams come true. Then things began to go sour in the marriage and speedily deteriorate to the point when, ten years later, when both are stressfully planning for divorce. The damage manifests in different forms – in him as depression and in her as incessant bitterness. Add to that an environment saturated with insecurity for the two young children. Bliss for sometime, then distress.

---

[6] All names used are for the purpose of illustration only, with no connection to real persons, except for cases that have already been highly publicized through the media – for example, Nelson Mandela's story (Chapter 3) to illustrate victory over adversity.

Colin and Fabian are neighbors. A case of the Midas' touch, success has followed success for Colin in his career and he always seems so happy. Fabian just cannot understand why similar success and happiness has evaded him, in spite of the effort he puts into life to make it joyous. What else can Fabian be but jealous to the point of sickness? One person happier than another.

Colin, the only breadwinner of the family suddenly loses his job of twenty-five years when his company filed for bankruptcy and just ten months later he was diagnosed with malignant colon cancer. Now Colin feels worse than Fabian. Reversal of fortune.

Augustina was very attached to Grandma. When Granny passed away, Augustina was distraught and continued to mourn for weeks. Five years later, while at dinner with the rest of the family, she affectionately recalls funny things Granny used to do and they all join in laughter. One time grief, another time laughter.

As illustrated by the above narratives, we discover that there is no person who is *totally* happy or totally unhappy all his or her life; happiness alternates with unhappiness. Also it varies from person to person. Undoubtedly, all this variability leaves a common thread of dissatisfaction through human existence. It is this dissatisfaction that creates in us our basic *quest for lasting happiness,* the driving force behind everything that we energetically do in life.

We begin the search as children, intensify it in adult life and continue, in many cases into old age and death, not having found the real thing (lasting happiness), like the experience of most men digging for gems. Why for that long? Because, innumerable times along the journey we feel that we have found it, but then each time to our utter disappointment we find it is not the real thing, and we move to the next. Each time the experience has three clear phases. First, there is the feeling "This is it!" Second, it is tried out. Third, there is the realization, exactly opposite to the first phase, that "This is really *not* it", for it turns out to be either a total disappointment or just transient happiness. So with frustration, the helpless seeker continues the endless quest.

The young child, in the unconscious search for this elusive entity of lasting happiness, takes refuge in playthings. The older child may try out things such as a la mode clothing, dyed hair or shaven heads, girl/boy friends and even alcohol and drugs. The same old story. Not the real thing, so we try the next. Then as adults our hopes move onto sports cars, university degrees, the stock market, marriage, children, the dream home and so on. After all these have been realized, we still find the thing we are seeking – unchanging happiness – is missing. "How come," we ask "even after all this time and effort?" Now we are not only frustrated, but begin to get disillusioned with the whole idea of worldly accomplishments. Looking back, we realize the nature of the problem from childhood onwards has one common theme: with some things tried out, it has been total disappointment and with the others, transient happiness at most. We find something missing at the very core of being, though the surface may be glittering with acquisitions, with adornments.

On each occasion it is discovered the thing tried out for happiness also causes unhappiness – from the disappointment that Barny experienced to Barnaby's impending divorce from 'soul-mate' Adeline. And every time each is convinced that their distress is someone else's fault. Little Barny's fun in the park was spoilt because Mom did not bring along a pack of lunch. Barnaby is now going through the trauma brought on by the looming divorce, all because of the insensitivity of Adeline. Adeline, for her part, is convinced that her life was ruined because Barnaby trapped her into marrying him; otherwise she would have been a happy single woman today and rising up the executive ladder to ever greater things in the corporation which she left to get married. Always it is someone else's fault. So it seems to be with all our worldly problems. Ironically that strategy does not solve the problems for anyone but drags all involved deeper into the mire. It is at this point in our desperation and impasse that Buddhism comes to help, like a lamp does for one lost in a deep and dark cave.

Taking the Barnaby/Adeline example, Buddhism would point out to Barnaby that Adeline is not the *root* cause of his marital chaos. Whatever Adeline may have done, whatever she may be as a person, all that Barnaby went through emotionally was created by his perception of Adeline and her actions. Adeline's actions, at most, are to be *associated* with what Barnaby has gone through, but *letting* her actions ruin him happened completely within his own mind. To Adeline, Buddhism will bring the same revelation, in principle. So the work both have to do, if they want to eradicate their mental distress, is to learn how to change the way they perceive the world, so they can be in touch with reality; in Dhamma terms, purify the minds. And showing the way to do it is essentially what Buddhism is all about. That effort will enable both to live with inner peace. It may even save their marriage.

We started this chapter by quoting one of the most profound insights discovered by the Buddha and gifted to the human race. Worth repeating, it is: *A person's present thoughts build his/her life of tomorrow; a person's life is the creation of his/her own mind.* In practice, this insight translates into the fundamental principle on which the Buddhist doctrine of personal transformation was based by the Buddha 2500 years ago and fully concurs with modern day science. It carries two corollaries of immense significance that are invaluable tools for extricating ourselves from existential distress.

These corollaries are:

1. *Our thoughts come first; related feelings and actions follow. Therefore, to change the way we feel and act, that is, to alter the direction of our life, we need to change our thinking.* We cannot *directly* access our feelings but we can change our thinking so that *indirectly* we have the means to cause our feelings to change. It therefore follows that if we change our thoughts to be in touch with reality, the accompanying feelings are in touch with reality. Feelings in touch with reality are feelings of inner peace, as we will discover later on. Thus, this corollary points to the Buddhist *technique* of personal transformation, i.e., change one's thinking (views).

2. *It is a person's own thinking that shapes his/her life, not the thinking or action or behavior of anyone else or, in general terms, the 'world out there'.* In other words, it is my view of the world, not the world itself that forges my life. This corollary, which correctly *places the scene of effective action in one's own mind*, has far-reaching implications for our daily lives. For example, it clearly establishes the common practice of blaming as a meaningless aspect of human behavior. We will explore a lot more along these lines later in the book.

Having extracted the above two corollaries, now we are a step closer to the solution in our search for lasting peace. Let's illustrate the above corollaries with two examples.

First example. Two people wake up in adjoining apartments and see snow falling outside. One curses the snowfall and goes to bed again, a miserable man. The other is thrilled because he can go cross-country skiing with his family. Without detailed analysis, we can see that it was not the snow ('the world out there') that was responsible for the contrasting feelings, because it was the same snowfall that both observed, but the thinking that went on inside the two minds.

The second example.   Ganya is at home in Boston and her boyfriend Patrick is in the Cayman Islands on business.   A happy Ganya is preparing for their upcoming wedding.   On Monday morning, Patrick meets with a fatal car crash.   Ganya gets the bad news on Wednesday evening and immediately dips into severe mental distress.   Was it the fatal car crash or her thinking that caused her distress?   If it was the car crash, then she should have been distressed from Monday morning.   So the crash did not cause the distress.   Her thinking about the tragedy started only on Wednesday evening, so it has to be the thinking process that brought the distress (though, admittedly, the crash was the *trigger* for the thinking).   We could say 'it is human for Ganya to react as she did'.   Yes, it is human, but not in touch with reality.   Wait until later chapters for further clarification with scientific details and thence the development of the path to inner peace.

Five hundred years after the Buddha, the Greek philosopher Epictetus conveyed the same deep meaning about thoughts and feelings when he said, "It is not the events that cause our feelings but the view that we take of them".   Eleanor Roosevelt put it very simply thus: "No one can make you feel inferior *without your consent*."   So all that happens to us, as far as our feelings go, are not caused by the Adelines or Barnabys of this world or other things external to us, but by ourselves in our own minds. That applies not just to our unwholesome emotions, but also to our wholesome emotions (happiness[7] and peace).   Hence, while the problem is in our minds, the solution is in our minds too.

Buddhism explains in clear detail very systematically and scientifically the method of moving from unhappiness into lasting peace – an emotional state that is not transient but far surpassing the highest emotional state we have ever experienced through sensory contact.   That method is the Noble Eightfold Path[8].   For now, instead of venturing into any aspects of the

---

[7] In Buddhism, happiness and peace have distinctly different meanings.   Happiness is a condition associated with the senses and is subject to change.   (So are other related emotions such as joy and unhappiness.)   Peace is a condition realized upon transcending the senses, therefore lasting.   Perfected, unchanging, ultimate peace is Sublime Peace.   More exploration of these terms will follow later in the book.

[8] The Nobel Eightfold Path is Buddha's way that leads to Sublime Peace.   The formal list of the eight steps are: 1. Right Understanding 2. Right Thought 3. Right Speech, 4. Right Action, 5. Right Livelihood, 6. Right Effort, 7. Right Mindfulness and 8. Right Concentration.   In this book we will cover the 8 steps in a manner and practical detail that makes the most meaning for daily living in today's world, rather than strictly follow the classical treatment of the Path.   The reader interested in a formal treatment of the subject

Eightfold Path in detail, let's first try to get a preview of Dhamma practice in a 'nutshell', for which we move to the next chapter.

▶ *Digression*

FROM THE OUTER WORLD

TO THE INNER WORLD

Before moving onto the next chapter, we may put into practice the important insight we have just learnt. Once we fully understand the deep meaning of the insight 'It is not the *events* that cause our *feelings* but the *view* that we take of them' we can integrate this new thinking into our lives relating to what we consider as distress-producing existential 'events' of our world. In the process we will accrue substantial therapeutic benefits. Thus for example, of *criticism*, contemplate: It is not her criticism that caused my anxiety, but the view I took of her criticism. Similarly, of *aging*: It is not my aging that causes my emotional distress, but the view I take of aging. Likewise for all other existential 'events' that seemingly cause havoc in our emotional lives.

Chapter Insights and Highlights

1.   It is a person's own thoughts (views) that shape his/her life, not the thoughts or behavior of anyone else or events of the 'world out there'.

2.   Our thinking happens first, emotions (and actions) follow.

3.   Usually, happiness and unhappiness alternate in any person's life. Happiness and unhappiness are dependent on one's sensory interaction with the world.

4.   Buddhism provides us with a way to realize unchanging peace, a state surpassing happiness, by transcending the senses and choosing to think in touch with reality.

---

may refer to "Noble Eightfold Path" Wheel Publication No. 308/311 by Bhikku Bodhi. Buddhist Publication Society, 1984.

2

Dhamma In A Nutshell

Not to do any evil,
to cultivate good,
to purify one's mind –
this is the teaching of the Buddhas.

- The Dhammapada 183

The Buddha showed that there is a way to realize the lasting happiness that we are after and also that we can go beyond what we ordinarily mean by happiness to a point of culmination referred to as Sublime Peace[9]. He went on to assure us that the goal could be realized in this very life if we do our part properly.

The Buddha referred to his universal 'prescription' as Dhamma, meaning teachings (doctrine, laws) pertaining to existence. In a more practical sense, Dhamma may be viewed as the Buddha's gospel for deliverance from distress. Dhamma as originally taught by the Buddha is essentially a way of wholesome living, with no religious connotations, which guides the practitioner to use his/her mind to its fullest potential. It is a set of scientific laws applicable to the existence of beings as Newton's and Einstein's laws are for the physical universe. In fact, as science (particularly neuroscience) advances, an ever-increasing convergence between scientific thought and Dhamma becomes evident.

After the Buddha passed away, outsiders began to call Dhamma by the name 'Buddhism' (meaning teachings of the person called the Buddha) and the followers themselves began using the term. With the passage of time, various cultural coatings, rituals, symbolism and the like came to be added to the original Dhamma. These additions arose for a number of

---

[9] We are using the term *Sublime Peace* as English equivalent of Sanskrit *Nirvana* (and Pali *Nibbana)*. This is the highest and ultimate goal of Buddhist aspiration – realized through extinction of craving, aversion and delusion. As we will see later, craving, aversion and delusion are all rooted in the false belief in an abiding self. Hence, as a single, converged point of action, complete extinction of the belief in a self is, in the final analysis, the clear path to Nirvana.

reasons, such as community needs and sometimes also misunderstanding of the Buddha's teachings on the part of some followers. It would be more appropriate to refer to the Buddha's teaching as the most scientific self-help psychotherapy ever, rather than religion. Given all these factors, for the purposes of our discussions we will henceforth use the term Dhamma whenever we need to refer to the doctrine as originally taught by the Buddha.

And who was this person called The Buddha? At this juncture it is suffice for us to know that he was not a creator but an astute observer and discoverer of crucial phenomena relating to life, particularly emotional life, that had evaded the perceptive reach of other humans before him. In that respect, he was to the understanding of the human mind what Newton and Einstein were to the understanding of the physical universe. The Buddha was born, lived, attained full enlightenment and died as a human being.

When the Buddha was once asked to explain his teaching in a few simple words, he answered thus: "Cease to do evil[10]; learn to do good; purify your own mind." An assignment simply stated, but a lifetime's undertaking and worth every moment spent in implementing it. As noted earlier, the pinnacle of achievement in Dhamma practice is purification of the mind. However, one needs to create a conducive environment for that mind-purification by practicing good living as a prerequisite. Hence the reason "cease to do evil, learn to do good" precedes "purify your own mind" in the Buddha's formula for realizing inner peace.

A closer examination of the message "Cease to do evil; learn to do good; purify your own mind" reveals a further factor essential to the means by which the goal can be realized – that is to focus on the present moment. This becomes clear if we add the implied word *now* to each part of the message. Let's examine each part in that context.

Cease to do evil *now*. This implies no self-blame or guilt (for wrongs one may have done up until now) and no sin (Dhamma knows no sin, only ignorance). The past is to be used, if at all, for growth now, through knowledge of mistakes made through ignorance.

Learn to do good *now*. Now – the present – is the only opportunity there is to change the direction of one' s destiny, stay on the Path and head

---

[10] Definitions of good and bad (evil), within the context of this book are as follows. *Good* is intentional action that causes no harm to self or other beings. *Bad (evil)* is intentional action that causes harm to self or other beings.

towards the goal of Sublime Peace by wholesome action. This opportunity to do good now also enables us to pay back any dues for any unwholesome deeds done in the past.

Purify your own mind *now*. Again, dwelling in memories of past experiences is not going to help a person with spiritual advancement. The prime factor that will determine progress towards Sublime Peace is what one does *now* to purify one's mind. The means is meditation. This part of the Buddha's message also emphasizes purification of one's *own* mind, not another's – the real cure for all problems that exist between people. It comes as a correction to our usual erroneous tendency to blame others.

Having got a glimpse of the building blocks of Dhamma, let's now touch on a few salient points about the journey on the Path itself.

First, *there is no coercion*. While Dhamma promises a path that delivers us from unhappiness into Sublime Peace, it does not coerce anyone to follow the Path. It is a try-it-and-see-it-yourself offering. This important point about Dhamma is the essence of the Buddha's admonition to one audience conveyed to us via the *Kalama Sutta*[11]:

> One day, the Buddha visited a city called Kesaputta. Some princes of a clan named Kalama came to the Buddha and the leader of the clan said: "Venerable Sir, various teachers come to our town from time to time and expound different teachings. One teacher says one thing and another teaches something quite contradictory. This happens over and over again. When we listen to these various teachers we get puzzled, and we cannot fathom which one is correct and which one is wrong."
>
> Thereupon, the Buddha said:
>
> "It is no wonder that a person gets puzzled and confused when that person hears teachings contradictory to each other, but I tell you this:
> Don't accept a thing merely because it is handed down by tradition.
> Don't accept a thing merely because many people repeat it.
> Don't accept a thing merely on the authority of the sage who teaches it
> Don't accept a thing merely because it is found in the so-called scriptures.
> Don't accept a thing merely because probability is in its favor.
> Don't accept a thing merely because you have imagined it, or that it is inspired by some supernormal agency.
>
> After examination, after testing it for yourself, if you find it reasonable and is in conformity with your well-being and the well-being of others as well, then accept it and follow it"

---

[11] Discourses of the Buddha are called *Suttas* in Pali.

There we have a wonderful litmus test to check the efficacy of any belief system, religion, faith, healing agency etc. before we accept it and follow it. Let's try the Buddha's litmus test on his own teaching, the Dhamma.

> Don't accept Dhamma teachings merely because they are handed down by tradition. (In particular, "Born Buddhists" amongst us need to note this.)
> Don't accept Dhamma teachings merely because many people repeat them.
> Don't accept Dhamma teachings merely on the authority of the Buddha.
> Don't accept Dhamma teachings merely because they are found in the so-called scriptures (e.g., the Pali Canon).
> Don't accept Dhamma teachings merely because probability is in their favor.
> Don't accept Dhamma teachings merely because you have imagined them, or that they are inspired by some supernormal agency.
>
> **After examination, after testing Dhamma teachings (Buddhism) for yourself, if you find them reasonable and are in conformity with your well-being and the well-being of others as well, then accept Dhamma teachings and follow them"**

So the Buddha himself emphasized complete freedom of thought in one's exploration of Dhamma. What greater encouragement and confidence does one need to explore a promised path to salvation? There is total freedom to enter, walk or quit the path as it pleases the individual. The only thing that keeps one on the path is personal satisfaction with the results of each step taken. Those who have earnestly entered the Path and did their part properly tell us that the only thing that ever brought them to a halt was the destination.

Second, *Dhamma is for all.* If one were to ask the simple question "Who can benefit from Dhamma?' from our discussion so far we know that the equally simple answer is "Anyone who has a mind". One's religious and other leanings should not stand in the way of straightening out views that are not in touch with reality. Our personal leanings do not come into the question when we try to understand, live with or use Newton's laws of the physical world. The same should hold true for Dhamma, the natural laws that pertain to existence of beings.

Third, we have to *do our own work.* Again the Buddha's advice was: "You yourself must make the effort – the Buddhas only show the way." Self-reliance is the key. No different from sensible advice on everything else of significance in our lives. The High School teacher will show you how, but you have to study and pass the exam yourself if you need the High School Diploma.

Fourth, *the work is hard but is achievable.* To change wrong views that have taken root in the deep crevices of the mind over a whole lifetime, and move against further resistance offered by forces unique to the individual (karmic forces) and societal impositions is indeed hard work.

But many have done it and the reward of Sublime Peace is worth the effort. It requires diligence, dedication and patience from the traveler. Cleaning one's wound is painful, but once cleaned and the medicine is applied, a pain-free existence follows. The same applies to the journey of liberation.

Finally, *the results are verifiable in this very life.* One does not have to wait until heaven or hell, or reach another life to see 'the test results'. The results of 'ceasing to do evil, learning to do good and purifying one's own mind' can be seen right in this life.

In summary, at a practical level what is in Dhamma for us, is a time-tested and well-proven method to help us eradicate unhappiness for good. The method shows us how to achieve this by dealing with the root cause of the problems, namely, wrong views. If the doctor tells you that the root cause of your pain is a potentially cancerous tumor, you would go all out to get the tumor removed. Shouldn't we do the same for our minds? After all, happiness and peace reside in the mind and, as the reader will discover during the course of this book, the greatest self-help program available to humankind for achieving inner peace is Dhamma.

Chapter Insights and Highlights

1. The Buddha's teachings are called Dhamma – laws or truths that pertain to the existence of beings as Newton's laws pertain to the physical universe.

2. The meaningful way to view Dhamma is as a self-help psychotherapy that is based on scientific principles, rather than a religion.

3. The essence of Dhamma may be stated in these simple words as: "Cease to do evil; learn to do good; purify your own mind." Details of the teachings explain how to realize that essence.

4. Some salient points about the Dhamma path are:

- There is no coercion. ("Try it yourself. If you find it works, i.e., helps the wellbeing of yourself and others, integrate it into your life").
- Dhamma laws apply to all, just as Newton's laws of gravity apply to all.
- We have to do our own work as the Buddhas only show the way to peace.
- The work is hard but achievable, and
- The results are verifiable in this very life.

3

Teachers in Disguise

In the middle of difficulty lies opportunity.

Albert Einstein

The glory is not in never failing,

But in rising every time you fail.

Chinese Proverb

A man walks down a footpath and encounters an ugly stone. He curses the stone for being in his way and walks on, an angry man. Later, another man, a sculptor with a creative mind, encounters the same stone and promptly recognizes amazing potential in it. Next day, he returns with a wheelbarrow, takes the ugly stone with him, and eventually turns out a prized work of art from it.

In our daily life, we encounter many "ugly stones" in the form of problems, mistakes, sickness and so forth, all of which are contributors to some form of *distress*[12] (*dukkha* in Pali), as in the examples quoted in Chapter 1. We usually look at these, in the same manner as the first man in our little story above. What we need to do is change our view to that of the second man, the sculptor and see the amazing potential in the things in our lives that we normally wish were not there. They are all our teachers in disguise. Developing such a view is an integral part of the Dhamma path. Let's now investigate a little further and see in what disguised forms our teachers appear.

The first view we have to develop is not only that *distress for us worldlings is a fact of life* (the First Noble Truth[13]) but also that it is a *necessity*. Just as much as the ugly stone was necessary for our sculptor to build his prized work of art, we can only realize Sublime Peace by working with our "ugly" distress. Without distress there is no foundation on which to begin our work towards that Sublime Peace. From this

---

[12] The subject of distress is addressed in greater detail in Chapter 6.

[13] The Buddha's Dhamma is contained in the Four Noble Truths: (1) There is distress, (2) There is the origin of that distress, (3) Distress can be eradicated and (4) There is a Path that leads to its eradication. The Path is the Noble 8-Fold Path, defined earlier.

realization emerge two further insights: firstly, to *accept* distress as a part of worldly existence and secondly, to view distress as a friend (who helps us progress towards Sublime Peace). This is a complete turnaround from our usual viewpoint – a transcendental[14] way of thinking – because it requires us to go beyond sensory perception. Thus distress is our principal teacher in disguise. Given that a major contributor to the resilience of distress is aversion to distress itself, creating a vicious cycle, such a changed view can become therapeutic, as we begin to accept that embedded in *everything* that happens to us there is the seed of a noble mission. Hence the Buddha teaches us within his Four Noble Truths to use distress to overcome distress – no different to using, in the form of a vaccine, the very virus that causes influenza to fight influenza.

Those who make our life miserable, particularly those who create the worst times in our lives, are our next group of teachers in disguise. As attempts to change others often end up as futile exercises, the Dhamma way urges us to *look at ourselves,* more precisely to look within, and identify changes needed, using the other person's reaction(s) as our mirror. With that new approach, we will invariably be motivated to take some wholesome action, aimed at changing ourselves, specifically how we view the world around us. That is within our control and will benefit not only ourselves but the other person as well.

Ironically, enlightenment is usually offered to us in the palm of the enemy, not of the friend. It's usually the gust of adversity, not the gentle wind of joy that carries to us the aroma of peace. Why? Because these adversities make us come face to face with reality and to see reality is to be enlightened.

The boss one finds impossible to get along with may be the blessing in disguise that causes a person to find another job that is more satisfying. A person who always blames you and never praises you provides a wonderful opportunity to practice the art of survival independent of praise and blame, thereby developing the priceless quality of equanimity. ("Even as a rock is not shaken by the wind, the wise man is not shaken by praise or blame" – The Dhammapada 81). The rebelliousness of a child may be a hidden message for us to re-examine some erroneous beliefs or values we are trying to impose on the child. The spouse who doesn't do things for you may be the one propelling you on to a path of self-reliance that will one day be your greatest savior. Someone (our "worst enemy")

---

[14] The word *transcend* (and its adjective *transcendental*) has many meanings. In this book it is used to mean "go beyond the limits of sensory perception", exclusively. The reason will become clear in later chapters.

who pushes us to the brink may be just the trigger that catapults us from a life of transient pleasures into the true Dhammic path leading to full enlightenment. What better gift can we receive from anyone?

So we must be thankful to those who cause the greatest grief in our lives. We can do this only with a complete shift in our attitude, from the easy and ordinary way of focusing on negativity and blame to one of deep introspection and viewing all that happens as lessons facilitating onward progress.

Moving from disagreeable persons to disagreeable *events*, we can consider the latter as our third category of teachers in our school called Life. Every tragedy has built into it the seed for the germination of a higher purpose, a nobler cause and a gain far surpassing the loss. Numerous are the examples of extraordinary men and women who realized such greater gain over their losses, providing inspiration for the rest of us.

Of those great ones, some are no longer with us at the time of writing this book. Terry Fox, the one-legged runner, raised millions of dollars for cancer research, after his own affliction with cancer. Then there is Victor Frankl[15], prisoner in a World War II Nazi concentration camp, whose entire family, except for his sister, perished in captivity. After regaining freedom, Frankl became one of Europe's leading psychiatrists. Helen Keller, who became blind and deaf at the age of two after an attack of scarlet fever, left a legacy of contributions to humankind.

Two illustrious examples of human beings still amongst us who turned adversity into gold are Nelson Mandela and Stephen Hawking. Mandela kept his sanity during 27 years behind bars as a political prisoner to become the President of his country (South Africa), Nobel Prize winner and an internationally revered hero. At age 20, Hawking was struck with a wasting disease (called motor neuron disease, also referred to as Lou Gehrig's disease). It gradually took away most of the functionality of his nervous and muscular systems, making him look like a sick and frail old man in the last stages of his life. After initially capitulating to the ravages of the disease in the form of emotional setbacks, Hawking changed his destiny completely (with some help from other compassionate human

---

[15] Certain aspects of Victor Frankl's story are not too different from those of Patacara, a woman who lived during Buddha's time. She lost her husband, the two children, mother, father and brother in one day. Though she temporarily lost her sanity, Buddha's intervention and a profound exposition by the Enlightened One brought Patacara to the Path and eventual deliverance.

beings, especially the person who later became his wife). Using his mind and with hardly a body, Stephen Hawking – an almost completely cerebral human being – became the greatest physicist of our time, positioned on the same platform as Einstein by many.

Such are the capabilities of human beings when they make the determination to transcend their misfortunes. And the Buddha demonstrated the pinnacle of such potential when, shaken by the sight of human distress, he discovered the very remedy – the Dhamma – to transcend all distress, and made it available to humankind for all time to come.

While we have listed famous names in our examples, it must be stated that persons who have turned ugly stones into beautiful sculptures can be found amongst 'ordinary people'. Of primary importance is not the fact that a person is famous, but the act of transcending adversity in our own way using our will power, given the unique circumstances prevailing in our individual lives. It is what we do with what we have that matters. In that sense, for example, a single mother, who with meager means raises her four children to become illustrious citizens is a 'Nelson Mandela' too.

Our fourth teacher is Nature. We normally speed through life just *encountering* Nature, but seldom *learning* from it. For example, take a fruit tree in our garden. We see leaves at one time, buds later and fruits still later. We pluck the fruits, eat them and we are happy. But the teacher disguised as the tree can teach us the whole world of Dhamma, if we care to look more deeply. The birth, decay, old age and death of the leaves and the fruits – just the normal process of Nature, is equally applicable to us (although we usually pretend it is not) and happens in front of our eyes in each complete cycle of seasons. Likewise Nature encountered in our daily lives (animals, clouds, our breathing, a feeling of anger, a sick man and so forth) can teach us all the principles of Dhamma, but only if we care to slow down and contemplate. That is Insight Meditation (*Vipassana* in Pali)[16] in action.

Our fifth category of teachers in disguise are our mistakes and our failures. We are worldlings because we are not perfect, which is another

---

[16] The original Pali term of *Vipassana* is rendered in English as Insight Meditation and sometimes as Mindfulness Meditation. We prefer the term Insight because the crux of the practice is the replacement of an erroneous view with a view in touch with reality, i.e., an insight. In this book, for Pali words we will provide English words that best serve the objective of conveying the essence of Buddha's teaching to the man and woman of today's English speaking world, to benefit in their daily living. We will use English words appearing in classical Pali-English dictionaries only when that objective is served.

way of saying we are here to make mistakes until we attain full enlightenment. The common way is to blame ourselves for our mistakes and feel guilty, and blame others for their mistakes and get angry. Dhamma trains us to treat our mistakes as our teachers, never to assign blame, take corrective action where possible and accept what we cannot change. A similar attitude applies to our failures. In reality, there are no mistakes, no failures, no problems but just *happenings* governed by eternal laws of nature. These happenings provide us with the basis for the next action, with the potential to change our own destiny, if only we choose to use them so.

From now on, whenever we confront a problem, however severe it may appear to be we can train ourselves to think of the problem as a teacher in disguise. Then we can proceed to ask the question "What is the lesson this is trying to teach me?" Now, with the help of the teachers in disguise, we will be able to transform the 'ugly stones' of our lives to 'prized works of art'. Perhaps there is no greater leap we can take on our path to Sublime Peace. The tools and techniques for the 'sculpturing work' will be described in the rest of the book.

Chapter Insights and Highlights

1) In what another perceives as an 'ugly stone', a sculptor sees tremendous potential for a prized work of art. The two choices we have for viewing our problems in life are similar. Between the two lies a world of a difference. One view leads to misery, the other to inner peace.

2) The potentials hidden in our problems are our 'teachers in disguise'.

3) The disguise can appear in many forms, such as Mother Nature, distressing events, our mistakes and failures, those who create misery in our lives and mere distress itself.

4) It's usually in the palm of the enemy, not of the friend, that enlightenment is offered to us. It's usually the gust of adversity, not the gentle wind of joy that carries to us the aroma of peace. By beginning to view problems as teachers in disguise we can take a great leap towards inner peace.

4

Living Through Change

Impermanent, subject to change, are component things. Strive on with mindfulness.

- *The Buddha* (Final admonition to disciples)

Nothing is permanent but change.

- *Heraclitus (c. 500 B.C.)*

The one single fact on which the whole philosophy of Dhamma hinges is the fact of *impermanence*[17] or simply, change.

We all know various changes occur around us but this is often a casual recognition. Rarely do we gain a deeper, insightful, awareness of change as intended in Dhamma, to benefit daily living. It is to realize that deeper awareness that we make impermanence a subject of meditation. Training to gain the *deepest* possible realization of the impermanence of things (first intellectually, then experientially) should be the foremost endeavor of our Dhamma training.

Everything from the tiny atom to the universe itself is constantly undergoing change. In particular, the form of, and the thoughts and feelings within, the human being are constantly changing.

The key to effective living with change lies in developing awareness of the possibility of change *before the change actually takes place.* When we face the actual change, if we were not pre-conditioned to its possibility, then it will lead to more distress than it should. We should always be ready for change, rather than let change surprise us – this is one objective of meditation on impermanence. When things are going well for us, it pays to remind ourselves once in a while that this will not last forever, then get back to enjoying the good fortune we presently have.

---

[17] Two other facts, which *follow* from the fact of impermanence (*anicca* in Pali) are also key to the discussion of Buddhist philosophy. These are distress (*dukkha*) and no-self (*anatta*). These will be addressed in detail in the next two chapters.

Then, when things do change, as they surely will, we can accept the change with equanimity.

All the teachings of the Buddha eventually contribute to one objective – to help us live our daily lives in such a way that we advance towards the spiritual goal of Sublime Peace. Hence, let's see what corollaries result from the fact of impermanence that may help us in daily living – corollaries that we can contemplate once in a while (or during meditation on impermanence) to help ease the burden of change when change does occur.

1. *We normally tend to live as though things do not change.* For example, when we face a difficult situation or a crisis, we often tend to feel the situation will never pass away. But the reality is that, even while we are thinking so, changes are taking place. Given time, the turbulence will settle down to a new situation that is more amenable to problem resolution, or as it often happens, it resolves on its own, just as turbulent water eventually finds its own level of stability. In times like these, one can seek refuge in the profoundly healing message contained in a beautiful story from the East, which has been retold many times with different flavors. The following rendition brings out its essential message:

There was a king whose life was a 'roller-coaster' with regard to everything about him – wealth, kingdoms, family and personal issues. One day a gain, another day a loss. One moment happiness, another moment sadness. The king couldn't continue anymore in this fashion, as he was being emotionally drained. He wanted a life of equanimity but did not know how to realize it. So he called his seven sages – the senior advisors. He asked them to come up with the answer by the following day. He told them that he would call them one by one and each advisor who failed to produce a viable solution would be sent to a desolate island.

Next day dawned. The king called the first sage. The solution he proposed was not viable. So he was sent to the island. He called the second – the same outcome. So on it was up to the sixth. Finally, very angry and frustrated, he called the last sage. The sage handed over a ring to the king. The king looked at it and found no relevance to what he was seeking. He became more angry and shouted at his advisor asking him how a ring would solve his problem. To which, the sage responded by respectfully asking the king to read the inscription on the ring. It read "This too will pass." The meaning of the words (that is impermanence of all conditioned phenomena) so deeply penetrated the king's mind, that it immediately imparted a spark of deep tranquility he had never experienced before. As a result of that deep realization, the king wore the ring for the rest of his life and the inscription always reminded him to view all things and events (the 'good' and the 'bad') with the insight of impermanence. His life rapidly evolved into one of equanimity. In gratitude he promoted the sage to the highest rank of advisors and arranged for all comforts that could be bestowed on a citizen. The four words "This too will pass" is a jewel for all of us to carry in our minds right through our lives.

Before we conclude this sub-topic, let's also note that we often cling to our attachments as though they will not change and when they do change, the resulting disappointment strikes us down. In fact, being impermanent themselves, when people cling to objects (which always are impermanent, be they mental or physical), their distress is always compounded. Again, awareness developed ahead of the occurrence – that both object and subject will change – helps to soften the disappointment. Practiced over a period of time, this contemplation perhaps will help one to completely let go of attachments, which is even better.

2. *No relationship is the same forever.* The nature of parent-child, employment, marriage or any other relationship changes with the passage of time, due to inevitable change in the parties to the relationship or the surroundings. Insightful awareness of this will help us to tide over change and partings. "Meetings always end in partings".

3. *Our thoughts and feelings change as do physical entities.* Our thoughts and feelings are triggered by phenomena subject to the law of impermanence, and therefore are subject to change themselves. Neither good feelings, nor unfavorable feelings are permanent. Often when we are feeling poorly, all that is required is patience (sometimes patience with perseverance) and the feeling passes away on its own. At such times let's again recall the words: "This too will pass".

Time and again Dhamma advises us to not allow sensory pleasures to get the better of us. What is so 'bad' about sensory pleasures? It is that these pleasures are subject to change and when they do change, we suffer because we crave for the earlier known pleasure.

4. *There is no lasting security in life.* Lasting security implies no change. For example, we wish our health to be as good in the future as it is today. But the incessant and moment-to-moment change taking place within us as well as outside us ensures that we will be subject to illness and decay – so it helps to train ourselves to accept this truth. The only meaningful

security that one can have during a lifetime is an inner (mental) security – a resolve – that one shall deal effectively, in touch with reality, with every worldly insecurity as it arises. This, in other words, is self-confidence, based on reality.

5. *Everything in this universe is unique.* Imagine a wave in the ocean as seen in an instant in time.   In its make-up, such as composition, movement and shape it is unique. It is unlike any other wave that has ever existed from the beginning of time and will be unlike any other wave that will ever exist until the end of time. This uniqueness was brought about by the moment-to-moment change in all the components of its make-up. The same applies to humans and every identifiable thing in the universe. *Acceptance of the uniqueness* of all things can lead to profound healing in many aspects of living, such as overcoming jealousy.

6. *The only worldly reality is what happens in the present moment.* Using the example above, the wave was reality at the moment it was observed. The next moment, that wave, exactly as seen in the previous moment, is no longer reality, but just a memory in the mind of the observer.

7. *Everything in the universe affects everything else in the universe.* Again getting back to our wave, we note that after a few seconds, even the perceptive human eye cannot locate the wave that once was – its components (molecules) have become parts of other waves. After a long time, its components are spread across the world – in waves in the Indian Ocean, in the Atlantic Ocean, in the Great Lakes, some may be in a well, some in a tree and so on.

The fate of the human being is no different from that of the wave. Further, thoughts, feelings and actions of one human being affect all others within his/her reach. In turn, their thoughts, feelings and actions, now influenced to whatever small degree, affect others and the cycle continues. The message here, for daily living, is that all we think and do should be wholesome, so that our living contributes to a harmonious world.

Impermanence – we cannot stop it, though it is the primary cause of all our distress.   However, if we insightfully understand it and learn to anticipate and accept it without fear as inevitable reality, then we can harmoniously grow alongside it as we walk on the path towards deliverance from distress and realization of inner peace.

Chapter Insights and Highlights

1) Everything in the world, without exception, changes.

2) Typically, we maintain a casual, superficial and occasional recognition of change. To realize inner healing from existential distress, we need to develop a deeper and insightful awareness of change, which is a crucial aspect of Dhamma practice.

3) Some important corollaries to note regarding the fact of impermanence, that will help develop inner peace are:

- We normally, and erroneously, tend to live as though things do not change.
- Since people and their environment are subject to change, no relationship remains the same over time.
- Our thoughts and feelings change just like physical entities.
- There is no lasting security in life. A strong resolve to deal with any insecurity as it arises, in touch with reality, is about as far as we can meaningfully go towards security.
- Everything in this universe is unique.
- The only worldly reality is what happens in the present moment.
- Everything in the universe affects everything else in the universe.

4) If we learn to accept without fear the fact that it is in the nature of all worldly things to change, we will be able to triumph over distress and move towards inner peace.

5

Me and Mine
(The Ego)

Mere suffering exists, no sufferer is found,
The deed is, but no doer of the deed is there.
Nibbana is, but not the man that enters it.
The path is, but no traveler on it is seen.

- *The Path of Purification*[18] *XVI*

The primary factor that differentiates Buddhism from other philosophies of life (including religions) is the doctrine of *no-self*[19] (*anatta* in Pali). The discovery of the fact of no-self by the Buddha using his mind alone, at a time when meaningful scientific investigation was unavailable, places the Buddha as a being above all beings in his mental incisiveness. Today, thanks to all the recent groundbreaking discoveries made by science, particularly neuroscience, one can easily see the congruency of the two knowledge bases and readily conclude that science corroborates the doctrine of no-self.

While our intention in this chapter is not an analysis of all the far-reaching implications of no-self, our present objectives would be satisfied if we look at no-self through the eyes of science. In addition, we will discuss just one early hurdle encountered by most, if not all, who embark on a serious inquiry into the subject. The hurdle is the dilemma wherein we need to, on the one hand, insightfully understand and accept that the self does not exist in reality, while on the other hand, refer to self constantly in daily life, even after insightfully understanding the concept of no-self.

---

[18] *The Path of Purification* is the English translation (by Bhikku Nanamoli) of the original Pali publication titled *Visuddhi-Magga*. *The Path of Purification* (1991) is available from the publisher, the Buddhist Publication Society, Kandy, Sri Lanka.
[19] Other English terms used for *anatta* are *egolessness* and *substancelessness*.

In later chapters we will explore no-self in-depth, and from different angles, in view of its utmost importance in Dhamma practice and therefore attainment of inner peace.

Let's begin our investigation by reviewing the basic fact of impermanence, particularly as it relates to the human being, since no-self is an immediate corollary of impermanence.

The human being is made up of matter (body) and mind. First, we will consider the body. The best way to do this is to look at the cell, which is the basic unit of life. The human body is made up of billions of cells, most of which are so tiny they can be seen only with a powerful microscope. Understanding what goes on inside the tiny cell is a fascinating way of understanding life. Let's do just that.

Within the cells, there is incessant bustling activity, which effectively makes each cell a stand-alone life. The cells absorb substances from outside. They burn fuels derived from food, generating energy, which in turn enables various body functions to be carried out. Then there is waste product elimination. The cells regenerate themselves through division. They synthesize complex substances. Hormones and enzymes, which control vital body functions, are made in the cells. It is the collective (and harmonious) "living together" of the billions of these "little lives" that give rise to what we refer to as the life of the individual. Thus the body is in constant flux.

Next, let's consider the mind, for which the platform of action is the rapid electro-chemical activity taking place in the multi-billion-cell (neuron) network of the brain. The changes taking place in the mind are infinitely faster than in the body. We all know how our thoughts change from one to another to another in never ending rapid succession. Since our emotions are primarily influenced by our thoughts (and to a relatively lesser degree by body conditions such as nutrition), our emotions are constantly being updated by the new experiences of each additional moment lived. Thus our minds too are in flux.

We can summarize this discussion by saying both mind and body are (and therefore the whole being is) subject to incessant change. Therefore both mind and body are made up of ever changing processes and not fixed entities, although the limitations of our senses create the illusion of permanency. *Therefore there is no permanent entity called the self or the ego.* This is the same observation that the Buddha made 2500 years ago. The difference is that we needed electron microscopes and other high tech support as well as combined efforts of thousands of scientists over many years to reach that conclusion. The Buddha, alone, and without the help of even one simple external adjunct, observed the same fact and further extended that to explain the truth (of life) with his profound philosophy. His extraordinary electron microscope was his fully enlightened, intuitive and deeply penetrating mind. However, it is comforting to know that today's science corroborates the Buddha's discovery of impermanence and no-self.

Although both science and Dhamma tell us that we should not realistically think of the mind-body combination (that is, the whole human being) as a non-changing entity even for a moment, in daily living we do. To start with, this is because our imperfect senses ask our minds to believe as reality what is 'seen' by the senses. Then, as we proceed to assign labels such as 'I', 'Me', 'Mine', 'Rex', 'You' and 'Patsy' to what is seen, we compound the error. Having assigned these arbitrary mental anchors (the labels), we live as though the 'I' or 'Rex' is a non-changing entity (that is, self). In reality, the only thing that does not change is *the label* 'I', or any other that we create in our minds. Thus we have created an illusion (not consciously, but through ignorance of reality and *worldly* necessity) of a non-existent permanent entity which we, as a species, have got used to calling the 'self' or 'I'.

So, when Patsy welcomes her husband Rex after a week away on a business trip, they think they are seeing the same spouse of a week ago. From the discussion on cells, we now know that in reality, it is a different Patsy and a different Rex, in both body and mind. To be precise, we can go further, and say that Rex who was entering the house is not the same as Rex who is now in the house.

(The preceding analysis pertained to the self because our interest is about life, distress and inner peace. However, it wouldn't take much to realize that a similar analysis would apply to everything else in the universe. Thus, the universally applicable insight should be 'no-entity' with 'no-self' being its specific application to life phenomena.)

Since the erroneous idea of an abiding self has existed from time immemorial, not only has it become ingrained in the mechanics of human communication but also is *essential* in society, primarily for communication. It will very likely continue to be so, as long as the human species exists on this planet.

It is no different from saying the "sun rises" and the "sun sets" giving the impression the sun moves around the earth. Just as a self *appears* to exist, to our sensory mechanism, the sun appears to rise and set. That appearance is what everyone believed to be also the truth up until 16th and 17th century astronomers such as Copernicus[20] and Galileo demonstrated that in reality it is the exact opposite that happens, i.e., the earth rotates on its own axis and moves around the sun. Thanks to these great minds, we now know that the sun neither rises nor sets though it continues to *appear* to our imperfect senses (and will appear for all time to come) that it does. It is the revolving movement of the earth on its axis that gives us the impression (illusion) that it is the sun that moves.

Unfortunately, the new understanding (of reality) as to which moves and which doesn't, still will not allow us to now change our ways of communication amongst fellow beings. That is due to two reasons: (1) the appearance continues and (2) the terminology has got too deeply ingrained over time. We will continue to say, "the sun rises", although it is based on illusion. We will continue to say "heartfelt[21]" when we know the reality is 'mindfelt' – the heart is just a pump whereas it is the mind that feels. Likewise, we will continue to use 'I' and related labels as we have done before.

The most profound healing begins on the day a person insightfully understands this thing called 'self' does not really exist (as a permanent entity). The most we can rightly say is that a self exists only for an *infinitesimal* moment in time, which of course is the same as saying that we are constantly changing. So we are back to *impermanence*, the primary law of the universe.

Science helps us to understand no-self thus: because, a certain grouping of cells works in harmony, there is a process, for example, that of breathing, but there is *no I* that is doing the breathing – echoing the words of the profound Dhamma quotation with which we started the chapter. Breathing is a natural process with no doer, no ownership. Similarly there is the feeling of sadness or happiness, but there is no 'I' that feels. There is dying, but no 'I' that dies.

---

[20] The first person to believe that the earth rotates on its own axis and revolves around the sun was the Greek astronomer Aristarchus of Samos (280 B.C.) but his thinking did not make any significant impact amongst others because of strongly held contrary beliefs based on the supernatural.

[21] This erroneous usage had it beginnings in the proclamation by the Greek philosopher Aristotle (384 – 322 B.C.) that the center of thinking and emotions is the heart.

As a person progresses in Dhamma practice, it is essential that he/she understands the truth of no-self without ambiguity, if the person is to experience the higher layers of inner peace that Dhamma offers. Once acquired, that understanding may initially be accompanied by a feeling that an enormous amount of one's life has been wasted trying to protect a self that did not, and does not exist in reality. That feeling will soon be replaced by a profound sense of relief, inner peace and true mental freedom as never before felt, upon realizing that the formidable burden of self has at last been unloaded from one's mind. That is a giant step taken on the Dhamma Way.

A person who has realized the truth of no-self in completeness, i.e., attained enlightenment, will still continue to use the 'self labels' to communicate with fellow beings who have not yet come upon that realization, because it is the only way they will understand worldly issues. Even the sentence "There is *no self* in *me*" seems contradictory, but it is not. The only way we can communicate in society is with sentences like this – we have no choice. Evolution of language has brought us to a point of no return; correcting the incongruity is not possible and we have to continue to accept and live with the problem. Even the Buddha, who based his teaching on the fact of no-self, faced the same problem to his last days and used the common terminology of self, as illustrated in this extract from the *Maha Parinibbana Sutta:* "*I* have now grown old and full of years. *My* journey is drawing to a close. *I* have now turned eighty years of age and am now reaching the sum of *my* days. Have *I* not often declared to *you* that it is the nature of things, ……………"

Once we have intellectually understood the concept of *no-self*, the mind still needs more work before the concept penetrates the deepest levels of one's psyche and uproots not only the core belief in the self, but also every other belief or behavior which was based on that core belief. This is realized by including contemplation of *no-self* in one's Insight Meditation practice and in daily living.

Having approached *no-self* from the angle of science, let's now briefly review a classical rebuttal of the belief in a self. An abiding self, capable of regulating our existence, should be able to ensure that our body and mind do things that we like. For example, if there is this self, and I have some abdominal pain, the self should be able to order and ensure that the pain ceases. Yet we know it cannot be done. Likewise, if a person feels depressed, the self should be able to order its cessation and replace it instantly with a feeling of joy. Again it cannot be done. Examples like these endlessly establish beyond any doubt the non-existence of a self.

Let's conclude this chapter with an analogy. It is 2 a.m. and Brian is having a dream. He sees his dearest brother drowning but cannot help him because Brian does not know how to swim. So in desperation he shouts for help. At that point his wife wakes him and says, "Brian, you had a nightmare. What did you see?"

Now awake, Brian realizes that it was all a dream – an illusion. There was no brother that drowned. There was no dear brother to be rescued.

In real life (to be more precise, 'worldly life' in contrast to 'transcendental life'), when we think of a self (ego), it is like thinking of that dearest brother in Brian's dream. Instead, now it is the 'dearest self'. We worry and 'sweat' through this worldly life thinking there is an all-important self that needs to be protected all the time. Often we think it is in trouble and frantically try to do things, day in and day out, to rescue it. If we can wake up from this long 'dream' of ours (worldly living), as the Buddha showed us, we will realize that there is no self to be protected or rescued at all. Then we will have all the life energy that we would have used to protect the non-existent self, freed to be channeled to useful and noble causes.

The *noble causes* are many and enough to keep all of us meaningfully busy during the balance of our lifetimes. The highest priority amongst these is to work towards perfecting one's own deliverance from existential distress. Following upon that are endless possibilities such as understanding and protecting nature, helping the needy through compassion and unconditional love and spreading the Dhamma so that others presently in darkness can realize inner peace.

Chapter Insights and Highlights

1) The primary factor that differentiates Dhamma from other philosophies of life (including religions) is the doctrine of no-self or egolessness *(anatta* in Pali).

2) Modern science corroborates the doctrine of no-self, for example via analysis of the human being down to its smallest building blocks of life (the cells and beyond).

3) To the imperfect senses it appears that there is a self. In reality, which is beyond human senses, there is no such self but mere

processes that arise and cease. The result for the human being is an existential dichotomy.

4) Since we need to use our senses for worldly survival, the dichotomy creates an ever-persistent conflict for the human mind resulting in distress.

5) The way out of the dilemma and distress is to:

- continue to communicate and interact with fellow beings using the self as we have no other choice,
- develop total awareness of (that is, insight into) the truth of no-self, and
- consistently integrate no-self into one's life.

6) Once we free the mind of the burden of self, there is an abundance of noble activities to which we can meaningfully direct our energies for the rest of our lives.

6

Focus on Distress

"Now this, monks, is the Noble Truth about dukkha. Birth is dukkha, sickness is dukkha, death is dukkha, likewise sorrow and grief, woe, lamentation and despair. To be conjoined with things we dislike, to be separated from things we like – that is also dukkha. Not to get what one wants, that also is dukkha. In a word, this body, this fivefold mass which is based on grasping, that is dukkha."

Samyutta Nikaya V

At the start, we need to resolve a word-problem relating to Pali-English translation. Various English words, such as *distress, stress*[22], *existential stress, existential angst, dissatisfaction, suffering,* and *unhappiness* have been used in English works on Buddhism as equivalent to the Pali term *dukkha*. Yet, as we can see from the all-encompassing definition in the ancient Buddhist scripture Samyutta Nikaya, none of these words deliver the full meaning that the word dukkha intends to convey.

The Random House Dictionary of the English Language includes the following descriptors for the word *distress*:

- Great pain, anxiety or sorrow; acute physical or mental suffering; affliction; trouble
- State of extreme necessity or misfortune
- That which causes pain, suffering, trouble, danger etc.

Comparing the Samyutta Nikaya definition of *dukkha* and the dictionary definition of *distress*, the latter word is as good as any available in the English language. Therefore, we will use the English word distress as though equivalent to the Pali dukkha, but implying the Samyutta Nikaya meaning.

---

[22] Due to its very widespread usage today, one may infer that *stress* (as a word in medical lexicon) has been in use for a long time. However, the term was coined only a haf-century ago (in 1956) by the world-renowned Canadian doctor Hans Selye, who conducted pioneering research into "adaptation syndrome". Selye borrowed the term from another discipline - engineering - where it had been in use for a longer term.

The theme of distress runs through the whole of the Buddha's teaching. After all, it is the First Noble Truth.   Accordingly, the reader will encounter throughout this book direct or indirect reference to this basic fact of existence, as well as means for its eradication based on the teachings of the All Enlightened One. In this chapter, we will review the salient points of the subject, only briefly mentioning those covered in greater detail elsewhere.

A closer examination of the Samyutta Nikaya definition reveals that distress falls into two categories – physical and mental. Let's first discuss these in some detail.

(a) Physical Distress

The most common manifestation of physical distress is as *pain* resulting from injury, sickness, hunger or thirst. Pain is a physiological mechanism and exists to serve a purpose in beings. That is, to alert the mind to a need for attention somewhere in the body. So pain is something that cannot, and should not, be totally eliminated from the body. Pain can be temporarily relieved with painkillers or Calming Meditation (*Samatha* in Pali)[23]. The other manifestations of physical distress are the general deterioration of the body and death, which may be postponed a little using healthcare, but which cannot be eliminated. So there is little we can do to alter the course of physical distress.

The important message here is that we need to *learn to accept most physical distress as an inevitable part of existence.*   After such acceptance, in some situations we could proceed to take action to alleviate or postpone the physical distress, where such action is possible and desirable. For example, if we have an injury, we can initiate action to have the damage repaired, but we cannot totally prevent the body from being vulnerable to injury in the future.

To the extent that physical distress is the disturbance of the status quo, we could say that physical distress is inherent in the inanimate universe too. This depends on the finer meaning we wish to attach to 'physical distress'. Viewed thus, physical distress merges into the meaning of

---

[23] The original Pali term *Samatha* has been rendered in English as Meditation of Concentration in some writings. However, we prefer the term Calming Meditation because the net result of the practice is calming of the mind by drastically reducing, from six to one, the sensory load (input) imposed on the mind. This is clarified in Chapter 12: *Calming the Mind.*

impermanence itself. Then we can say that physical distress (disturbance of the status quo) is inherent in the whole universe.

(b) Mental Distress

Most of our distress is mental and arises from the way we view (a) objects and events, that is, the external world through our senses and (b) imagined things, that is, all within our internal world. Except for the fully enlightened beings such as the Buddha, we all have mental distress, differing in degree and flavor from individual to individual.

First let's discuss in some detail how *the way we view objects and events* brings about our mental distress.

The first point to be covered in our discussion is the way we *view* physical distress. As noted earlier, if we learn to accept physical distress as an inevitable part of our existence, we have just physical distress and it stops at that. However, if we superimpose wrong thinking on physical distress, then our distress is unnecessarily amplified and we suffer more than we have to. This willful addition of mental distress to our physical distress is the reason why our existence becomes unbearable at times.

For example, let's say that Alicia feels a lower back pain. The nature of her distress can be one of two types depending on the way she reacts:

(1) Alicia accepts the pain as physical distress, knowing that the pain is present to alert her to something needing attention, so she seeks medical intervention. So far she has dealt with her physical distress rationally.

(2) Or, the moment Alicia feels the pain, she can jump to the conclusion that it is a slipped disk and imagine many other frightful thoughts beyond that, such as eventual nerve damage and partial paralysis in the future. Then *she has superimposed* mental distress on her actual physical distress and she will suffer much more than she really should.

When the medical reports are in, they may reveal the pain was due to a muscular strain or other minor condition that will heal over a short period of time – this, Alicia will handle objectively. On the other hand, the reports may reveal that in fact it is a slipped disk. At this stage, again her distress can take the route of one of the two types as before:

(1) If Alicia has trained herself to accept things as they really are, which is the outcome of intensive Insight Meditation (Chapters 13 and 14), she will be capable of first accepting a slipped disk as physical distress. Then she can proceed to take action, i.e., obtain whatever help is available to make the best of the situation. This is easier said than done and very few of us are trained to possess such nonchalant and stoic composure. Yet it's good for us to know the possibilities and Dhamma shows us how to (gradually) develop that mental strength. The dedication and effort one puts in to developing such mental capability, even if not perfected, will bestow significant benefits on the individual. Furthermore, it is prudent to embark on developing such capabilities *before* negative eventualities confront us, as mastery takes time.

(2) Or, Alicia can imagine all kinds of horrible things that follow a slipped disk and superimpose immense mental distress on the reality of the physical distress of the slipped disk.

So whether this whole situation will result in only physical distress or physical distress *and* mental distress will be determined by Alicia's mental attitude to things. The good news for all of us worldlings is that our mental attitude is something that we can gradually train to be in harmony with reality, using Insight Meditation.

Besides superimposing mental distress on physical distress, we humans often have a tendency to do the same over objects and events of the world in general and again cause unnecessary distress. An example would be how we perceive the existential hardships of a loved one. Later on we will look at some examples in detail as to how *the way we view objects and events* brings about mental distress.

Next let's consider how *the way we view imagined things* causes mental distress.

A thought suddenly arising from memory, with absolutely no physical association, can trigger an erroneous thinking pattern and cause us undue distress. For example, without examining the real likelihood of it happening, we can imagine such things as a terminal illness or loss of one's residence to fire and thereby trigger further thoughts that will cause undue distress. To be secure in the knowledge that if we do face these tragedies, we will handle them with equanimity, is the Dhamma way.

Now that we have discussed in general the two types of distress – physical and mental – let's review some features of distress that may provide us with some insights to ease the burden of having to live with distress.

Distress is universal – this is perhaps the first thing we need to realize. From the Samyutta Nikaya definition, it is easy to see there are many forms that distress can take. Though not all of them will comprise the distress of any one individual at a given time, distress is part of living for all *worldly* beings, just as breathing is. It is only when we have transcended worldly living that we will have transcended (mental) distress. Birth, sickness and death form a common denominator for all beings. So, while we are youthful and healthy, we may encounter few of the manifestations of distress, but it is only a matter of time before other forms confront us. In spite of all our technological and other advances, the fundamental distress that confronts us remains the same as it has always been, including in the Buddha's lifetime.

While one could easily accept sickness and death as distress, the question may be asked why birth is distress – after all, we are used to associating childhood with joy and happiness. The answer becomes abundantly clear if we look at these undeniable *facts*. (1) To start with, a child enters this world with a cry of pain at birth. (2) All other distress happens because one is born – if there is no birth[24], there is no distress. (3) Childhood is not all happiness but a mix of happiness and unhappiness. A child plays at the park and giggles with joy; the child also falls down, bruises himself/herself and cries. Children become sick, as do adults. However, all things considered, we can say that there is usually less mental distress in childhood than during other stages of life. (4) Childhood is impermanent – it becomes only a matter of time before the child moves into youth, old age and death with the attendant distresses.

Dhamma is based on absolute reality (truth) which causes initial discomfort in us because we are used to living in a world of relative reality or illusion. (Note: we will discuss absolute and relative realities in detail in later chapters). Why are we distressed? Because we don't know the truth. Therefore, if we want to transcend distress we should be prepared to face the truth, even if we have to endure some discomfort

---

[24] If birth and existence are laden with distress, one is likely to ask (a) Should people avoid having children and (b) Does Dhamma advocate suicide? The answer to both is 'no' and follow from the Buddhist teaching of *kamma* and rebirth. (a) The primary determinant of birth is the residual kamma of the one to be born and not of the future parents. (b) If one commits suicide, when he /she is reborn to pay back residual kamma, one will have the added burden of compensating the action of killing, in this case, oneself.

initially. Then, with time the discomfort gives way to a level of comfort and peace (based on truth) that we have not experienced before.

Therapy for distress is to train ourselves to acknowledge its existence but not own it.   This becomes obvious when we recall and deeply contemplate on (1) the fact of no-self and (2) the profound words of *The Path of Purification* quoted earlier "Mere suffering exists, no sufferer is found..."

Happiness always carries <u>latent</u> distress.   Due to the operation of the primary law of impermanence, with time what is now happiness will change to a state of distress, either as a direct manifestation now or as a latency to surface later. So there is always latent distress in worldly living. For example, I could be having an adorable pet dog now and enjoying its company. However, it is only a matter of time before the dog and I have to part company and then the present joy changes to distress. Another example is praise and blame. If we become happy in response to praise, it's just a matter of time before we become unhappy because praise is not forever and often changes places with blame.

Impermanence exists regardless of a perceiver. Impermanence viewed by a perceiver in a certain manner becomes mental distress.   Though every object or event in this universe is a manifestation of the primal cosmic law of impermanence, it inherently does not contain the property of mental distress. Impermanence is a neutral phenomenon in the universe at large. It is only when a perceiver interprets any manifestation of impermanence through ingrained views that are not in touch with reality (wrong views) that it turns into mental distress. It is like clear water in a lake that's neutral in color. However, if we look at the water through colored eyeglasses, the water too appears colored. So, to emphasize, any manifestation needs two conditions for it to be perceived as mental distress: (a) a perceiver and (b) wrong views through which the perceiver sees the manifestation.

In a way, we can say that we perceivers 'intrude' into manifestations of impermanence with our senses and thereafter view that manifestation with wrong views, thereby causing mental distress for ourselves. That is, sensory intrusions combined with wrong thinking cause mental distress. For example, I *see* rain (intrusion with my sight), then think, "What a lousy day it is" and I feel depressed (mental distress). Or, I *hear* the neighbor's dog bark (intrusion with my hearing), wish it didn't bark (wrong, futile thinking) and get angry (mental distress). So the way out would be to avoid sensory contact (which is not always possible) or change the way we view the manifestation to one that is in touch with reality (replace ignorance with wisdom). The latter always works, though it takes time to penetrate our lives. Thus, in our examples, we can learn to accept both the rain and the barking of the dogs as just the way things are at the moment and thereby alleviate our mental distress. The important message here is this: *if we train our mind to enable us to accept the things of the world we cannot change, then we can live in harmony with the world, and realize inner peace.* In contrast, if the mind is averse to a world not under our power to change, then we continue to suffer.

Our accustomed way is not to see impermanence (change) as such, but to interpret it as mental distress. This is primarily caused by the underlying wish in us for things that we like to remain as they are – the ego, our youth, good health, dear ones and so on. We do not like to see things change. To that extent, mental distress is inherent in unenlightened *human* existence, caused by our attachments. Hence Dhamma lists distress as one of the basic facts of existence – that is, *worldly* existence. Dhamma teaching shows us the transcendental way, that is, to see and accept impermanence as impermanence without aversion. Thus, whatever aspect of Dhamma we approach, we encounter the recurring emphasis to change our erroneous views (see things as they really are) in order to eradicate distress. Once we accept impermanence as impermanence and do not add our own coloring to it in interpretation, we have wisdom instead of ignorance and we are on our way to peace here and beyond. This point being of critical importance to our healing let's look at a few examples to help us solidify this principle in our minds.

In countries that experience the four seasons, generally people are happy when they see signs of spring and are overjoyed when summer arrives. In contrast, with the onset of fall, their moods wane and finally when winter arrives they are sad.

Now imagine that due to some cause, we the perceivers suddenly cease to exist on the planet. Will the seasonal changes – spring to summer to fall to winter – continue to happen? Of course! In fact, year after year. And that occurrence is caused by impermanence – the fact the sun and the planets don't stay in one place but are subject to constant change of position. Impermanence exists and continues to exist stubbornly and aloof, as a cosmic principle, whether we perceivers are there or not to interpret it as distress. Thus, to be precise, 'suffering' or 'distress' is a concept only in thinking beings.

So if we deeply accept the fact that the change in seasons (particularly onset of fall and winter) is exactly the way it is supposed to be, and not wish it to be otherwise, then we would have transcended our worldly (erroneous) way of thinking. With that, we would have transcended distress on this issue and we would be on our way to better moods and contentment in wintertime.

For the next example, consider the death of a loved one. This is something that we all have to face, some time or another in our lives. This, like the change of seasons, is a fact of nature dictated by impermanence and there is nothing we can do about it – what is born has to die. This natural event, when it happens, is usually transformed into one of much distress, in the minds of those still living. This is due to ignorance resulting in non-acceptance of impermanence of human existence and attachment to things. The remedy is to include the subject of impermanence in our daily meditation and practice it over a reasonable period of time. Then our minds will get conditioned to accept the reality of death and help us cope, with much less distress when the inevitable events do confront us.

For the third example, take the case of our feelings in general. Feelings shuttle between pleasant and unpleasant from time to time within a day and from day to day. This is due to (a) changes taking place in objects and events in the world around us, (b) the operation of our sensory mechanisms and (c) neuro-chemical activity in our brains primarily relating to the processing of sensory input. We create distress when we wish our pleasant feelings to stay (clinging) and the unpleasant feeling to vanish (aversion). However if we train ourselves to accept that both pleasant and unpleasant feelings are caused by impermanence and that whatever feeling we have will not stay the same for long, we will have alleviated a lot of distress in our lives.

With the focus on distress, Dhamma teaching starts with a realistic view of human existence. A common question that Buddhists are asked is: Since Dhamma refers to distress often, doesn't it teach a pessimistic world view? A simple and straight answer can be given in two parts. (1) Dhamma teaching is neither pessimistic nor optimistic but realistic – it pivots on truth and truth only. (2) While Dhamma starts off describing distress (because that is a fact of life), its lasting gift to humankind is a method (The Noble Eightfold Path) for the *eradication* of distress. In the Buddha's own words: "Not only the fact of suffering (distress) do I teach, but also the deliverance."[25] It is no different from a doctor first

---

[25] Anguttara Nikaya

telling a patient that he has a viral infection, and then that he will prescribe the medicine to cure it. It was not pessimism on the doctor's part to first tell the patient about his problem. Likewise, the Buddha has effectively told us all "You have distress. I will give you a prescription to cure it." There is absolutely no pessimism in that disclosure of truth and cure.

As a simple example to illustrate the above, take the case of aging. The usual worldly approach is to view aging with negativity – with pessimism. As opposed to that, some current 'optimistic' approaches are based on training adults to enact some desirable aspect of childhood that was missed in real childhood. This approach, although it may produce some transient mental benefits, is bound to fail eventually, because as a person gets older, the imaginary enactment of aspects of childhood becomes more and more impractical and finally impossible, creating a worsening dilemma with the passage of time.

The realistic approach of Dhamma views both birth and old age, as well as all stages in-between, as *equal* parts that constitute one process. That process is *existence,* laden with distress and Dhamma further proceeds to show how the distress can be eradicated. The focus is distress and its eradication and not age or age groups. Thus, old age is neither superior nor inferior to birth and childhood and vice versa. This is a stable and solid view for people in all phases of life to adopt   because it is based on absolute truth, instead of trying to mentally (and artificially) recreate a phase of life that is past and gone forever.

The root cause of distress is wrong views (erroneous thinking). Thinking (wrongly) is mental distress. Hence, meditation, which is the core of Dhamma is directed at changing our thinking from the accustomed, conditioned and erroneous ways to one of transcendental thinking ('seeing things as they really are'). Calming Meditation calms the mind by helping it to focus on a simple object such as one's breath and thereby bringing thinking to a virtual *stop* during meditation.

Once a person has mastered a reasonable degree of skill and confidence in Calming Meditation, one can proceed to Insight Meditation, where the (now-tamed) mind is willfully directed to see things as they really are, thus eradicating mental distress created by the earlier distorted perception. To see things as they really are, one trains to observe the impermanent and no-self nature of all things. That insight eventually helps to eradicate the attendant distress of *worldly* living. We will cover meditation in detail in upcoming chapters.

Distress is our principal teacher. When we deeply contemplate the truth of worldly existence and that it is laden with distress, that realization becomes our first step on the path of deliverance. It's like the discovery of a tumor, which is the first step that leads to its removal. The Buddha called the discovery that enables us to effectively say, "Aha! This existence is laden with distress" the First Noble Truth. So, distress is our principal teacher in disguise.

Rather than developing an aversion to distress, or wanting to run away from it, we need to learn to accept it and work with it. Distress is an opportunity for profound spiritual growth, provided we view it as such. In fact, often it turns out that extraordinary distress creates extraordinary opportunities, because it distils our essence and makes us look reality in the eye. The person, who utilizes his/her will to capitalize on such extraordinary opportunities, will see one's enlightenment process accelerated.

Chapter Insights and Highlights

1. Distress, according to Dhamma teaching, is one of the three fundamental facts of existence and can be subdivided into physical distress and mental distress.

2. Physical distress, most times, is inevitable. Therefore we need to train ourselves to accept it.

3. Mental distress can be alleviated, and eventually be completely overcome, by practicing meditation.

4. Some other characteristics of distress are:
   - It is universal
   - It is our principal teacher in disguise
   - We need to acknowledge its existence, but not own it.
   - Happiness always carries latent distress.
   - Impermanence transforms into distress when viewed by a perceiver in an erroneous manner.

7

Our Sensory World

Who is free from sense perceptions
In him no more bonds exist;
Who by insight freedom gains
All delusions cease in him;

But who clings to sense perceptions
And to viewpoints wrong and false
He lives wrangling in this world.

Sutta Nipata, Verse 847

Let us imagine for a moment that all our senses (sight, hearing, etc.) are disabled. Then, the world perceived by us immediately ceases to exist, even if all our other organs (such as the heart) and functions (such as blood circulation) are intact. Thus, the very foundation of our perceived existence – the 'world out there' and 'me' witnessing that world – is made possible by our senses, though, collectively the sensory mechanisms comprise a very small proportion of the human body. In fact, the most profound and significant teaching of the Buddha – that of Dependent Origination[26] – is formulated around our sensory system and not the rest of the body. Hence, to obtain a meaningful insight into Dhamma, we need to equip ourselves with at least a minimal understanding of our senses.

There are six senses in all. Of these, five are easily evident to us – they are sight, hearing, taste, smell and touch. Before we try to identify the sixth, let's take one of the five senses and get a glimpse into the sensory process by walking through the important events of that process from beginning to end. We will take the sense of sight for our illustration. First, let's try to understand the mechanics that help us see things. Consider light falling on a certain object ahead of us. The light rays reflected from this object enter our eyes and form an image on the retina. Then electrical (nerve) impulses carry information about the image from the retina to the part of the brain dedicated to the function of sight. From

---

[26] *Paticcasamuppada* in Pali

information received about this specific image, and by matching this information against existing data, the central processing part of the mind makes a series of quick associations at 'lightning' speed, aided by additional visual interactions with the object to gather supplementary information. All this happens with extreme rapidity.

We will now get an idea of the process of associations and their sequence, by looking at what is happening, in 'slow motion', or rather, as converted to the equivalent of a 'slide show'. Note that in real life the perceiver (we will call him Bertram) is unaware of the individual 'slides' because of the immense speed – he sees only the 'movie' and not the 'slide show'.

The first association is objective and close to reality – simply of form, movement and color and corresponds to what is referred to as the 'bare object' in meditation. This is the unadulterated view of the object. As we progress from this point on, the mental associations become more and more subjective (and judgmental). The events in the sequence are many; we will select only a few that are important for our discussion. In our present example, these associations (as perceived by Bertram) may be like this:

1.   It is an object, white, moving.
2.   It is a man.
3.   It is Cousin David.
4.   David is selfish, mean and obnoxious and he has never spoken a good word to me.
5.   I always end up in a confrontation with him.
6.   I hate David, the village bully.

Thus, it is easy to see how something that started as a simple sensory trigger (in this case sight of a moving form) eventually leads to the subjective reaction of hatred or aversion as it passes through, and is evaluated against, layers of existing data in Bertram's mind. In another case[27], the sequence of the 'slide show' as 'seen' by Bertram may be (1) It is food (2) The food is peach ice cream (3) Peach ice cream is delicious and (4) I want to eat peach ice cream (although I just finished eating a dessert of pudding!). Here Bertram ends up with craving.

The same kind of processing applies to the other senses – hearing, smell, taste and touch. In fact, each and every one of the innumerable sensory

---

[27] We will use the same examples to illustrate and clarify a number of other points as we progress through the book.

interactions we experience in a day passes through this process resulting in either aversion or craving.

The key points to note are:

(a) the five sensory contacts bring information about the world around us into our brain (we could use the term 'mind' in place of 'brain' as the process moves into the subjective phase),

(b) the mind processes that information,

(c) it compares this information to existing data, i.e. views, concepts, images etc. already rooted in the mind (from previous experiences),

(d) the mind makes judgements/conclusions about the object or event, and

(e) craving or aversion follows, and hence feelings. In passing, it is important at this point to recall (from Chapter 1) that first our thinking happens and *then* our feeling (of either distress or happiness).

Now what is the sixth sense? It is part of the mind itself – to be precise, the mind's storage area that feeds a triggering thought to its information processing area. The triggering thought in this case becomes the 'sensory' input, although it is not from a true sensory mechanism with physical parts and, more importantly, this sense does not interact with the external world. If you like, you may think of it as connecting to an 'internal' world, which is all within the mind. Let's consider an example to clarify and illustrate the sixth sense again with Bertram as the perceiver.

He is seated at the beach with his eyes closed. Suddenly a picture or thought of the peach ice cream arises in his mind – this is the 'sensory' trigger. Once the trigger is made, the processing is identical to the earlier example (where peach ice cream was actually sighted) and ends in craving. Likewise, a triggering thought about Cousin David may suddenly arise in Bertam's mind and as before he ends up with aversion, although this time Cousin David may be miles away. Thus, for craving or aversion to occur, we do not necessarily have to receive input from the world outside through the five senses that have physical appearances (eye, ear etc.), but they can be generated from within the mind itself – simply through imagination. In fact, if we look at all six senses together, the most important sense is the sixth – mental image. This is because we happen to cause more distress in ourselves through imaginations, than through the senses of sight, sound, taste, smell and touch.

We know the mind at times finds it difficult to cope with the incessant overloading of information by the six senses, often in competition, all seeking attention. When a person is really unable to cope with this overload, then it results in confusion and agitation, which is the starting point of many mental disorders.

The six senses may be compared to six[28] hyperactive tentacles of an octopus, all of which, in competition, are endlessly bringing in their collections to the octopus's body. Another analogy would be six rambunctious children who are driving their mother crazy. The Buddha compared this problem created by the six senses to a cow skinned alive. Flies settle on the bare body of the animal irritating (confusing) it endlessly, just as the information arriving via the six senses confuses the mind. The technique for overcoming this confusion is meditation.

Our eyes are designed to see continuity as permanency (the 'movie') and not impermanence (the 'slide show'). We see a tree today, and tomorrow we see the same tree, because our eyes cannot see the incessant cellular activity (change) that is taking place inside that tree. So the tree *appears* to us as a solid entity. The same applies to our other senses. This apparent continuity is then another 'reason' that supports our erroneous belief in an abiding self when there is no such thing.

Our senses are extremely limited in what they can do – for example, visible light is radiation that enables us to see, but it occupies a very small (relatively negligible) part of the total electromagnetic spectrum.[29] The rest of the spectrum can be 'sensed' and used only by instruments and machinery that belong to such technologies as radio, TV, microwave and X-rays. Nature has designed (and evolved) our senses for survival and not for us to see reality. Nature does not care whether we see reality or not, or for that matter, whether we suffer or not. So we have to consciously *transcend* our senses to see reality. Hence the need for meditation, which is a technique invented by human beings to get around the inherent handicap of sensory limitation that prevents us from perceiving reality.

The inherent limitations of our senses should caution us to be very careful when we try to impose on others as truth or reality our views, which are

---

[28] In passing, note that a real octopus has eight tentacles, but this is irrelevant to our analogy.
[29] The electromagnetic spectrum is zero to 10^{22} hertz which is an enormous span by any standards and visible light occupies less than a millionth of the spectrum. We will cover the electromagnetic spectrum in greater detail in later chapters.

based on our sensory observations. The same applies when we are at the receiving end of others' views. There is a lot going on in the universe that our senses cannot perceive and it takes humility to admit this. What we can know of this universe with our senses is truly negligible – a mere 'drop in the ocean' compared to what lies outside the grasp of the senses. We cannot discard possibilities outside our sensory detection as untrue. Of what we do not have the power to know (and that's a lot), it would be only prudent and realistic to say "maybe" and leave it at that.

The great physicist and mathematician, Sir Isaac Newton, displayed both wisdom and humility when he said: "I do not know what I may appear to the world, but to myself I seem to have been only a boy playing on the sea-shore, and diverting myself in now and then finding a smoother pebble or a prettier shell than ordinary, whilst the great ocean of truth lay all undiscovered before me."

Earlier, we saw how the six senses lead to craving or aversion. But why is craving or aversion the major existential 'sin'? For the answer let's look at an analogy.

Step outdoors at night and watch the activity around an intense light or flame. Insects such as moths and beetles head towards the source of light only to meet with suffering – to be roasted to death. Why do they move towards their destroyer? It's because the sensory interaction with the flame brings about a feeling of pleasure. The transient pleasure gives rise to craving, the insect is attracted to the object and it moves to its destruction. Thus, the transient pleasure is an illusion of permanent pleasure - a bait which succeeds in deceiving the insect.

The human predicament is identical to that of the insect, except for one very important difference. We humans are equipped with the power to think (to develop *wisdom*), if we care to use that capability, whereas that insect, lacking that capability, remains in *ignorance* and is doomed to move towards its own destruction. From the viewpoint of the paradox of basic existence, we are just 'moths given the ability to think' and therefore to realize the consequences of our actions. Unfortunately, it is a fact of humanity that we, in this worldly existence, let craving and aversion guide the course of our lives, fooled by the bait of transient pleasure and, like the ignorant moth, move towards our own demise, which awaits us at the end of that transient happiness.

Therefore, moving from ignorance to wisdom becomes our savior, and follows from link number one of Dependent Origination. A complete description of Dependent Origination and a thorough examination of its implications are obviously beyond the scope of this book[30]. Hence we will restrict ourselves to drawing out a formula from it to show us, in simple and practical terms, how we may apply it to resolve our day-to-day problems.

The doctrine of Dependent Origination explains the ramifications of existence of beings, the distress within that existence and how to bring about a cessation of that distress. It is based on the universal and scientific principle of cause and effect[31]. Its pivotal building block is a chain of twelve cause-effect links and is usually explained in terms of three consecutive lifetimes. However, a selection of the links can be used to explain every *individual event* that takes place within one lifetime – most importantly, this life of ours. We will restrict our present investigation to that.

A selection of the twelve links suffices in practical daily living because some of the links are primarily of theoretical interest. Thus, just as we can ignore the wiring and say the operation of a switch causes a light bulb to light, we can extract the practical portion of Dependent Origination:

(1) **Ignorance** causes Reaction to occur
(2) **Reaction** causes Sensory Contact to occur
(3) **Sensory Contact*** causes Craving** to occur
(4) **Craving** causes Clinging (attachment) to occur
(5) **Clinging (Attachment)** causes *distress* to occur

[* Here sensory contact does not imply physical contact as in touch, but the establishment of 'mental contact' wherein the three factors object, sense-faculty (also called sense-door or sense-base) and the mind jointly participate in the process of 'contact'.

Also note, in passing for now, that of the 12 steps of Dependent Origination the only step that involves a connection with the outer world is *Sensory Contact*. This is because, of the above-mentioned three factors, the *object* is in the outer world.

---

[30] Those interested in a deeper study of this doctrine are invited to consult "The Great Discourse on Causation. The *Mahanidana Sutta and Its Commentaries*" translated from the Pali by Bhikku Bodhi and published by the Buddhist Publication Society, 1983.
[31] The principle of cause and effect is discussed in detail in the next chapter, under the title 'Tolerance and Action'.

** Note that aversion too is usually considered a *craving* – craving for the non-existence of something.]

This simplified formula of Dependent Origination reveals two important insights into what we can do to eradicate distress:

(a) Eradication of Ignorance (primarily ignorance of the fact there is no-self) causes all the other links to cease and therefore eradicates distress for good. As we know, this takes time.

(b) Since ignorance is the root cause, even if we can sever any of the links 2 to 5, distress will be curtailed only temporarily. This is because ignorance will recreate links 2 to 5 (just as a tree pruned to the level of trunk just above its roots will eventually cause branches and leaves to reappear). Yet, this capability to willfully avoid or curtail our reactions, sensory contacts, craving and clinging gives us *temporary* relief from distress, while we are working to eradicate the root cause, that is, deep-rooted ignorance.

Our whole life is an enormous collection of individual events. Therefore, eradication of distress from our life requires the eradication of distress from each individual event lived through and experienced from moment to moment. Thus, Bertram's encounter with Cousin David was one of those events in Bertram's life and distress arose within Bertram due to the anger, anxiety and tension he created within himself by the way he thought about, and perceived Cousin David. So to get help from Dependent Origination as discussed above, the following actions are available to Bertram:

- For temporary relief he can: (1) *not react* to David's ways, for example, not talk back when David is obnoxious towards him, (2) go for a walk when David visits (*avoiding sensory contact of hearing and sight*), (3) go into a quiet place and do some breathing meditation (*avoiding 'sensory contact' of mental triggers*) and (4) remind himself that aversion is an unwholesome action.

- For lasting relief Bertram has to carefully identify which deep-rooted views have caused him to dislike Cousin David. Dhamma teaching shows clearly that the very fact he has an aversion towards Cousin David (and suffered), indicates he does harbor a set of basic wrong views that caused his averse perception of David.   We will pursue this aspect further in Chapters 13 and 14.

Dependent Origination applies to any and all of our life situations as in this simple example – it explains the problems and provides the solutions. As we can see, the replacement of basic wrong views with the corresponding right views becomes the crucial part of Dhamma practice. Specifics of how this is done, and what are wrong views and their corresponding right views, are provided in later chapters. For now, it is suffice to say that it is achieved through a *deep understanding:*

1.   Of impermanence and no-self and important corollaries that follow from them, solidified with the help of the practice of Insight Meditation.

2.   Of the knowledge that (a) our reaction to situations, objects and events leads to craving/aversion and (b) craving/aversion leads to our destruction, as it did for the moth.

Replacing wrong views with the corresponding right views for this one event is an example of moving from ignorance to wisdom for this *one event.* If we do likewise for all other events in our lives (the task becoming easier as our practice gathers momentum), then it becomes a *life* of wisdom – hence the vehicle to inner peace.

Chapter Insights and Highlights

1.   Knowledge of the sensory system is essential to an informed understanding of our existential distress and the means to its eradication.

2.   The six senses are sight, hearing, taste, smell, touch and mental trigger. The first five have physical organs (e.g., eye) and the last is an attribute of the mind with no physical organ.

3.   The profound doctrine of the Buddha called the Dependent Origination is formulated pivotally around the sensory process. Ignoring from the 12-link cyclic chain of Dependent Origination steps that are of academic interest, the linkage that is helpful in practice may be summarized as:

Ignorance → Reaction → Sensory Contact → Craving →
→ Clinging (Attachment) → Distress
(The symbol → stands for 'causes the occurrence of')

4. The process of Dependent Origination (including the component sensory process) takes place at immense speed and leads to craving for what is sensed and therefore to distress.

5. Temporary relief from distress can be realized by avoiding sensory contact, such as walking away from an object when sight and hearing are the triggers associated with the distress. Calming Meditation also helps.

6. Lasting relief can be realized by replacing ignorance with wisdom, that is, with Insight Meditation.

8

Tolerance and Action
(*Karma*)

"Undisturbed shall our minds remain, no evil words shall escape our lips; friendly and full of sympathy shall we remain, with heart full of love, and free from any hidden malice; and that person shall we penetrate with loving thoughts, wide, deep, boundless, freed from anger and hatred."

The Buddha (From the Majhima-Nikaya, No. 21)

"When a man has something to do, let him do it with all his might."

The Buddha (From the Dhammapada 313)

The doctrine of *karma* is one of the cornerstones of Buddhist teaching and its understanding is therefore essential to the proper practice of Dhamma. *Karma*[32] in Sanskrit (and *kamma* in Pali) means 'volitional (willed) action'. The most important aspect of volitional action, within the context of the doctrine, is its ability to produce results *(karmic results*[33]*)* that correspond to the moral nature of the deed. A key determinant of the moral nature is the *intention* contained in the volition. If the intention is wholesome the karmic result is wholesome. If the intention is unwholesome the karmic result is unwholesome. Thus the teaching of karma may be viewed as a doctrine of moral retribution.

Due to the inherent difficulty in understanding ramifications of moral retribution in detail, karma and its result applicable to beings is sometimes compared to cause and effect applicable to the physical universe, a concept to which we can easier relate. For the purposes of our discussion, we will follow that route, equating karma (volitional action) to cause and karmic result to effect. Once we add the factor of *intention* to the former, we have a reasonable equivalent.

---

[32] We have opted to use the Sanskrit word in the text because of its familiarity in today's world.

[33] *Vipaka* in Pali

'Cause produces effect' is a fundamental law of nature and easy to understand. If I do not eat healthy food, exercise and manage my stress (cause), then my health deteriorates (effect). Strictly speaking, what is usually at work is the collective action of multiple causes rather than a single cause and it is best to clarify this point first.

If we investigate thoroughly to determine what caused an event, we find one conspicuous cause and a number of relatively less apparent (supplementary) causes at play that collectively brought about the event. To illustrate let's take the case of a bonfire. We would usually be quick to say that fuel (firewood) is the cause of the existence of the bonfire. But if we contemplate for a while, we will identify other conditions such as oxygen (air) supply and dryness as essential for the fire to exist. Thus if we cut off the air supply by covering the fire with a large basin, the fire will die. It will also die if the dryness ceases due to rain.

We may call all these factors – firewood, air supply and dryness – *causes* or *conditions*. Alternatively, we may call the firewood (the conspicuous factor) the 'cause' and the other factors 'conditions' – this seems to be the common usage. Without getting any further entangled in the choice of English translations of Pali words, we will proceed with the essence of our discussion agreeing to use either word *(condition* or *cause)* depending on the best interests of context[34]. Words aside, what is important is that we should not lose sight of the principle that phenomena (things and events) arise because of prior conditions (causes). This principle is usually referred to as conditionality or causality. This is also the pivotal principle on which the Buddha's profound doctrine of Dependent Origination[35] is based.

Besides the fact that things happen due to multiple causes, another important conclusion of this principle is that there is no *'first* cause', or *the* cause, or the *only* cause for anything. Thus the bonfire we referred to above exists because of a set of immediately preceding conditions. Now if we take just one of those conditions, say the firewood, we know that it

---

[34] In discussing Buddhism, one of the common pitfalls one can get entrapped in is in the use of English words to represent the original Pali (or Sanskrit) terms. We have already seen a good example of this in the case of the Pali word *dukkha*. There is usually a tendency to cling to particular English words as 'gospel' simply because they have been already used elsewhere. That is a vain exercise if it degrades the intended meaning. Throughout this book, we will bypass that tendency by placing emphasis on conveying a clear and accurate message in context rather than rigidly cling to familiar words, unless a familiar word does help to convey the intended meaning.

[35] Dependent Origination was discussed earlier in Chapter 7: Our Sensory World.

exists because of a tree. This chain extends backward endlessly in time creating a maze of unfathomable complexity.

One important lesson that we can learn from this discussion on causality is that when it comes to dislikable events in our lives, it would be erroneous for us to blame immediate apparent causes. An example is to judge a blunder made by a family member as *the* cause of an unpleasant event. The reality is that it is one of a myriad of causes, though it may happen to be the closest to the event.

Now let's return to our discussion on karma. Divide karma into past and present and the essence of Buddhist teaching on karma shines through, as the sunlight beams through parting clouds.

Past karma and results, applied to human life, is the cause-effect chain up to this present moment. The facts about past karma and results are:

- They cannot be changed.
- They contribute to making each one of us (6 billion human beings) unique, and also each moment within one individual's life unique compared to every other moment of his or her life, as one progresses on one's karmic path.

What the above two facts clearly tell us is that, if our lives are at all to be rational and sane, we must totally and gracefully accept what has happened, that is, we must show *tolerance* towards what is. This is why Dhamma emphasizes "acceptance of the way things are" as an integral part of its teaching. This means a person accepts oneself, other human beings and all of nature for what has been, and what is, without judgement and without wishing that things should have been, and should now be, different. It also means we do not blame any person, event or nature for what has been and what is now. Here, to quote the Dhammapada (#50): "Let none find fault with others; let none see the omissions and commissions of others. But let one see one's own acts, done and undone". (To "see one's own acts" does not mean *blame* oneself, but be aware of one's own action.)

Tolerance is not a quality that can be developed directly but is a by-product of the deep understanding of, firstly, the uniqueness of all living beings and all things that make up this universe and, secondly, their right to that uniqueness. This understanding leads to acceptance and acceptance leads to tolerance. Thus, the practical means to acquiring the quality of tolerance is to insightfully understand the uniqueness of ourselves and of everything else in the world around us.

As did many other great thinkers and teachers, the Stoic Philosopher Epictetus echoed in summary (five hundred years after the Buddha) the Buddha's emphasis on the need for acceptance with these profound words: "True instruction is this: *To learn to wish that everything should come to pass exactly as it does*". The Buddha's advice on acceptance and tolerance surfaces in many of his teachings and nothing could be more appropriate for realignment of relationships – personal, social and regional – in today's world.

So far we have examined past karma and its results and how it inevitably leads to a need for tolerance in daily living. Having shown tolerance towards what is, do we stop at that? Absolutely not! This is where the second part of karma – *present karma* – comes in. It is the opportunity for willful **action** now, directed by wholesome intentions. Although we cannot change what has happened (past karmic results), and it determines our present, *we can influence our future by choosing our present action*. Thus our complete code for living is not passive acceptance of the way things were and are, but *acceptance followed by meaningful action* <u>*now*</u>.

The effect of past karma (and results) and present karma (willed action now) on one's destiny (direction of life) can be compared to the effect of the wheels of a front-wheel-drive car on its direction of movement. The rear and front wheels together provide for the movement of the car. Yet change of direction is possible only with the front wheels. Whether we end up in a safe destination or in the ditch will depend on the way the steering wheel is handled. The rear wheels are past karma (and karmic results) and the front wheels the present karma. The steering wheel is the intention. The safe destination and the ditch are the wholesome and unwholesome karmic results respectively.

Action entails determining what we can do about the situation we have accepted as reality, to make life better and to do it forthwith. But one needs to accept gracefully what is not within one's capability to change. Here one is reminded of words from the Christian prayer "...the serenity to accept the things I cannot change, the courage to change the things I can and the wisdom to know the difference."

We generally know the virtues of tolerance but usually find it difficult to practice it in daily living. Someone does something we do not like and we get upset and may even translate our feelings into verbal or physical expressions. An event that brings us difficulties or discomfort occurs, such as a snowstorm or job loss and we may grumble, get angry or depressed. Such reactions are counter-productive and negatively affect not only our long-term health through stress but also the world we interact with, our relationships, and our spiritual growth. The antidote is tolerance (acquired through understanding) followed by appropriate action.

We have so far seen how past and present karma translates into tolerance and action in daily living, in principle. Now let's see, with examples, how these principles actually apply to an individual's life, inter-personal relationships and nature.

If I have an altercation with my friend, and now I realize I have been unfair, I should first show tolerance and understanding to myself – no blame, no guilt, just compassionately understanding that I was at a unique karmic moment on my life's path (tolerance – of oneself). I phone my friend and say "sorry" (action). I also resolve to use this experience to act differently in the future (further action). The same should apply to everything else about me – be it cancer, poor personal finances or a mistake made – tolerance of what is, followed by action in the present moment to help make my continuing journey better.

A reckless driver speeds through a red light and crashes into Byron's car. First Byron accepts that it has happened – a karmic encounter between his path and the other driver's. It cannot be now "undone", so he does not waste his mental energy wishing that it should not have happened. He does not blame the other driver, since blame does not reverse the accident. And Byron does not get into a verbal encounter with the other driver (tolerance). Having accepted what is, Byron objectively proceeds to do what the society he lives in requires be done in these circumstances, for example, exchange insurance information (action). And so, tolerance and action work in harmony for all other interpersonal issues, to ensure peaceful movement through life for oneself and one's fellow travelers.

A seemingly endless snowstorm disrupts the day's planned activities. We accept the uniqueness of the snowstorm, and its 'right' to be nothing else but a snowstorm in the nature of things – it is neither bad, nor good. That also means we do not grumble or curse the storm. (Even if we do, the storm will continue until it finishes, and in the mean time we will have only increased our stress levels). That is tolerance of nature. Then we proceed to take action that is within our control – perhaps pick up the shovel and clear the driveway (and even hum a tune if we feel like it).

And so should our attitude be, to all of nature, our unavoidable and often unyielding companion, if we are to make life's journey enjoyable.

Given the cumulative power of our (erroneous) past conditioning, all this may perhaps (initially) be hard work, but worth every bit of effort.

Tolerance and willful action driven by good intention – the practical derivatives of karma and the essential ingredients for a life of reduced stress, peace and progress towards our desired spiritual destination.

Chapter Insights and Highlights

1. Karma (volitional action) produces karmic results on a moral scale similar to 'cause produces effect' in the physical universe.

2. A key determinant of the moral nature of the volitional action is the intention. Wholesome intentions produce wholesome karmic results; similarly for unwholesome intentions.

3. In reality, an effect (result) is not produced by one cause (condition) but many, going back endlessly in time.

4. Past karma and karmic results cannot be undone. This fact requires us to accept what was and is.

5. Present karma is volitional action now. Steered by wholesome intentions, herein lies our opportunity to guide our destiny towards peace.

9

To Have or Not to Have

From craving arises sorrow
And from craving arises fear
If a man is free from craving,
He is free from fear and sorrow.

The Dhammapada 216

Life is a bridge, therefore build no houses upon it.

An Indian ruler

We are advised, in Buddhist teachings, to get rid of *craving* (for things we would like to have) and *clinging* (to what we already have), *because craving and clinging give rise to distress,* sooner or later. Clinging and craving relate to *having*. But for daily living, we worldlings need to have some things. Thus, necessities for daily living on the one hand, and the doctrinal advice on the other, may appear to pose a conflict in the mind of the keen traveler of the Buddha's path. However, the conflict is resolved if one can obtain a clear answer to the question "Where do I draw the line between wholesome and unwholesome having, so that I can progress towards the goal?". In other words, when am I craving and clinging and when am I not?

The Dhammapada 204: "**Health is the greatest gain**. Contentment is the greatest wealth…..", helps towards finding that answer. If health is the greatest gain, then whatever acquisitions help one to maintain a healthy life would clearly be wholesome (i.e., not driven by craving or clinging). The further away we get from that point, the more our attempts move closer to what is implied in Dhamma as craving and clinging. Why is health the greatest gain? Because without basic health of body and mind, we will not be able to optimize our energies, to progress on the path to Sublime Peace. Put in simpler and practical terms, if the body and mind are healthy, contentment will follow. Let's now examine this subject of health a little further.

First, let's consider the health of the body. To maintain a healthy body we need nutritious food, physical activity, shelter, healthcare and (protective) clothing, and the means needed to acquire these. That gives us a baseline from which to determine which possessions we need to ensure physical health.

Thus, a 'litmus test' to determine if a current possession or a planned acquisition is wholesome or unwholesome, is to ask oneself the question "Do I really need this to lead a healthy life?". If the answer is no, Dhamma premise would advise us not to acquire the new thing or let go of what we already have – it belongs elsewhere, hopefully to help or support another who is helpless to obtain the 'greatest gain' – health. Lived on that basis, there is plenty on this planet to meet the *real* needs of all.

To let go of what we cling to is indeed not easy to do, because the attribute of clinging has been conditioned (erroneously) into our very existence right through our lifetime. But then, we need to understand the path to peace is not easy, yet with proper effort it can be traversed. To reach a gemstone, first one has to go through the hard labor of digging what is above. Then come the fruits of labor.

Next, let's consider health of the mind. Here, both the prescription and the medicine-supreme is in the package called The Buddha's Noble Eightfold Path, the essential aspects of which we will gradually cover as we progress through this book.

To summarize the discussion so far: to desire, and to have enough, to provide for a healthy body and mind is wholesome. This includes the needs of those one is responsible for due to their inability to fend for themselves, such as one's young children. Further away from that, we move deeper into the territory of craving and clinging. The means to wholesome having must always be, in Dhamma terms, 'right livelihood'.

Although in the final analysis all clinging is a feature of the mind driven by the root cause of ignorance, we can get a better appreciation of its impact on daily living if we subdivide clinging on the basis of the thing clung to:

(1) material things
(2) mental 'objects' – i.e., beliefs, values, ideas, labels, conventions etc., and
(3) relationships.

Any time one is in distress or is not feeling as happy as one wishes to be, invariably the immediate cause can be traced to clinging.

Common examples of (1) are "my house" and "my car". Examples of (2) are "my religion is the true religion" and " I am nothing without a university education". Examples of (3) are "our love affair" and "our business partnership". Clinging to any of these will precipitate distress in due course. For endless examples of distress caused by craving and clinging all we have to do is to pick up the daily newspaper. The pages are replete with reports of violence. It may be a murder committed by a spouse, lover or parent who believed he/she owned the other. Or it could be a case of international destruction of immense proportions because a group of people clung to the view "our religion and belief system is right and theirs is wrong". Or, it could be anything in-between.

The opposite of clinging is letting go. So the therapy for distress is to let go. In Dhamma language, it means eradication of the craving, which itself is dependent on the eradication of ignorance, primarily of the fact that there is no self, the root cause. When we consider our daily assertions "I want this", This is mine", "I think that ..." and so on, it is easy to see why ignorance of the fact of no-self - the belief in a self - is the root cause of craving and clinging.

That clinging causes distress and letting go frees one from the distress is illustrated in a beautiful parable from the East. It is the story of the monkey pot. The following rendition depicts the essence of the parable.

In India hunters use a pot to trap monkeys. The pot has a narrow neck, through which a monkey's hand can just pass. The hunter drops some favorite monkey food into the pot. He then leaves the pot on the ground tied to a tree, and hides behind some bushes to watch.

Soon monkeys descend from nearby trees, come near the pot and smell the food. One monkey puts a hand in the pot and grabs the food. Clinging to the food, it tries to walk away but the hand will not come out of the pot. The clenched fist containing the food is too big to pass through the neck of the pot. The animal keeps struggling to walk away to no avail while clinging to the food and it continues to suffer. Worse distress soon follows when the hunter takes possession of his captive. Moral of the story: All that the monkey had to do to gain its freedom was to simply *let go of its clinging*.

At this stage let's explore the fact that, in the final analysis, craving and clinging are attributes of the mind as this has an important bearing on the path to peace. To start with, here's our rendition of an ancient story about two monks and a woman that beautifully illustrates this crucial point about the mind.

Two monks paused at the bank of a river before crossing over to the other bank to continue with their journey. They saw a young woman standing on the bank, looking worried. Moments later the woman walked up to the monks and told them she had missed the last ferry, did not know to swim, is scared of being stranded and asked if they knew of any way she could get across before nightfall. To which the compassionate Monk A replied that he would carry her across, swimming. Monk A was aware of a rule in the Order that required monks to refrain from bodily contact with women, but deemed that in this special situation the safety of the woman had priority over adherence to the rule.

The monks and the woman reached the other bank within about five minutes. The woman thanked Monk A and they walked towards their different destinations. After the two monks had walked together quietly for a while, Monk A recalled that Monk B has been unusually edgy ever since they left the first riverbank. Then, with visible anger, Monk B suddenly burst out reproaching Monk A: "You carried that woman against the rules of the Order; you should be ashamed of yourself!" To which, Monk A in his usual calm manner replied, " I left that woman an hour ago, but you are still carrying her." Yes, Monk B was the one who was still carrying (clinging to) the woman *in his mind*. Monk A carried her only physically but not in his mind and when the compassionate deed was done, he promptly let go. Monk B suffered mentally, Monk A didn't.

In view of the importance of the message contained in the above story, let's solidify our understanding of that message, by moving from parable to two possible real life situations.

1. A poor shanty dweller lives a frugal life atop a mountain from which he can see the mansion of a very wealthy man. With this much information about the two men, we would most likely conclude that the poor man has no (or negligible) clinging whereas the degree of clinging of the wealthy man is 'sinfully' excessive.

    Now suppose we come upon some additional information. The poor man once happened to be one endowed with comfortable means but slid down to his present state due to drinking, gambling and others vices. The wealthy man inherited all his present wealth when his parents died in a fatal car accident.

The poor man is obsessed with envy of the wealthy man to the point where his sleep and health is affected. The wealthy man – an enlightened man – is of such mental disposition that if he lost all his wealth today he would be unshaken.

Contrary to our initial judgement, *in this particular case* it is the poor man, and not the wealthy man, who is clinging in an unwholesome way because the former is clinging *mentally* whereas the latter isn't.

2.   Jake, who has spent much of his last two years exploring spirituality, feels that he has reached the point where he should renounce lay life. He relinquishes all his property and other belongings and becomes a forest monk. From the day he enters the Order, his mind incessantly wanders back to what he owned, his relationships and the comforts he enjoyed.

Jake renounced his physical attachments but not his mental attachments. In fact his mental clinging is now intensified and he is in greater distress now than when he was studying spirituality as a lay person. Jake was mentally unequipped to enter monastic life.

Now we understand the emotional impact of clinging in general and the importance of mental clinging in particular. But *why* does clinging cause distress? Because clinging means to hold onto something so it will stay (with us). But we cannot do that because the pivotal law of the universe says that everything changes, so that in clinging we stand in the path of movement (change). So we suffer. It is no different from the man who suddenly clings to a moving train. Only a mad man or a drunkard would do that. The rest of us, witnessing such action and the tragic consequences, would perhaps think "What a fool!"

However, when we look at life, the rest of us are in the same plight. In our scenario, however, the action and consequences are not that obvious – in fact, they are often very subtle. We are all clinging to the massive train called Nature, which is forever in motion, and we suffer heavily because of that clinging. Furthermore, to go deeper into Buddhist philosophy, we can say from the fact of *no-self* that there is really no one to do the clinging after all. Thus we are wasting our life playing to an illusion by trying to cling, driven to satisfy an ego (self) that, in the final analysis, does not exist.

We came into this world with nothing. When the time comes to leave, we will have no choice but to leave with nothing. The peaceful way to prepare for the departure then is to gradually detach voluntarily because then there does not have to be the added painful struggle of freeing the knots of attachment to *my* things at exit time. And the most crucial of *my* 'things' are those that are mental, mainly views, and of views, the belief in an abiding self.

The discussion of the present subject would not be complete without answering the question "Is there anything at all one should crave for and cling to – for example, happiness?"

The answer to this is provided by the Buddha's characteristically simple wording (but with profound meaning and enormous impact): "Cling not to that which changes". And what changes? *Everything in the universe.* Thus, the Buddha's words, for practical purposes may be restated: "Do not cling to *anything*." Included are happiness and unhappiness as they, too, being dependent on the impermanent senses are ever changing phenomena. All we can do, wisely, is to observe and let go. Just be aware, then let go. Difficult to do, but achievable and easier as we gather momentum in the practice. And the reward? Peace, which is beyond the senses.

The specific craving for happiness is beautifully explained by the Buddha via a simile[36]. A log floating down a river will eventually find its way to the free, open ocean only if the log does not cling to either bank. The story of our life is similar. The log is the mind. The river is life. One bank is unhappiness (distress) and the other is happiness. The ocean is Sublime Peace. If the mind does not cling to either unhappiness or happiness, then it will eventually reach Sublime Peace.

Chapter Insights and Highlights

(1) *Craving* for, and *clinging* to things results in distress. In daily living, clinging and craving are closely related to *having*.

(2) Since we need to have some things to survive in this world, particularly to keep our minds in optimal condition, the criterion "having enough to maintain health of body and mind" helps us draw the line between unwholesome and wholesome having.

---

[36] Samyutta Nikaya, 35:200 (Salayatana Samyutta sutta)

(3) In the final analysis, craving and clinging are mental phenomena.

(4) The opposite of craving/clinging is letting go. Therefore the solution for distress is letting go, particularly of the underlying views. The self-view is foremost amongst the views.

10

Self-Reliance

Therefore, O Ananda, take the Self as a lamp;
Take the Self as a refuge.
Hold fast as a refuge to the truth.
Look not for refuge to anyone besides yourself.
Work out your own salvation with diligence.

The Buddha (Maha-Parinibbhana-Sutta)

It is one of the beautiful compensations of life,
That no man can sincerely help another,
Without helping himself.

Ralph Waldo Emerson

Having traversed the Path of Peace to its destination, the pioneer explorer, the Buddha, advised another explorer Ananda who was eagerly seeking the same destination, thus: "Look not for refuge to anyone besides yourself. Work out your own salvation with diligence". In this gem of advice, the key message is *self-reliance*. In any effort we take to keep ourselves on the right track, moving in the right direction, ensuring progress all the way to our destination, we should pay heed to the Buddha's advice on self-reliance, which he emphasized throughout his teachings. All-round existential self-reliance is something we need to develop, not partially or half-heartedly but with the utmost determination, our full commitment and our iron will.

For purposes of discussing self-reliance within the context of this book we may think of the Noble Eightfold Path as being comprised of two stages of development, that is mundane (worldly) and supra-mundane (higher spiritual) development. The latter relates to aspects such as meditation and is well documented in available existing literature and also elsewhere in this book. The former relates to aspects of ordinary day-to-day living such as livelihood, and seems to be inadequately addressed elsewhere and was therefore chosen for treatment in this chapter.

The importance of developing self-reliance in mundane aspects is easy to recognize.   That is, if our minds are cluttered and pre-occupied with worry, anxiety and other unhealthy emotions over ordinary issues of daily living, imposed by various types of mundane dependencies, will we have any space left in our minds for higher spiritual development under the Noble Eightfold Path? The answer to that question, which is an obvious "No", explains why many 'Buddhists' do not have the time, energy, determination and patience to practice Dhamma. Thus self-reliance at the mundane level becomes a pre-requisite for any higher spiritual development.   The solution therefore, is for us to first develop the maximum possible self-reliance in every conceivable aspect of ordinary day-to-day living.   That alone will alleviate or eradicate unhealthy emotions that stand in the way of the realization of our higher aspirations.

In passing, let's note that it is easier for monks to move onto higher spiritual practice than it is for lay people. This is because factors (such as family responsibilities, ownership problems and employment issues) which are the breeding grounds of obstacles (dependency) for laypersons are by design not present in the traditional monastic life.   So it is incumbent upon us laity to work harder than the monks to enter (and maybe even to maintain the momentum as we tread) the truly spiritual part of the Noble Eightfold Path.

It is harder to develop self-reliance in ordinary day-to-day living, than in higher spiritual living, because the former entails first *unlearning* and then learning, whereas the latter needs only learning. In mundane daily living we invariably are dependent on others or on worldly things, as a result of erroneous conditioning throughout our lifetime. This is where we need to work hard to discard old habits of dependency and gradually let habits of self-reliance take their place. In the following paragraphs we will first discuss the salient points about self-reliance in general. Then we will proceed to examine distinct areas of self-reliance in which we may have problems and what we can do about them.

As a first point, let's recognize that dependency is rooted in the conditioned erroneous view that other people or external things are responsible for one's happiness and wellbeing. Such an attitude in adults, apart from being an obstacle to spiritual progress by creating dependency, is the main cause of all interpersonal problems in relationships, as it invariably results in blame and interference in others' affairs, and is compounded when others have the same attitude. The diametrically opposite view, which is in touch with reality and healthy, is "I am responsible for my happiness and well-being." That is the Dhamma approach and the self-reliant way. It gets one moving on the Noble Eightfold Path. A person living according to that rational view, if capable of providing guidance to others, may provide such guidance *if and when asked for*, yet the actual work has to be done by the seeker.

Second, let's note that self-reliance is not something we can produce on demand when a crisis hits us. It has to be nurtured gradually over time and developed with patience, so when a crisis occurs, we are already equipped to cope, with calmness of mind. We should learn to change a tire as soon as we acquire a car, not when we have a flat tire on the highway at 2 am in frigid winter weather. The same applies for self-reliance.

Third, it would be useful to recognize that a great aid to self-reliance is a life that is simple because simplicity implies fewer things in one's life to depend on. Hence the built-in simplicity of a monk's life.

Fourth, the only true and lasting antidote for loneliness is not the presence of other people, but self-reliance.

As a last point let's note that while self-reliance is something we develop for ourselves, and that implies a lack of dependency on others (adults), we can in reverse compassionately help others to be independent of *us*. Since the other person's self-reliance, which in this case we have facilitated, helps that person to accelerate his/her own journey on the Noble Eightfold Path, our action can only be considered as good karma that will bring merit to ourselves.

Now let's examine some distinct aspects of self-reliance. For practical purposes we may view our dependencies as falling in three areas: (1) *physical* (2) *livelihood*, and (3) *mental* dependencies. We will proceed to examine each type in some detail. But before we do that let's state one important but obvious point: by self-reliance we do not imply the ability always do the work by oneself. To get work done by someone else but recompense with money earned by oneself through 'right livelihood' is self-reliance, not dependency. Thus for 25-year old Tom to pay for the unexpected plumbing repair in his house by working overtime is self-reliance, whereas requesting his mother to pay the bill would obviously be a dependency on the mother!

PHYSICAL SELF-RELIANCE

The most important aspect here is what one does to maintain one's body in optimum health. Instead of living an unhealthy lifestyle and being dependent regularly on the healthcare system including the family doctor, medications, and caregivers at home, we can help ourselves enormously through regular exercise, proper nutrition and by doing our utmost to manage our daily stresses. The cost of healthy exercise is almost negligible. Activities such as a daily brisk walk for 30 minutes, a swim or bicycling are within the reach of all of us. So is healthy eating that entails a balanced diet comprised of grain products, vegetables, milk products and sources of protein. And a healthy body weight is achieved easily with proper exercise and nutrition. The cumulative benefit we receive from these inexpensive practices of preventive healthcare is far greater than that received from any medication, medical help or any combination of these.

All the above is not to say that we can prevent all illness, decay and death. The law of impermanence still prevails, but while alive, we can live each day with the optimum health available to each one of us. That is, without being a burden on externals, and with the utmost self-reliance enabling our minds to focus on the important task of achieving Sublime Peace rather than spending mental energies on aches and pains. However, if we do have physical maladies already, then we still can provide much help for the rest of the physical self, with practices of self-reliance.

Besides taking care of the health of our bodies, we need to look at a long array of physical things and activities on which we are dependent, the non-availability of which has the potential to cripple us. A simple example is the total dependency of one spouse on another for meals or other mundane household affairs. Another common example is the continuing dependency of children grown to adulthood, on their parents for things that were only appropriate when they were younger.

SELF-RELIANCE FOR LIVELIHOOD

Lack of self-reliance can create a potential 'time-bomb', particularly in difficult economic times. This is apparent when a breadwinner is dependent on one employer, on one type of career, or on dwindling resources for one's sustenance. It is also present in situations in which one spouse is totally or largely dependent on the other for essentials. Eventualities such as serious illness, injury or death of the provider or simply unjust behavior of the provider may leave the dependent person helpless and distressed. In some such cases of dependency there is also the potential that the dependent person may have to live in subjection to, and at the mercy of, the provider, which in turn would lead to distress for the dependent person.

In all these cases the solution is to prepare oneself for eventualities by developing self-reliance. Thus, as an example take the case of the spouse who is dependent on the other for daily sustenance. No one can predict what the future holds for any relationship – the earning spouse may lose the job, there can be incapacitation due to an accident and so on. Therefore it is wise for the dependent spouse to take steps to develop the *potential* to earn a living, if not actual earning just now, for example by enrolling in a part-time study program in a subject area where the opportunities for earning a livelihood are good.

MENTAL SELF-RELIANCE

Because the ultimate driver of all modes of dependency and self-reliance is the mind, it is very important that we understand what mental self-reliance means. This understanding may be obtained by examining some of the more obvious manifestations of mental self-reliance as discussed below.

(a) *Emotional self-reliance*. When we were infants and children it made sense to be emotionally dependent on others (especially parents), but this is not valid in the adult world. Nevertheless, there are many of us who have been unable to grow out of that dependency.   One common example of an erroneous belief, which causes this emotional dependency to continue, is that an adult *needs* love and praise from others to feel good. Another common mistaken belief is that it is terrible to be alone. Here we need to ponder over these erroneous views and replace them with the corresponding right views – this can be achieved most effectively via Insight Meditation.

Another example of emotional dependency is to look for sympathy from others. "It must be awful to have gone through what you have. But I am sure all this will pass soon". We may feel temporarily relieved upon hearing such "poor you!" statements but very likely will sink into greater distress when the next sympathy is long in coming or we find that the expression of sympathy failed to help solve our present problem. The Dhamma way is to take the problem in own hands, act to correct things where we can and equally important, learn to accept what we cannot change. We just don't need others' sympathy. In fact dependency on sympathy can worsen things in the long run.

(b) *Decision-Making.* Sometimes some of us depend on others such as family members and friends to think and make decisions for us. We stand to benefit in the long term by weaning out that dependency. We have a mind of our own and we need to keep it sharpened all the time by using it. "Use it or lose it!"

(c) *Spiritual Self-reliance.* As emphasized by the Buddha right through his teachings (see quote from Kalama sutta in Chapter 2 and the quotation at the start of this chapter), it is very important to watch our attachments to, and dependencies on, spiritual teachings and teachers. Examples are gurus[37] (especially the charismatic ones) and other teachers, retreats and other group-based practices and communication media.

It may be said that an All-Enlightened-Being (e.g., the Buddha or an Arahant) is totally self-reliant. A person less developed than an Arahant will need guidance from well-screened outside sources, the degree being determined by how far the person has progressed on the Path, a beginner needing the greatest help. However, it is very important that we constantly watch ourselves and discontinue this temporary help when the adjunct tends to become a chronic dependency.

No guru can save us from our existential distress. Even a Buddha cannot. A wise teacher (who has understood and walked the path ahead of us) can only show us how. For our liberation, we have to understand and traverse the path ourselves.

(d) *Relationships.* A relationship is comprised of two parties, both of which are subject to the law of impermanence. When we are not mindful of the fact of impermanence, relationships lead to distress. In practice this manifests in the form of rigid adherence (clinging) to views such as:
- One partner's definition of the relationship
- How the *other* party should behave
- The belief that those relational rules are absolute reality, when in fact they are all human-made (worldly).

---

[37] *Guru* (a word from Hinduism, now in fairly common use in the West), means 'A guide or teacher in philosophical or spiritual matters'.

The way out of the distress is to let go of the rigid adherence, or clinging, to these individual views and in the end the view of the relationship in total.

A general strategy for developing self-reliance is as follows. For each area ask "On whom or on what external thing am I dependent and for what purpose?" and write down the answer on paper. Next dig deep into your mental resources and obtain specific answers to the question "What can I do to eliminate these dependencies (to be self-reliant)?" and again write the answers. Then, most importantly, proceed without postponement to DO what has been identified as needing to be done – this *doing*, as always, is the most crucial part of our self-development.

For example, a sedentary person now bent on self-improvement recognizes a chronic dependency on doctors and medications for ordinary day-to-day health and to feel good. This person has identified that, to be self-reliant in this aspect he/she must (1) walk 30 minutes per day and (2) enroll in a nutrition course at the community college to learn the latest facts on healthy nutrition and (3) potentially benefit from a certain stress management book that helped a friend. By the end of the following week, this person has enrolled in the nutrition course, has bought the book on stress management, read it and begun to practice effective stress management techniques and exercises five days a week. It will not be long before this person has moved from dependency on the doctor and medications to self-reliance for ordinary day-to-day well-being – a giant step forward.

Another example, is the person who, dependent for his/her daily living on unstable employment, tries one's own business on a part-time basis as a fallback, so that if the need arises, the person is better prepared to adjust.

In this chapter we examined how self-reliance can be developed in our mundane day-to-day existence, as a prerequisite for higher spiritual endeavors. Once we are past that hurdle, we can develop self-reliance for onward progress on the Path, which is addressed in later chapters (to the extent allowed by the objective of the present book).

If we are to undertake a long journey to a wonderful destination on another continent, we will obviously need a suitable means of transportation to take us to that destination. On a spiritual scale, the Noble Eightfold Path entails such a journey, the destination being Sublime Peace. Here our means of transportation is self-reliance. There is no other way to reach the destination.

Chapter Insights and Highlights

(1) The key to freedom, both worldly and beyond, is self-reliance. In the words of the Buddha, "Look not for refuge to anyone besides yourself. Work out your own salvation with diligence".

(2) The unhealthy attribute of dependency is rooted in the conditioned erroneous view that other people or external things are responsible for one's happiness and wellbeing.

(3) The healthy attribute of self-reliance is based on the diametrically opposite and reality-based view that each person is responsible for his or her own happiness and wellbeing.

(4) Self-reliance needs to be nurtured gradually over time and with patience so when a crisis hits us, we are ready to face it with the necessary skills.

(5) For practical purposes the self-reliance we need to develop may be considered as falling into three areas, i.e., physical, livelihood and mental.

(6) Again for practical purposes, mental self-reliance may in turn be sub-divided into a number of categories such as emotional self-reliance, decision-making, relationships and spiritual self-reliance.

(7) We can take stock of our current dependencies and work out a strategy for gradual elimination of them. That action will help enormously towards reaching the goal of inner peace in our lives.

11

Right and Wrong Views

What we are today comes from our thoughts of yesterday,
And our present thoughts build our life of tomorrow:
Our life is the creation of our mind.

From The Dhammapada 1

It is best to start this topic with the reader pondering over the question "At a given moment in time, what is my existential essence or in simpler terms, my personality?". Or even better, "Why am I what I am?"

The answer to that question, for our present purpose, is that it is composed of two components, namely:

1. An *inherited* component, which may be subdivided into
    - genetic inheritance
    - karmic inheritance, and

2. An *acquired* component, which is the result of one's *sensory interaction* with the environment, during one's lifetime.

Now let's discuss these components – genetic inheritance, karmic inheritance and what we have acquired (mentally) during our lifetime through sensory interaction with our environment.

Genetic material is passed down through one's lineage in a physical format via the genes. Examples of our genetic inheritance are skin color, physical appearance and predisposition to certain disorders such as Hemophilia and Huntington's chorea[38]. Generally, our genetic inheritance is something we have to learn to live with, or cope with – we do not seem to have much of a choice here.

---

[38] A rare disease in which degeneration of certain cell clusters in the brain causes *chorea* (jerky, rapid, involuntary movements) and dementia (mental impairment).

We humans have recently begun to experiment, and sometimes tamper, with the genetic material of animals and human beings. Discussion of that involved subject is outside the scope of this book, except to make two comments as a digression (see box) because they have some bearing on our subject of distress and inner peace.

While one's genetic material is passed through other people, karmic inheritance is purely one's own, so genetics and karma operate on different planes. Unlike the genes, karma is not passed on in a physical format – at least not physical in the way we perceive things through our senses as being physical– but rather in the nature of energy vibrations[39]. Yet, karma influences genetic inheritance, to the extent that Buddhist doctrine teaches that one's karma will determine where one is to be born.

The consequence of past karma is something one has to live with and live through. Therefore, with regard to unwholesome past karma, it is wise to do whatever we have to do without complaint and resistance, pay back dues and 'get it over with' to help us with our onward journey with no more hindrance. What we don't pay back now will have to be paid back with interest later, like bank loans. For that reason, if I have to move garbage to make a living and for some reason I don't like doing it (though intrinsically there is nothing wrong with moving garbage), I might as well teach myself now to change my attitude and do it with acceptance and contentment. Why? Because the karma created by myself and no other, placed me in a situation where I have to move garbage. While engaged in moving garbage to earn a living, if I so desire I can use the power of my *present* karma (will) to take action to change my lot, with wisdom and patience. The same holds true for all kinds of other unpleasant experiences we have to go through in life, including tragedies.

(To be accurate, in place of karma, we should consider the more general *bundle of conditions* that affect us each moment of our existence, karma being one of the conditions within the bundle. However, we will keep it simple for now, considering only the factor of karma – this makes sense because karma is a dominant condition within the bundle of conditions. We will embark on a detailed and fascinating exploration of the subject of *conditions* later in the book).

---

[39] The distinction between matter and energy becomes hazy as we proceed to look at things at deeper sub-atomic levels.

▶ *Digression*

GENETIC STUFF

It can be stated with certainty that genetic science and technology *will never* be able to *eliminate* sickness, injury, aging and death simply because these are manifestations of the primary law of the universe – impermanence. But if the goals of science and technology are of a different nature, we can look towards affirmative answers in the years to come. Improvements to longevity? Yes. More cures for the injured and the sick? Yes. Novel forms of help for the dying? Yes. Achievement of some extension to the maximum life span? May be. *Elimination* of sickness, injury, aging and death? NO. So the message is clear: given impermanence, our generation and the ones to come will continue to need Dhamma to help make a peaceful journey through one's existence because the core existential problems – sickness, injury, aging and death – will continue.

The second point about genetic tampering that may be worth noting in passing is one that applies to all technology in general.

Nature evolves (changes) at what we may call evolutionary speed – a very slow pace that has existed from beginning of life forms on the planet. That slowness of pace ensures that any change in any life form will accommodate changes necessary to all the (hundreds, perhaps thousands of) interdependent factors in a synchronized and harmonious fashion. Technological change (which is brought about by human beings), on the other hand, is very speedy and generally focuses on the one product of interest to the developer with no attention paid to interdependencies. Often the developer simply does not have the knowledge to identify all the interdependencies, in contrast to the wisdom of Mother Nature. The result is disharmony inflicted by human beings upon Nature and distress brought upon all living beings. An example is automobiles. We developed and perfected the automobile at technological speed focusing all efforts only on the automobile, but ended in poisoning the environment. The result? Amongst other things, negatively impacting the health of humans and other life forms – in other words, distress. Genetic tampering using technology is open to similar dangers. Therefore we need to be very cautious in tampering with Nature in general and our genes in particular.

Next let's discuss what we have mentally *acquired* during our sensory interaction with the world around us from birth to now. Let's start by noting at the outset that of these mental acquisitions, the *views* that were inculcated into our minds are the most influential.
What makes of us criminals or Buddhas or anything in between are primarily these views. Fortunately for us, *views happen to be also the only mental phenomena we have the power to alter, throughout the*

balance of our lives and that can change the direction of our existence - call it destiny *if you will.*

That means that each and every one of us (including the worst amongst us) have the *potential* to be Buddhas. After all, a Buddha is no more and no less than one who has realized perfected right views[40], that is, views that are totally in touch with reality. Hence the reason why 'purification of the mind (views)' becomes the essence of Dhamma. Therefore, what is of real interest to us in the present chapter are *the acquired views from birth to the present time. Views* is a general term we are using here to include concepts, ideas, prejudices, biases, notions of traditions and culture and any other entities akin to those. Just as we have acquired these since birth, we can also get rid of them when necessary (though with much effort), if we develop the necessary skills to do so and are prepared to work diligently at the task.

The first question we need to answer is how we acquired these views. We got them from the many influential environments that we grew up in, or associated with, at different stages of our lives. These include our parents, the rest of our immediate family, day-care and baby-sitters, relatives, our community, clergy, educational institutions and work environments. We should also include inanimate information sources such as books and, in today's world, communications media such as television and the Internet. The greatest influence on inculcation of views is during our formative years – from birth to about six years of age.

The views we acquired may have had significance at the level of our community, small or large, but may not be true in an absolute sense. Let's explore that proposition further with an example, which will also throw some new light on a factor of prime importance in Dhamma philosophy which we encountered earlier – that of *no-self.*

Let's say a baby girl has just been born. She is given the name Ramona. The name Ramona is an arbitrary 'fixture' we assign to the baby due to societal needs of identification. For the rest of her life she will be referred to by that name, so that she becomes anchored to the 'fixture' Ramona for a lifetime. This is just one example of a multitude of anchors

---

[40] This will be an appropriate point to define *right* and *wrong* within the context of this book. *Wrong* is that which is not in touch with reality, that is, perceived with our truth-distorting six senses – which also means 'worldly". *Right* is that which is in touch with reality, that is, upon transcending the six senses. Pali for right view is *samma ditthi* and for wrong view (= false belief) is *miccha ditthi.*

that will 'fix' Ramona as another self – for example that she is the granddaughter of Harvey (anchor 2) and Hazel (anchor 3). Ramona lives at 2261 Iroquois Crescent (anchor 4) and so on, to an endless number of anchors (fixtures) – all our own creations, to serve some purpose of worldly existence.

The net effect of this multiple anchoring is that Ramona and others perceive her as an abiding self. But we know from our thorough analysis in earlier chapters that Ramona is an incessantly changing entity and there is no abiding self in that entity. This, then, is the dilemma created by the anchoring to the fixtures. While that process helps to fill a societal need, it leads to the wrong view of an abiding ego (self). The belief in a self that initially was triggered by external influences (anchors) will become so ingrained in Ramona as she grows up that it will be second nature to her. Everything she does and perceives will be colored by that wrong view of self, now an influence of which she is not even aware. The only way in which this wrong view can be uprooted in the adult Ramona is through un-learning, with the help of meditation, as we other adults are also painstakingly attempting to do.

An analogy – of a spark and a bucket full of fluid – will enable us to appreciate the important difference in results produced in a human being, by right and wrong views. The owner of a quiet house in a peaceful neighborhood vacuums the garage not realizing that the vacuum cleaner, though functional, emanates sparks due to an electrical problem. A bucket full of water stands in a corner of the garage. Nothing unusual happens and the environment continues to be calm. Next, while repairing his car, the owner fills the bucket with contaminated gasoline. At the end of the repair job, he proceeds to vacuum the fresh accumulation of dirt, having forgotten the bucket of gasoline he placed in the corner. Boom! An explosion, destruction of property, injury and distress and a devastated environment are now the unfortunate consequences.

Sensory input is to the contents of one's memory as a spark is to the contents of a bucket. If the bucket contains water, calm persists. Equally so, if the mind (memory) contains right views, peace persists. If the bucket contains gasoline, the result is an explosion, destruction, injury and distress. Equally so, if the mind (memory) contains wrong views, distress is the inevitable result. The important message to us is that to move from distress to inner peace, we need to fill our mind with right views instead of wrong views.

What are generally referred to as wrong views in Dhamma are (1) the view of an abiding self, (2) the view of permanency of things and (3) all corollaries that follow from (1) and (2). Let's look at a sampling of wrong views and the corresponding right views organized in a table format reflecting the majority of the key points discussed in the previous chapters. They are stated here in simple language and somewhat different from the manner in which they are presented in doctrinal writings[41], in order to focus on their application to day-to-day living.

---

[41] Readers interested in a study of the classical description may consult "The Discourse on *The All-Embracing Net of Views:* The Brahmajala Sutta and its Commentaries" translated from the Pali by Bhikku Bodhi. Buddhist Publication Society, 1978 and "*The Discourse on Right View:* The Sammadithhi Sutta and Its Commentaries" translated from the Pali by Bhikku Nanamoli, revised by Bhikku Bodhi, BPS 1992.

Table 1: Right and Wrong Views

A	B
Wrong View (Worldly)	**Right View** (Transcendental)
View of permanence	All things are impermanent (subject to change). Some change slowly, some rapidly. *(Impermanence)*. For perspective, I can reflect on "This too will pass" and ponder on "What will be of this present happening or thing, say, 100 or 1000 years from now?"
View of an abiding self (ego).	There *is* a self only as seen through our senses, which are utterly deficient for perceiving reality. Upon transcending the senses, i.e., in reality, there is no such thing as a 'Self'. "I", "Me", "Mine", "You" etc. are mere conventional terms needed for human communication *(No-self)*.
It would be possible to sustain happiness with sensory gratification.	Sensory stimuli sometimes result in transient pleasures but invariably lead to unhappiness when the object (stimuli) or subject (perceiving mechanism - senses) undergoes inevitable change *(Impermanence)*.

Table 1: Right and Wrong Views (continued)

A	B
Wrong View (Worldly)	**Right View** (Transcendental)
I should welcome praise and be averse to blame.	I should be unaffected by praise and blame as both are transient[42] (*Impermanence*)
The world is responsible for my distress.	I am responsible for both my inner peace and distress. The root-cause of my distress is my own ignorance of reality (wrong views) (*Karma, Dependent Origination*).
Life is full of problems and they distress me.	Every so-called 'problem' is a teacher in disguise. With that attitude we can gracefully transcend the problems and create inner peace.
I should not have to suffer.	Physical distress (pain) is inherent in change (impermanence) and so I have to accept it. Some pain may be temporarily abated, but many times during my life, I will have to confront pain. Mental distress can be eliminated by replacing ignorance (wrong views) with wisdom (right views) (*Impermanence*).
My mind and my body belong to me. So do my children, spouse and wealth.	In reality they belong to nature, and to me only by convention[43] (*No-self*).

---

[42] "Even as a rock is not shaken by the wind, the wise man is not shaken by praise or blame." – The Dhammapada 81

[43] "'These are my sons. This is my wealth.' In this way the fool troubles himself. He is not even the owner of himself: how much less of his sons and his wealth." – The Dhammapada 62

Table 1: Right and Wrong Views (continued)

A	B
Wrong View (Worldly)	**Right View** (Transcendental)
Birth must be celebrated and death mourned.	Birth and death are equal spokes of the same Wheel of Life. Treat them as equals. Develop wisdom to transcend both *(Impermanence)*.
My unpleasant feelings will not go away.	They will. Feelings (in fact all mental activities) are subject to impermanence. They change faster than physical constituents of the body *(Impermanence)*.
The key to inner peace is amassing wealth, being famous and powerful.	The key to inner peace is purification of the mind, that is, to move from ignorance to wisdom *(Link 1 of Dependent Origination)*.
I should develop affection for my dear ones and they in turn should show affection to me. The rest of the world is not really important.	Affection for a select few (dear ones) causes attachment, which in turn brings distress when parting occurs[44]. So develop unconditional love for *all*, including the 'dear ones.' It is a far superior love. *(Impermanence)*

---

[44] "From affection springs grief, from affection springs fear; for him who is wholly free from affection there is no grief, much less fear." – The Dhammapada 213

Table 1: Right and Wrong Views (continued)

A	B
Wrong View (Worldly)	**Right View** (Transcendental)
All I am going through is my fate. There is nothing I can do about it.	My past karma is a determinant of what I have been through and what I am going through now. However I have the power to change the direction of my existence from this point on, in the way I take **action now**, i.e., in the way I generate fresh karma *(Karma)*.
Bad things always happen to me although I don't understand why me, of all people. I have always been a good person. It is not fair.	Things happen dependent on nature's laws of conditionality only – a cause/effect linkage going back endlessly in time. Comparison with others is not a condition for what happens. Neither is 'good' and 'bad'.
Some things (and people) in this world are good, others bad.	Everything in the world just *is* – neither bad nor good. Good and bad are human labels (conventions). Cause and effect chains have brought things (and people) to what and where they are *(Impermanence and karma)*.

The above list is not exhaustive, yet it is a significant part of a very long list of right and wrong views that we can compose to cover every imaginable facet of human existence. The list of examples reveals clearly that every one of our views can be carefully examined to see if it is right or wrong. If it is a wrong view, the corresponding right view can always be deduced in terms of two of the three basic facts of existence – impermanence *(anicca* in Pali) and no-self *(anatta).*   Karma and Dependent Origination, which we have used above to explain some views, are in the final analysis themselves dependent on impermanence. The reader may add to this list as he/she progresses through his/her studies of Dhamma, as the list will become valuable preparatory material for Insight meditation. In any event, in Table 2 appearing at the end of the book we will provide a collection of additional views that will be discussed in the chapters to follow.

Now let's observe a few insights using the information in Table 1.

1. *The Worldly Way and Transcendal Way.* To live with the views of Column A is worldly living. That is a life of sensory gratification, with transient pleasures that fade, leaving behind confusion and distress. Living according to the views of Column B is the transcendental path, the way that leads to Sublime Peace – the Dhamma way. Our problems cannot be solved in the world of Column A, because that is where the problems are – we are submerged in distress there and we cannot see. So we have to be like the Coast Guard pilot who leaves the host ship and flies the rescue helicopter above the ocean to find a missing person. We have to step out into world B (in our mind) and look at what is happening in world A to understand, and find solutions, for our distress. That is the Buddha's way and needless to say, it goes exactly opposite to the worldly way to which we are accustomed.   Hence the inherent difficulty in moving from the The Worldly Way to The Transcendental Way.

2. *The Worldly Views Inculcated into Us Prepared Us to Undergo Distress.* It is clear from the examples in Table 1 that as we were growing up we were not taught views based on the basic facts of existence (impermanence and no-self). On the contrary we were taught to do practically everything to support the ego and on the illusion that things, particularly those that we like, remain more or less unchanged. Few, if any, amongst us grew up truly understanding the realities of *impermanence* and *no-self*.

For example, how many of us grew up being able to treat death as an event occupying a place in par with birth? We learned to celebrate birth and abhor death. The result? The irrational fear of death. On the other hand, think of the immense peace we would have in life if we would have learned to interact with a person with unconditional love *(metta)* while alive, and then when the person dies, to treat the passing away with equanimity? After all, in the eyes of impermanence the passing away of a human being is no different to the passing away of a seasonal flowering plant, say the petunia, as the summer comes to an end. What is born *has to* die (and that includes us). To be in touch with reality (and therefore to be really at peace) we need to accept that fact. Then our actions and feelings relating to human death should ideally be no different from those we demonstrate at the passing away of the petunia. But we cannot act in that manner because of the deep-rooted erroneous views (conditioning) that now controls our emotions involuntarily, until we are able to eradicate them with intensive Insight meditation.

As another example, take the case of praise and blame. How wonderful life would be if we could live unaffected by both praise and blame, except for judiciously selecting constructive feedback to enhance our growth. Instead we are usually on an emotional roller coaster driven by our sensitivity to what others think of us, or say to us. Again, this is the way we were taught to view, and react to, praise and blame.

In general, how many of us can truly claim that our lives are based on *all* views akin to those in column B (and similar transcendental views on other issues of life that are not listed)? If we do, we don't need to struggle to master and practice Dhamma!

3. Be Here Now. In our readings on Dhamma we often encounter advice on the need to live in the present moment or, to use a popular phrase, to 'be here now'. This is because it is only in the present moment that our senses are active and we can interact with reality. The past, though real when it was the present, is now totally imagination. Likewise, though the future may turn out to be real when it becomes the present, it is at the moment total imagination. So it makes sense to live in the present moment and be in touch with reality. However, our discussion on views so far reveals a very important additional factor. Since views can be right or wrong, we need to process the present-moment information received through our senses with *right* views, not wrong views, if we are to 'see things as they really are.'

Thus, in the example we had about Cousin David in Chapter 7 "Our Sensory World', Bertram developed an aversion towards David because of wrong views (as in Column A). However, if Bertram perceives him through right views (as in Column B), then he will see the reality of Cousin David and, instead of being averse, he will be compassionate towards David. So our formula for living in the present moment is not 'be here now' but 'be here now *with right views*'.

4. Conventional Reality and Absolute Reality. Except for the few actions such as eating and breathing needed for survival, our ordinary day-to-day living centers on a vast array of conventions (rules, guidelines, names, labels, symbols, values etc.) *of our own making.* In contrast, absolute reality refers to things as they are in Nature and outside of the conventions created by people, that is, outside our sensory perception. For example, consider the proliferation of anniversary dates we have to live with – Mother's Day, Father's Day, Grandparent's Day, birthdays, Halloween, Boxing Day and so on. Promoted endlessly by commercial interests, these days are deeply entrenched in our society, seemingly as significant events reflecting reality. In today's hectic lives, these events often turn out to be mechanical routines after some time. In the eyes of absolute reality all these days are the same – each of them no more than just another sunrise followed by just another sunset.

Convention is useful, necessary and only valid for the purpose, or society or geographical area and the time frame for which it is made. Thus Adrienne, a 100 mph speed, money, a beautiful hairstyle, oxcart, an ugly man, a good boy, Professional Engineer and tragedy are all examples of the endless list of conventions, that we humans create to manage our transient lives on this planet. Outside of the human mind, they don't exist.

Absolute reality has no judgements, boundaries or time limits. In contrast, when viewed through convention, we pass judgement on the world, usually labeling things as good or bad or with some other dichotomy. Thus, a "crooked tree" makes sense within convention, and enables one human being to convey some idea to another. However, a "crooked tree" does not exist in an absolute sense. The tree exists simply as an integral part of nature, of the universe, not as a *crooked* tree. "Crooked" is a unilateral judgement we human beings try to impose on nature (on absolute reality). Though it satisfies us, nature moves on like an insensitive giant totally unaffected and aloof – it will probably make the offspring of the crooked tree also a crooked tree, in spite of what we think or say! Likewise, the need to arrange dinnerware on the dining table according to a specific layout is simply convention, but in an absolute sense it has no meaning. And so it is with all convention.

Many of our problems and distress in life arise not because of conventions, but because we fail to realize that:

(1) for every conventional reality there is an absolute reality,
(2) there is a fundamental difference between the two realities, often being opposites, and
(3) while conventional reality is needed for our transient existence within transient societal boundaries, it is absolute truth that matters for progress on the spiritual path, attainment of enduring inner peace for oneself and harmony amongst all.

On a specific note, it is the lack of the above realizations - ignorance - that causes one to think that his convention (view) is right, the other's wrong and therefore the justification to impose one's convention on the other. Such erroneous thinking is the cause of all our hatred, conflicts and hostile confrontations, whether between two individuals, two ethnic groups or two countries.

5. No One Can be Blamed for Our Wrong Views. Views that we acquire as we grow up are not all wrong, but most generally are. We cannot blame anyone for inculcating wrong views in us simply because they were ignorant as we are. Most people do what they do with good intentions but also through ignorance – the mix of ignorance and wisdom is unique to each one of us. We were taught what our 'influential others' knew. We have taught and continue to teach what we know. If the 'teacher' is ignorant, what is imparted is ignorance. If the 'teacher' is wise, what is imparted is wisdom. That is how things are. The only way to break the vicious cycle is to recognize our ignorance and work diligently to eradicate our distress with the help of the precious gift that the Buddha left for us – the unsurpassed Dhamma.

Every generation, through ignorance, passes on wrong views to the next. Most of us will find that by the time we get around to insightfully grasping Dhamma, we have already passed on wrong views to those we have influenced and now they are outside our range of influence for corrective action. So they in turn pass on wrong views to the next generation and the cycle continues. No wonder 2500 years have elapsed since the Buddha passed away, yet we as a generation are in the same predicament of illusion as the ignorant people who lived in the Buddha's time. However, in each generation, "there are beings whose eyes are only a *little* covered with dust; they will understand the truth[45]" and they sustain the relay to keep the flame of Dhamma from being extinguished forever.

Chapter Insights and Highlights

1.   Our personality can be thought of as being comprised of :

    (a) An *inherited* component, which may be subdivided into
- genetic inheritance
- karmic inheritance, and

---

[45] The Buddha (from Majjhima Nikaya 26)

(b) An *acquired* component, which is the result of one's *sensory interaction* with the environment, during one's lifetime.

2. Of the acquired component, the predominantly influential factor is the collection of views stored in our memory.

3. Views can be categorized as 'right' or 'wrong' depending on whether they are in touch with reality or not. Wrong views lead to distress whereas right views lead to peace.

4. Views happen to be the only mental phenomena we have the power to alter, throughout our lives, and therefore become the tool with which we can change the direction of our lives (destiny).

12

Calming the Mind

The mind is fickle and flighty,
It flies after fancies wherever it likes;
It is difficult to restrain.
But it is a great good to control the mind;
A mind self-controlled is a source of great joy.

The Dhammapada 35

Before we embark on a discussion of Buddhist meditation let's do a very simple exercise. Pick up a small object (a pencil, pen, cup – anything) with your hand, look at it and put it away. Then close your eyes and for the next ten minutes try to focus your attention on the mental image of that object. For timing, use a clock or wristwatch alarm or go by your internal alarm (feel). Whenever you stray away from that image try to bring back your concentration to the object.

What is the most striking thing that we notice during the exercise? It is that the mind does not stay focused on the object. It wanders as it fancies – to sounds, bodily pains, other thoughts and so on. It is like a constantly rebellious and hyperactive child. Except for the small minority amongst us who have become accomplished meditators, this nature of wandering about is the way of the untrained mind. This is a universal human problem. The mind jumps from thought to thought because by habit that is what it knows, and likes, to do. The purpose behind *Calming Meditation* is to tame this discursive mind, gently guiding it to focus its attention on one object and eventually make that a habit. Thus, Calming Meditation may be looked upon as a method of breaking a bad, or unhealthy, habit (of a wandering mind) and replacing it with a good habit (of a focused mind).

Calming Meditation capitalizes on the scientific fact that the mind cannot think of two things at the same time (that is during the same 'thought moment'). So when we induce the mind to think of a neutral object such as the breath, then during each thought moment of that thinking process it cannot think of other things which agitate it. Through repetition of that process, when we succeed in guiding the mind to concentrate on one thing at the exclusion of all else, for a reasonable length of time, the net effect is calming of the mind. The tranquility (calmness) realized will be in stark contrast to the usual state of the mind resulting from its habitual discursiveness. Of course, a calmed mind leads to the calming of many bodily activities (such as lowering the blood pressure) and calming one's entire life rhythm, contributing to better overall health. Note that concentration (on the chosen object) is the practice; calmness is the result.

Buddhist meditation comprises two types, *Calming Meditation*, which as we have seen develops calmness through concentration and *Insight Meditation,* which enables one to perceive things without distortion ('see things as they are'). For optimum effectiveness, Insight Meditation needs a mind that is calm, a mind that has been prepared by Calming Meditation. Thus Calming Meditation is a prerequisite for effective Insight Meditation, if one is to realize the best results with the latter. Insight Meditation will be discussed in some detail in the next two chapters.

The objects of focus available for Calming Meditation practice are many. We will use our natural breath as the object and restrict our discussion and practice to that, to keep things simple. The breath is one of the most popular objects of meditation. The scriptures tell us that the Buddha himself used it the night of his enlightenment. The main advantage to using the breath is its natural (guaranteed) availability twenty-four hours a day for a lifetime, so that one does not have to depend on externals for objects of meditation. Another advantage is that it may also be used as a model and a 'home base' for Insight practice.

Calming Meditation carried out with the breath as the object of focus is called Breathing Meditation (*anapanasati*[46] in Pali, *sati* meaning mindfulness and *ana* and *apana* meaning inhalation and exhalation respectively). So strictly speaking, Breathing Meditation is mindfulness (Insight practice) of breathing. However, it is common practice to use the term anapanasati when referring to breathing meditation, whether it is used for Calming Meditation or for Insight practice.

We can get a good idea of what we are trying to achieve with Calming Meditation if we go back to the analogy[47] of the six rambunctious kids

---

[46] We will render the Pali term *Anapanasati* as Breathing Meditation in English.
[47] Another useful analogy to get a feel for the combined effect of the six senses on the mind is to compare the former to wind and the mind to a tree full of leaves. When there is no

who were driving their mother crazy (Chapter 7: Our Sensory World) and extend that analogy a bit. An immediate consequence for the mother is that it is simply impossible for her to concentrate on helping the eldest child prepare for a school test. Now let's say, after dinner the mother puts the kids, starting from the youngest, to bed one by one, except for the eldest. As each child goes to sleep, the home atmosphere becomes more peaceful and the mother's situation improves proportionately. Once the fifth child has retired for the night, the mother is able to focus (concentrate) on helping the eldest. Her own anxiety gradually diminishes as she concentrates on helping the child and she is completely calm by the time she finishes helping.

The mother is analogous to the mind and the six children to the six senses. In Calming Meditation what we try to do is 'put to sleep' five of the six senses and focus our attention on just one activity associated with the sixth – the sense that is 'awake'. In the case of breathing meditation, the sense that is awake is the sense of touch. So our focus is the sense (or sensation) of the breath *touch*ing the nostrils.

The procedure for the Breathing Meditation is as follows:

- Sit comfortably in the cross-legged position (if you are comfortable with this posture) or simply in a chair with hands cupped and resting on the lap. Keep the back straight with the chin drawn in slightly. Breathe normally and close the eyes.
- With awareness note the in-breath and out-breath as they pass through the tip of the nostrils, as a security guard watches people entering and leaving a building through the main door. Do not follow the breath into the body or out of the body.
- Each time the mind is distracted by a thought, simply acknowledge that (with no aversion or craving) and gently come back to the anchor, that is the breath at the tip of the nostrils. Do this with patience however many times necessary.
- Practice for ten minutes the first day and very gradually increase the duration to a maximum of one hour (usually considered to be an optimal duration for one sitting). The increase in duration is determined by your own estimation of how comfortable you feel with the progress.

---

wind, the leaves are still (calm), therefore the tree is calm. When there is wind, the leaves are agitated.

That is all there is to the essentials of Calming Meditation practice. Now we will cover some noteworthy points of clarification regarding this practice.

1. *Distractions*. The mind *is* going to wander into other thoughts. That is the nature of the untrained mind and that is also the very reason why we have undertaken Calming Meditation practice. So we must accept the discursiveness of the mind and after acknowledging the distraction, gently return to the breath. In accepting its wandering nature, we are for the first time beginning to understand the nature of our own mind, which is a great step in itself. It may help the meditator to mentally note any negative distractions such as "physical pain" or "mental (emotional) distress" and any feelings of joy as "joy" and get back to the breath. After the meditator has acquired some mastery over the practice, this supplementary aid of labeling could be eliminated.

2. *Counting*. Counting the breath could help the beginning meditator to better stay focused on the breath. There are many ways of counting, but for our present purpose the following is suggested. Count the first breath as "one, one". That is, "one" at in-breathing, "one" at out-breathing. Count the second breath as "two, two", the third breath as "three, three" and so on up to "ten, ten". Do not count beyond "ten, ten" as the attention then tends to get diverted to numbers rather than the breath; instead start all over again at "one, one". A very effective alternative to counting is to use the word "Buddho". Use "Bud" at in-breathing and "dho" at out-breathing.

3. *Absorptions*. When the concentration becomes sufficiently deep, the meditator may notice a sign (*nimitta* in Pali) arising, as a mental image. This may take the form of a puff of smoke, a cloud, an image of the Buddha, a gentle touch of breeze or some other form indicative of peacefulness. The arising of this mental image is an indication that the meditator has reached the stage of calmness called 'neighborhood concentration' (*upacara-samadhi* in Pali). This stage is the entry 'door' leading to two paths, one of which must be chosen by the meditator at this point.

    One path leads to various higher stages of 'absorptions' or ecstatic trances (*jhanas* in Pali), intensifying the tranquility realized so far – this path[48] is really continuation of Calming Meditation. The trances

---

[48] Those interested in pursuing the subject of *jhanas* may consult the book *The Jhanas in Theravada Buddhist Meditation* by Mahathera Henepola Gunaratna (Wheel Publication No. 351/353, Buddhist Publication Society, 1988)

will enable the meditator to enjoy spiritual 'highs' which are *transient*. However, they will not take the person one step closer to liberation from existential distress. The other path is Insight meditation, which alone is the way to deliverance from existential distress. Our interest, in the context of this book, is the Insight route, discussed in the next two chapters.

So, what have we gained by doing Calming Meditation up to the point of 'neighborhood concentration'? Two things:

(1) We have brought some degree of calmness to an otherwise agitated mind, so we can proceed to perform the function of rational thinking required in Insight Meditation, and

(2) Though not directly relating to Insight practice, we have developed a skill that can be called upon any time to calm the mind whenever it becomes restless and confused in conducting the 'business' of daily living. This means Calming Meditation can be used for temporary relief of distress, while developing the skill of Insight Meditation for lasting relief.

It is important to bear in mind at this stage that Calming Meditation is a desirable preparatory base for Insight Meditation, but is *not mandatory*. Calming Meditation makes the practice of Insight so much easier. Yet, one can practice Insight Meditation without Calming Meditation, but will find it so much harder. It is like climbing a mountain (in warm weather). One can climb with or without shoes, but proper shoes will certainly make the climb much easier.

Also note that for our purpose of using Calming Meditation as a preparatory base for Insight Meditation, it is not essential that we see a nimitta, but if we *feel* an unusually good sense of peacefulness without seeing things, that is good enough.

4.   *Place and time of day.* It helps to select a place that is quiet, as Calming Meditation is an exercise in concentration. The ideal is a quiet room where you are the only occupant. When this is not possible, meditating in a group in fine, so long as everyone maintains silence. With experience and proficiency, the meditator will be able to practice even within noise and common distractions. Silence is very important for beginning meditators. With regard to time of day,

it is best to allocate a specific time for Calming Meditation practice and adhere to that time slot daily, so that meditation practice becomes part of one's routine like dinner.

5. *Effort.* The effort applied in Calming Meditation is mental only and minimal. All the effort needed is to gently bring the thinking (concentration) back from a discursive thought to the breath at the tip of the nostrils. This is where Calming Meditation primarily differs from *Pranayama* of Yoga practice, where physical effort is applied to the breath and respiratory system to alter the characteristics of one's breath. In *Breathing Meditation* we use the breath itself as is.

6. *Results.* Since meditation is an art in 'going with the flow', one must not expect anything from the practice. The only rule for successful meditation is: start and continue. If you look for results and do not find them, you will get restless and defeat the purpose of the exercise. Don't look for tranquility. When the time is up, tranquility will come as a reward for your doing your part with consistency and dedication. Remember that the initial part of any significant change is allowing the body and mind to get used to a new habit. The mind has been used to running amok all the time to this point, and now we are trying to teach it to stay still and focus on just one thing. It is like learning to drive a standard car after being used to driving an automatic or learning touch typing after being used to one-finger typing. It takes time to change any habit and the same principle applies to changing the behavior of the mind from discursiveness to calmness.

7. *Duration.* Do not be concerned as to the number of minutes you have been able to focus on the breath. Each single thought-moment you are able to focus on the breath is a moment of peace for the mind. So go by the smaller thought-moments, not minutes. So, as far as progress goes, every attempt at meditation by a meditator contains many thought-moments of success, which are not measurable with a clock, but still comprise success.

8. *Comparison.* Finally, do not compare your performance with that of others. Meditation is unique to the individual because each mind is unique. There is no competition or comparison in meditation. When you reach enlightenment, only you will know because it all happens inside *your* mind.

Chapter Insights and Highlights

1) It is in the nature of our untrained minds to wander about restlessly.

2) The objective of Calming Meditation (Pali: *Samatha*) is to tame the restless mind.

3) The calming effect is realized by focusing the mind on one object using only one of the six senses so the mind is not open to the other five senses. The sensory traffic to the mind being vastly reduced, the mind becomes calm.

4) The most popular object of focus is our natural breath. This particular form of Calming Meditation is called Breathing Meditation (Pali: *Anapanasati*).

5) Calming Meditation is used to calm the mind as preparation for Insight Meditation.

6) An additional use of Calming Meditation is as a *temporary* relief for distress. (Insight Meditation provides *lasting* relief for distress).

13

A Preparatory Technique for Insight Meditation

The objective of Insight Meditation is to perceive things without distortion. Put differently, we can say that we want to perceive with right views the things we now perceive with wrong views. This is realized in two stages, namely:

(1) an *intellectual understanding* of precisely what the wrong view is and also understanding what the corresponding right view is (that is, 'right understanding' in formal Dhamma terms), and

(2) *experientially integrating* the right view as a deep meditative insight, the prerequisite for which is the intellectual understanding in (1)

In the present chapter we will see how we can realize the first stage. (The second stage will be covered in the next chapter). To that end, we will become familiar with a technique that has been successfully tried by the author, students in his meditation and stress management classes and also readers of the first edition of the book.

In addition to serving the purpose of an effective stepping stone for Insight Meditation practice, the technique was found to provide significant healing benefits on its own, even before we moved on to, and practiced, the corresponding experiential phase of Insight Meditation.

The technique entails written work, for which the worksheet form shown has proven to be most effective. Before we use the steps of the technique we may need to get some *temporary relief* as the enduring benefits from Insight Meditation take time to ensue. Therefore let's discuss temporary relief first. The objective of temporary relief is to calm the mind sufficiently so it can work on the steps towards abiding peace. To give a practical perspective to the issue of temporary relief, we can state the following:

- Beginners must practice Insight Meditation on incidents of distress <u>after</u> (as opposed to during) the incident whilst using measures of temporary relief to tide themselves over.

- When new views have had time to get rooted in the mind the meditator (who by now is no longer a beginner) will realize the healing effects of Insight Meditation while incidents (that carry the potential for distress) are happening, because the new views are now controlling *involuntary* reactions.

The temporary relief can be obtained by using any one of a number of methods all based on temporary sensory control. Examples are (1) Calming Meditation, particularly the breathing version *(Breathing Meditation)* which is the best, (2) counting to ten and (3) walking away from a stress-triggering situation.

Now we can go through the steps of the technique involving the worksheet:

1) When you are emotionally distressed (or stressed, if you can relate to that term better) following an incident, describe your distress clearly in box (A) in simple language, as if you are speaking to your best friend and confidante. Do not try to analyze or rationalize but 'pour out your mind' onto paper. This write-up will contain a mix of *thoughts* and *feelings*.

2) Read over carefully what you have written in box (A). You will identify a number of distinct *thoughts* (views) connected with your stress, as distinguishable from *feelings*. These are worldly views that are circulating involuntarily ('free running') inside your mind. They are the hurricane winds causing emotional havoc inside you. Extract the distinct thoughts and write them down in Box B as Worldly View 1, Worldly View 2, Worldly View 3 and so on. Leave space below each worldly view for a further entry, as described in the next step.

3) Refer to Table 1 in Chapter 11: Right and Wrong Views. Try to locate, in Table 1, entries closest in meaning to the worldly views listed by you in Box B. Select Right (Transcendental) views that correspond to each worldly view and write them (not necessarily

Worksheet:

(A) <u>STATEMENT OF MY DISTRESS:</u>
(B) <u>ANALYSIS OF MY VIEWS (THOUGHTS)</u> *Worldly View 1:*   *Transcendental Views:*
Worldly View 2:   *Transcendental Views:*
Worldly View 3:   *Transcendental Views:*
(C) <u>ACTION (PRESENT *KARMA*)</u>

verbatim off Table 1 but the meaning) below the corresponding worldly view, as a forceful (willed) challenge to the worldly view. *This is the most important step in the method.   You have just rebutted, in a down-to-earth practical way, the distress-causing worldly thinking with peace-promoting transcendental thinking based on the Dhamma,* i.e., views in touch with reality.   It's a giant step towards attaining peace on this particular distress that you described in Box A.

In terms of modern day neuroscience, given that every thought of ours causes some *change* somewhere in the immense neural network of our brain, you have begun the process of 're-wiring' the brain with peace-promoting thinking, regarding this particular view.   We will explore the fascinating subject of brain re-wiring later in the book.

If Table 1 does not list a particular worldly view you are trying to locate, and therefore the corresponding transcendental view, deduce the latter from the principles of *impermanence, no-self, Dependent Origination* and *cause and effect (karma)* discussed earlier.   If necessary go back to the relevant chapters and read about these subjects again.   Filling in the worksheet is not intended to be a mechanical   operation   but   one   that   requires   thinking   and contemplation from the person filling in the form.

Contemplatively   compare   the   transcendental   view   against   the worldly view for a moment.

4)   Repeat steps 2) and 3) for all other worldly views associated with this particular distress.

5)   The concluding step – very important in its own right – is the *action* step.   After steering the mind to look at the situation in touch with reality in Box (B), now it is time to identify, and take, meaningful action.   This, in Dhamma terms, is the act of doing wholesome karma in the present moment.   The criteria in determining this action are:
   ♦   It should be feasible.
   ♦   It should contribute to the wellbeing, and alleviation of distress, of oneself and/or others.

This   action   step   is   in   Box   (C).   That   completes   filling   in   the worksheet.

Whenever this specific distress resurfaces, read over what you have written regarding it in the worksheet, particularly the transcendental views. *Take action on items listed in Box (C)* – this is of crucial importance. As you do this repeatedly, you will feel the distress abating, first partially, then significantly and with practice completely, as the mind realizes inner peace through the wisdom of Dhamma. A degree of soothing relief is felt. Pitting the right view against the wrong view is like throwing water on a fire burning out of control. It is as though the Buddha's divine influence suddenly appears in our irrationally thinking mind and imbues it with rationality and wisdom and therefore peace. In fact, what we have done is to allow the Buddha's Dhamma to penetrate our mind, since the Buddha is not with us today to help us in person.

It is important that this preparatory technique be carried out *on paper* as we discussed, and not just mentally, because we need to *focus* on our views, but the mind has not yet been trained to focus properly. By writing things, we are forcing the otherwise wandering and perhaps confused mind to stay focused during the exercise. In that sense, we can think of this technique as serving a key purpose of Calming Meditation, that is, as the prerequisite for Insight Meditation.

Let's illustrate the technique with two examples. To keep things simple, we will use two cases that we referred to earlier, that of Alicia's lower back pain (in chapter 6: "Focus on Distress") and Bertram's aversion towards Cousin David (in chapter 7: "Our Sensory World"). The first is an individual problem and the second relational. Let's first re-state the situations briefly.

Example 1: Alicia recently suffered some severe lower back pains. After medical diagnosis, the doctor reported that she has a slipped disk. The doctor explained the possible courses of action, but Alicia became apprehensive.

Example 2: Bertram's relationship with Cousin David has always been unpleasant. He feels David is mean and obnoxious. David visited Bertram's family recently. After meeting David, once again Bertram's mind was like an active volcano. He was burning with so much anger that he continued to be upset even long after David left.

Example 1 (Worksheet as filled by Alicia)

(A) <u>STATEMENT OF MY DISTRESS:</u>

I feel worried and hopeless after the news of the medical diagnosis. Why do these things have to always happen to me? Really, I am to blame because I should have been more careful in the way I used my body in the past; if I had been, this probably would not have happened.

(B) <u>ANALYSIS OF MY VIEWS (THOUGHTS)</u>

Worldly View 1:   Bad things always happen to me. But why me, of all people?

Transcendental Views:

(a) Things happen dependent on nature's law of conditionality only – a cause/effect linkage going back endlessly in time. (One's past karma is one of the operative conditions). Hence, existential distress is universal and has not exclusively chosen me. The law of conditionality does not operate on factors such as the comparison of one person with others or on labels of 'good' and 'bad', which are mere human-devised practices and labels.

So, I have to *accept* the physical distress resulting from the slipped disk but I need not overburden myself with *mental* distress with irrational thoughts such as labeling a happening (slipped disk) as 'bad', asking "why me?" and comparing my distress to that of others.
(Impermanence, Conditionality and Karma)

Worldly View 2:   I should have been more careful in the way I used my body in the past; if I had, this probably would not have happened.

Transcendental Views:
(a) Things happen exactly the way they are supposed to. An unfathomable cause-effect linkage that goes back in endless time determines any happening. So I cannot blame myself for what I did or didn't do up until now. Neither can I visit the past to change what has happened. And I could only do what I knew to do at each moment in my life dependent on the unique mix of ignorance and wisdom prevailing at each moment. *(Dependent Origination, Past Karma)*
(b) However I can take the most sensible action in the present moment to improve things. *(Present Karma)*

(C) ACTION (PRESENT *KARMA*)

I will:
   (a)   Accept any physical distress that is beyond help as 'the way it is'.
   (b)   Facilitate eradication of mental distress by not entertaining such meaningless views as "Why me?"
   (c)   Abstain from self-blame, as all that is done is done.
   (d)   Consult medical experts to determine what's best for me now.

And after consulting medical professionals:

   (e)   Now I have the following possibilities from which to choose an action plan for recovery, subject to discussion with my family and supplementary medical consultation:

   1.   Bed rest for a number of weeks, and pain relieving drugs when necessary – to be followed by wearing a corset or supportive collar. This may turn out to be all I need for full recovery.

   2.   If (1) fails and compression on the nerve root produces muscle weakness (which is not present now), I can consider surgery to relieve the pressure. *(Action – present karma)*

Things are, after all, not as bad as I thought earlier. Now I can see how I over-burdened myself with self-induced and unnecessary mental distress.

Example 2 (Worksheet as filled by Bertram)

(A) <u>STATEMENT OF MY DISTRESS:</u>

By coming here today Cousin David made me infuriated again. I think he shouldn't have visited us. What annoying ways this insolent rascal has!

(B) <u>ASSOCIATED VIEWS:</u>

Worldly View 1: He infuriated me.

Transcendental Views:

(a) It's not others or their behavior that causes me to be upset, but how I perceive them. I need to identify, as I am doing now filling out this form, the wrong views (ignorance) in me that caused me to get upset and with the help of Insight, gradually work to eradicate them. *(Dependent Origination)*

(b) Anger first destroys the one who harbors it, like hot coal picked up with one's hands to be thrown at someone *(karma)*. Furthermore, if the one at whom it is directed is clever enough to duck, he escapes totally unscathed.

(c) In absolute reality there is no 'me" to be upset. So why am I causing unnecessary mental distress for myself trying to protect a self that does not exist? *(No-self)*

Worldly View 2: He shouldn't have visited us today.

Transcendental Views:

(a) The changing nature of everything in the universe, including that of time, has put the incident behind us – it is past. My saying "he shouldn't have visited us today" a million times will not alter the fact that he visited us today. *(Impermanence)*

(b) For the same reason, given time, all that is now existing or happening (Cousin David, myself, and my feelings etc.) will come to pass – into insignificance. So why not think "This too will pass" at the present moment and unload the burden from my mind? *(Impermanence)*

Worldly View 3: He has annoying ways.

Transcendental Views:

(a) He can be anything he wants to, be it wholesome or unwholesome. All I can do is take care of *my* mind (thoughts) and actions. *(Dependent Origination)*

(C)   ACTION (PRESENT _KARMA_)

Now I realize that my emotional distress is caused by a number of wrong views held by me.   To eradicate this distress I will steadfastly contemplate on the corresponding right views in touch with reality as identified above until this particular distress is no more.

It is clear that all we have done on the worksheet is put in writing right Dhammic views to counteract irrational worldly views in an organized manner.   Thereby, we force the otherwise wandering mind to stay focused on the realities of the distress-causing issue.   Remember that thoughts cause feelings, meaning our thoughts arise first and feelings follow.   Hence wrong views cause distress and right views peace.   Replacing wrong views with right views, as we have done in filling in the worksheet, should always help in our efforts to shift the feelings from distress to peace.

The technique indicated in these two illustrative examples can be applied to any other existential problem.   To every imaginable human condition, we can find a solution, once we step out of worldly living and thinking.   Then, we can come back to our worldly living armed with the solution for implementation.

In this chapter we have familiarized ourselves with an effective technique for the _intellectual understanding_ of right views.   That in itself is a beneficial and necessary step on the Path, yet it is a stepping stone.   With the intellectual understanding alone we have not been able to eradicate the old erroneous views _from their roots_ embedded in the deep crevices of the mind.   Therefore, we need to move on to the second phase – the experiential realization of right view in order to obtain the full benefits of our endeavor.

At this stage, the reader is encouraged to fill in the worksheet as it applies to some existential stress he/she is encountering at present, for use in Insight Meditation practice, explained in the next chapter.

Chapter Insights and Highlights

1) Since the nature of the untrained mind is to wander and be restless, entrusting any corrective action to the mind alone tends to end in failure. The untrained mind will wander while being on the very task of correction!

2) The solution is to write things on paper, thereby effectively forcing the mind to stay focused.

3) The written work is done on a worksheet containing three elements:
   a) A statement of the distressing situation.
   b) Associated worldly views and corresponding transcendental views.
   c) Action steps.

4) Steps b) and c) help alleviate the emotional distress.

5) The (beginning meditator) must fill in the worksheet *after* the occurrence of the incident linked to the distress.

6) When new views resulting from the Insight Meditation practice get rooted in one's mind, they will fuel involuntary thinking preventing emotional distress from forming in the first place.

14

Using Insight

Better than a hundred years
Lived in ignorance,
Without contemplation,
Is one single day of life
Lived in wisdom
And deep contemplation.

The Dhammapada 111

In this chapter, we will discuss a fairly simple and practical way in which Insight Meditation can be effectively used in daily living. Therefore our objective is neither a classical[49] treatment of Insight Meditation nor an in-depth analysis of the subject aimed at attaining the higher reaches described in Buddhist scriptures, but a means to realize significant benefits in daily living.

What is Insight Meditation, in practical terms? Let's start with an analogy. If the glass in a window is covered with dirt it will prevent us from getting a clear view of what is outside. In countries that experience sub-zero temperatures, patches of ice can form on the glass, so we get a reduced view of the outside. If there is a wet snowfall on a windy day, a layer of snow can cover the glass. With all these impediments – the dirt, the ice, and the snow – we will barely be able to see the outside or we may get a hazy, distorted view. If we want to get a really clear view of the outside, we need to remove the impediments.

What invariably happens when we ordinarily perceive things is similar to looking through that window. Here our impediments are wrong views – they are the dust, ice and snow of the mind. Our mind cleared of wrong views is like the glass that is cleared of the impediments. So the purpose of Insight Meditation is to clear the mind of wrong views (by experiential

---

[49] The reader interested in pursuing an in-depth study and practice beyond the scope of the present book may consult *Satipatthana Vipassana:* Insight through Mindfulness and/or *Practical Insight Meditation*: Basic and Progressive Stages. Both are by Ven. Mahasi Sayadaw and are published by the Buddhist Publication Society.

means), in order that we have an undistorted view of nature, especially our existence. In other words, see reality. When we perceive things as they really are, our minds are in harmony with nature and truth. Then there is no confusion, restlessness or worry. Instead, our minds become clear and peaceful.

At this point let's review the main difference in technique between Calming Meditation and Insight Meditation. In Calming Meditation our objective is to keep the mind's attention focused on one object via one sense so we cut off sensory input from all other senses. In contrast, in Insight Meditation we let the mind move from object to object or event to event ordinarily encountered in daily living, but observe these phenomena in the light of the basic facts of existence, namely impermanence, no-self and existential distress. In the final analysis, no-self and existential distress are dependent on impermanence, the incontrovertible characteristic of the universe. Hence, to 'see' through impermanence is to 'see' things not the way our senses perceive them (which is invariably subject to inherent distortion) but by transcending the senses with mind-only penetration, i.e., *insight* – hence the reason why the term *Insight Meditation* is used in English for *Vipassana* of Pali.

Diligent and regular practice of Calming Meditation (Chapter 12) makes the mind calm. And a calmed mind has the capability to penetrate what it looks at, contemplate beyond superficial sensory perception and see things that the mind cannot otherwise see. It's similar to the way a microscope helps one to see the details of human tissue that the naked eye cannot see. Furthermore, the preparatory technique described in Chapter 13 helps the mind to *intellectually* identify (a) wrong views through which we look at issues that confront us in our daily lives and (b) the corresponding right views. Armed with these two aids, the mind is prepared and ready to overcome its last hurdle – to *experientially* realize right views as deep meditative insights.

Given diligent practice, this experiential practice will complete the process of dislodging the wrong views from their roots (and substitute right views in their place). With that, peace settles in, as the root causes of agitation no longer exist.

So, the complete sequence of Buddhist meditation can be listed, for our practical purposes, in four steps as follows:

1. An intellectual understanding of right and wrong views pertaining to the issues likely to come up during meditation.

2. Breathing Meditation carried out in *Calming Meditation mode* to bring the mind to the point of 'neighborhood concentration'.

3. Breathing Meditation carried out in *Insight mode* to prepare the breath as 'home base', and model, for Insight practice.

4. Insight, one at a time, into *all objects and events* that the mind moves into in daily living. When we are finished with one particular object or event, we can either proceed to the next object or event of daily living or go back to the 'home base'

Now we will expand on these four steps to obtain a procedure and illustrate the application with examples.

Step 1: Intellectual understanding. The general background to this step was covered in Chapter 13. Review the chapter if needed, particularly during the early days of practice. Go over the contents of the worksheets of the two examples in that chapter and note wrong (worldly) views and the right (transcendental) views. Also, go over the worksheets you filled in at the conclusion of Chapter 13 for evident distress *in your own life* and again note the wrong views and the right views you used to rebut them.

As you progress in practice over a reasonable period of time, this information will become familiar to you and the paper work can be gradually phased out.

Step 2:   Reaching neighborhood concentration. This was described in Chapter 12. Practice Breathing Meditation in Calming Meditation mode (i.e. with the focus on the breath) until you reach neighborhood concentration (perhaps appearance of a mental image[50] - *nimitta;* or feel an unusual sense of calm). Now you are ready to move into mindfulness mode.

Step 3:   Mindfulness of breath ('home base'). Instead of one-pointed focusing on the breath at the tip of the nostrils, we follow and contemplate the whole breath with its movement, without imposing any

---

[50] While neighborhood concentration (a by-product of Calming Meditation) is necessary as a prerequisite to gain *optimal* benefits from Insight Meditation, one can realize substantial benefits from it while still a beginning practitioner of Calming Meditation. In other words, developing Calming Meditation skills and practicing Insight can happen in parallel, though the effectiveness of the latter will be at a reduced level.

restraints or force of even minimal intensity. In our deep contemplation we become mindful of:

- Impermanency of the breath – there is first the birth of the in-breath, then there is a life span of that in-breath and then it dies. We note that what is born dies - what arises ceases. We note the same regarding the out-breath. We observe that the death of one (in-breath) gives rise to birth of another (out-breath). We note the arising of a full breath, its life span, cessation, death and the birth of another full breath. Insightfully, we realize that the same is true of our own lives through *samsara*[51] and that all phenomena in the universe are in incessant flux.

- *No-self.* We observe that breathing happens as a process and does not belong to us. Although we call it *my* breath for purposes of communication, in reality there is no abiding entity that it can belong to – the breath is a part of nature. We also note that there is no abiding entity within the breath itself (although, again, we call it the 'breath' for purposes of communication.)

- *Distress*[52]. There is constant effort needed to support the breath and so there is distress associated with it.

- *Corollaries* that follow from the three basic facts. For example, we observe that we cannot hold on to an in-breath or out-breath, for we will die; we learn, therefore, that if we cling to things subject to the law of impermanence (and all things are), we have to suffer. So we understand the need to constantly let go of things.

Step 4: Mindfulness of objects/events. When we have established mindfulness of the breath (our 'home base'), then we follow the mind and be aware of whatever the mind moves on to – it can be an object (examples: a tree or a cloud or a person) or event (examples: a feeling of anger or pounding of ocean waves or the sound made by a lawnmower). We observe the phenomena in deep contemplation, insightfully realizing things in relation to the basic facts of existence – impermanence, distress, no-self. The details of procedure are similar to those in step 3.

---

[51] *Samsara* (Pali) is the continuous process of ever again and again being born, growing old, suffering and dying.
[52] Insight appplies not only to situations of distress but also happiness. However, states of happiness are transient and invariably return to distress.

To illustrate, let's assume that each one of us meditators is Bertram of example 2[53] in Chapter 13. Sometime after we are mindfully established on the breath, let's say our thoughts go to Cousin David resulting in feelings of aversion (anger etc.). As each wrong (worldly) view arises in the mind, we contemplate and deeply realize the corresponding transcendental truth that surfaces when we consider the basic facts of existence, as filled in on the worksheet of example 2.

When we see things as they really are, that is against the backdrop of the basic facts of existence, we are able, with the power of the mind prepared by Calming Meditation, to intercept sensory impingements *before* the information gets colored by wrong views. This is *bare attention* – that is, the bare object seen as it really is. Now we have the basis for seeing the object, or event with insight (wisdom). We have then realized what we earlier referred to as *experiential* knowledge, the step above intellectual knowledge.

To illustrate, recall the following 'slide show' steps (Chapter 7):
1. It is an object, white, moving.
2. It is a man.
3. It is Cousin David.
4. David is a selfish, mean and obnoxious person, who has never spoken a good word to me.
5. I always end up in a confrontation with him.
6. I hate David, the village bully.

As a base for seeing things as they really are (with the mind at 'neighborhood concentration'), our meditative grasp should be able to intercept the sensory data just after step 1 in this example. Then we have objectively seen form, color and movement only, and it is before the slightest subjective interpretation has arisen. Now we insightfully contemplate what is seen until the truths penetrate us in the light of the basic facts of existence.

As we begin to see David in the light of impermanence, no-self and distress, our whole perspective and attitude change from negativity (illusion) to reality. Anger and aversion are replaced by compassion and unconditional love for David because we no longer see him as an entity (self) separate from us, but we are one (universe). The earlier biased view of Cousin David in isolation now changes to one that merges with a universal unbiased view applicable to all beings. Our own mental state changes from agitation to peace.

---

[53] The reader may also want to try out example 1 for practice.

When the mind moves to another object or event (a feeling, a sight, a noise, etc.), we repeat the same process looking at it insightfully against the backdrop of impermanence, no-self and distress. Then we move onto either the next object/event or 'home base' and so on covering every aspect of daily living. Where worksheets have been filled in and reviewed before the practice was begun, recall the thoughts recorded on them to facilitate contemplation, in the early stages of the practice. As we become more adept at the practice, we may do away with the adjunct of worksheets.

As one progresses in the practice of Insight Meditation, applying it to everything that comes up in life, one's whole outlook on life, one's behavior and the manner of interaction with others and the world take on a totally different and increasingly wholesome flavor. The meditator's whole life begins to gradually move from dissatisfaction to joy. The culmination[54] of continued practice is the realization of a blissful state of mind hitherto not experienced, where everything without exception is seen exactly as it is, that is, in the light of impermanence and no-self. The mind settles into a state of calmness and awareness where no fresh karma is produced. When there is no karma, there can be no birth; the cycle of birth and death comes to an end and the meditator realizes Sublime Peace.

Chapter Insights and Highlights

1) All *emotional* distress in our lives is the result of how we view the world, which in turn depends on views we hold in our minds, which are not in touch with reality.

2) Insight meditation enables us to replace these wrong views with views in touch with reality, therefore moving from distress to inner peace.

3) Insight practice may be thought of as comprising four steps:

- An intellectual understanding of wrong and right views.
- Breathing Meditation in Calming Meditation mode to calm the mind as preparation for Insight Meditation.

---

[54] This may happen in this lifetime or in a future life dependent on the refinement of one's practice and the dedication and effort the meditator puts into the practice. The reader interested in a detailed treatment of this phase of the practice should consult an acclaimed classic such as *The Heart of Buddhist Meditation* by Nyanaponika Thera and/or *The Path of Purification* by Bhikkhu Nanamoli and/or *Practical Insight Meditation* by Ven. Mahasi Sayadaw. They are published by the Buddhist Publication Society.

- Breathing Meditation in Insight Meditation mode to prepare the breath as 'home base' and model for Insight practice.
- Advancing Insight Meditation to all objects and events that the mind moves to in daily living.

15

Gratitude

In this Part A of the book we have covered some of the key principles of Dhamma and explored ways and means to apply them to our daily living. While the principles of the Buddha's teachings are universal and timeless in their applicability, their actual application to an individual has to become, in the final analysis, a personal endeavor. The Buddha's Dhamma is an accurate road map[55] but it's up to the seeker to do the walking, using it until the destination is reached. This personal endeavor takes the form of diligent practice of the Dhamma. To quote the Buddha's last words[56]: *"Strive with earnestness"*. In those three words lie the secret to the difference between continued distress and inner peace in our lives.

To strive with earnestness one needs a strong inner conviction that purification of one's own mind is the most important mission in his or her life from the present moment onward. That conviction must be followed with persistent effort in the practice of Dhamma in daily life with a degree of determination reflected in the following words of the Buddha[57]: "...I shall not give up my efforts till I have attained whatever is attainable by manly perseverance, energy and endeavor." Yet there must be the patience and understanding that the progress on the path will be gradual.[58]

It is not uncommon for a Buddhist facing seemingly unsolvable adversity to think, in desperation: "If only the Buddha was alive today, I would not be going through this." At times like these, one should recall the Buddha's advice to disciple Ananda prior to his passing away: "For that which I have proclaimed and made known as the Dhamma and the Discipline, that shall be your Master when I am gone"

---

[55] "It is you who must make the effort. The Buddhas only show the way." From The Dhammapada 276
[56] From the Maha Parinibbana Sutta
[57] Majhima Nikaya, Sutta 70
[58] "Bhikkhus, I do not say that final knowledge is achieved all at once. On the contrary, final knowledge is achieved by *gradual* training, by *gradual* practice, by *gradual* progress." Majhima Nikaya, Sutta 70.

The Buddha is not with us today, but the Dhamma is alive and well. So we need not use the fact of the Buddha's absence as an excuse to sink into hopelessness, whatever our adversity may be. In fact, in certain aspects, the Dhamma is doing much better today than it was in the Buddha's time. During the Buddha's lifetime one had to be in his presence (in India) to benefit from his wisdom, as there were no books on Dhamma at the time. Very few of the world's population were indeed fortunate to be able to listen to the Buddha (and with the passage of time, his knowledgeable disciples). In contrast, today the Dhamma is, or can be made, easily accessible to any person anywhere in the world. So today's world is really more fortunate than that of the Buddha's era. All that is required of us today is a keenness to study and understand the principles of Dhamma and to practice diligently.

Also, the struggle we face is small compared to the Buddha's, thanks to the Buddha himself. There was no Dhamma when he began his search – the monumental struggle to find the solution to existential distress. There was no one to show him the way – no guiding light ahead of him. During his days of searching, groping in the dark for six years, he knew only what the problem was but not the solution. All he had was hope, determination, courage and absolute self-confidence that he will find the solution. Eventually he did find it - the unsurpassed Dhamma. The Buddha had to *discover and apply.* We have only to *apply.*

Within the spectrum of Dhamma exists the means to transcend any human distress, whether caused by a little irritant or the worst human tragedy. The Dhamma principles covered in this book should provide us with a solid basis from which to build the necessary individualized practice. With the right effort and discipline injected into that practice, we can gradually transcend distress and make constant progress toward inner peace, feeling the healing effects in our daily lives as we progress. Along the way, at some point, we will know we are at the start of the last lap. Then, with further help from the Buddha's teachings, we will begin to tread that last lap with confidence, and hopefully in this very life, reach the state of Sublime Peace.

When we realize the unsurpassed gift that the Buddha left for us, we feel equally unsurpassed awe, respect and everlasting gratitude to him. The best that we can do to demonstrate that gratitude is to diligently practice Dhamma in our lives and do all in our power to keep the Dhamma alive for the benefit of future generations. That would be the noblest mission we can ever hope to undertake in this life.

So let's begin now and *strive with earnestness.*

~

Homo Sapiens Under Distress

~

Sub-Preface to Part B

This part is a somewhat deeper exploration of some of the more important aspects that were either briefly mentioned or penetrated to a lesser degree in Part A. These aspects are:

- The important concept of *reality* (Chapters 16 – 18).

- The biological mechanism that underlies distress (19 – 24).

- The neural basis of emotions (25, 26).

- A scientific examination of *the self* (27, 28).

- A hitherto unexplored aspect of conditionality that has important ramifications on daily living (29)

In a way, we might say that Part B attempts to explain *why* we said some of the things we did say in Part A. Thus most of Part B is an attempt to establish rationale for critical premises relating to the Path of Inner Peace.

But why is it important to know rationale? The answer is simple. The human mind will accept new ideas and suggestions best and retain them well when the 'whys' are known, in contrast to when it is asked to accept things on faith.

In spite of the appearance of some scientific and philosophical concepts, for example *neural communication* and *reality* respectively, the reader will find the subject matter of Part B becoming meaningful and interesting (and even fascinating) as we gradually progress through the material. Also, Part B is an essential pre-requisite for appreciating the all-important Part C that deals with our common daily problems and their resolution.

The reader not familiar with science will encounter some new terms, which we had no choice but to use, to explain some essential topics. We advise the reader not to get too bogged down in these terms, but proceed with the exploration absorbing meanings in context.

.

16

Perception and Reality

"Up to the 20th century, reality was everything humans could touch, smell, see, (taste) and hear. Since the initial publication of the chart of the electromagnetic spectrum, humans have learnt that what they can touch, smell, see, (taste) and hear is **less than one-millionth of reality.** ...."

Buckminster Fuller
Famous Engineer, Architect and Inventor

Reality (or the synonym *truth[59]*) is a term that we encounter throughout our lives. Sometimes its meaning seems crystal clear to the user's mind, as when a mother says to her child, "Now tell me the real truth, Natalie – did you take your brother's book or not?" Here the truth lies in a simple 'yes' or 'no'. This is one meaning of the word *truth* – the easy one. The other – the one to be addressed in this chapter - is when the term is applied in a profoundly philosophical context. Here the meaning is usually hazy and the term refers to something profound in which clarity is being sought, such as the truth of distress (a 'Noble Truth' in Dhamma) or the truth of the origin of life (science).

At this stage one might ask, "Why bother with truth? Why can't we carry on living without all these investigations about truth and absolute reality?"

The answer is: "In the final analysis, all the important things that happen to us during our existence, the good and the bad, are caused and controlled by truths operating as *undercurrents*." For a tangible analogy let's consider earthquakes. In earthquake-prone regions, before an earthquake occurs, everything appears normal on the surface but the undercurrents beneath are building towards the event. If the

---

[59] Because of established usage, the three terms *truth, reality* (used without adjective) and *absolute reality* are used in this book as synonyms implying that which is beyond sensory perception. In contrast, the term *worldly reality* is used to imply that which is perceived with our six senses. These terms are discussed in greater detail in Chapter 18: *Reality in Perspective*

undercurrents (truth) are known in advance, much destruction of life can be averted. Such was the case of the 1987 California earthquake that was correctly predicted by measuring underground pressure waves. Thus it was not the sensory perception of Californians that foresaw what was to come but the undercurrents which were detected by extra-sensory means (scientific instruments). The message here is that the truth prevails over human sensory perception in determining the course of our existence. Therefore, the closer[60] we can get to understanding the truth behind the phenomena that affect us, the closer we will be to guiding our own destiny, including mitigation of existential distress.   Two further examples will illustrate this.

Annabelle used to be emotionally devastated at the death of close friends and relatives. Then she participated in a meditation retreat at which the truth of the impermanence of things was effectively established in the minds of the participants. Since then, Annabelle has been able to accept death as the way things are. Now she is able to handle death in a more accepting and realistic manner.

Brad is a seemingly healthy man of 38. He ate and drank well and enjoyed the 'good life'. He never bothered to visit the doctor for his annual check-up because he felt he was in good health. Then suddenly he had a stroke. Upon investigation medical personnel discovered that Brad has high blood pressure (HBP) and elevated cholesterol and no doubt has had for a long time. If Brad had known the truth about his health, the stroke would have been averted. Now, what is the truth about his health? It is that both HBP and elevated cholesterol:

a)   are risk factors for cardiovascular disease,
b)   generally do not produce symptoms (hence they are referred to as "silent killers"),
c)   can only be detected by clinical means (measuring HBP and testing blood cholesterol levels)
d)   can both be brought down to safe levels with lifestyle changes and/or medication.

What is not the truth is Brad's conclusion that his health is fine because he felt fine.

Just like the truths ('undercurrents') that were behind the perceivable events in the above examples, in the final analysis all other perceivable

---

[60] In practice, 'closer to the truth' becomes a more meaningful term to use than 'truth', because of the difficulty ordinary humans have in transcending sensory perception completely to realize truth (absolute reality).

things that happen to us during this existence (cancer, winning the lottery, death of a loved one etc.) are similarly caused by appropriate truths. Hence, if we are to really know our existence, the distress within it, and how to overcome that distress, we have to investigate and know the truth, and where truth is impractical to reach, at least get as close as we can get to truth. It is important. It is practical. The search for truth is not a mere exercise for academics and philosophers.

Now, let's start our investigation of the subject of Perception and Reality. In order to be aware of anything, three entities must be present:

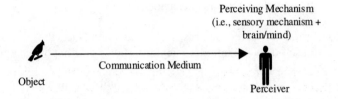

1. The *object* (e.g., bird) or phenomenon (e.g., thunder). For brevity we will refer to either as the object. Then, what each individual perceives as the 'world out there' is made up of objects.

2. The *communication medium*, which is external to the observer. In the example of the bird, it will be *light* reflected from the bird and reaching the eyes of the perceiver.

3. The *perceiving mechanism* comprising of:

   (a) the sensory organ (in our example, *the eye* of the perceiver) and
   (b) relevant parts of the *brain/mind* mechanism (in the example, that which is involved with the sense of seeing and perceiving the particular object as a bird).

   (For brevity in writing, we will often refer to the brain/mind component as the *mind; also* the term *sensory mechanism* to mean *perceiving mechanism* because the former is a more familiar term than the latter.)

1 and 2 are external to the perceiver and 3 is internal.

In our daily lives we experience *the world* (of colors, shapes, sounds etc.) by focusing all our attention on the external objects with our sensory mechanisms. Thus, we see a bird, hear the sound of a car, taste ice cream and so on. While we perceive these objects, we do not pay attention to what is happening in *our* sensory mechanisms (associated with the eye, ear, tongue etc.) or in *our* minds. Normally, we do not even think of the presence of such mechanisms in us because they were there from the day we were born and therefore their use is now habit. Thus, *we take what is perceived to be reality.* If significant to the perceiver, this 'reality' is committed to memory and becomes one more perception added to a myriad of other perceptions of a lifetime, that uniquely make up, and influence, an individual's life and behavior.

The conclusion of perception as reality assumes that the sensory mechanism itself does not introduce any distortion. This implies that the mechanism is adequate for perceiving reality (i.e., for seeing[61] things as they really are). But is this so? If not, then is reality one thing and what we perceive another? Do we actually perceive a 'shadow' (illusion) while reality is outside our range of perception? If we are to know the true nature of the world and ourselves, then it is important that we answer these questions by investigating and understanding our biological mechanisms. In order to come up with the answers, we will now explore a number of avenues. In later chapters we will discuss in some detail, the part played by the mind.

If our purpose in life is not merely to procreate, but to realize the truth behind our existence, then the investigations we are about to embark on will show that *our sensory mechanisms are inadequate for that purpose.* In fact, often what our senses and the mind provide us with is mostly a *distorted* view of truth (reality), so that we may rightly refer to our senses as *'truth-distorting senses'* and the complementary (untrained) mind as the *'truth-distorting mind'*.

If we are to overcome the deficiencies, or extend the capabilities, of sensation and perception, it is clear that this has to be achieved by the sensory mechanism, that is by (a) the senses and (b) the mind. (a) can be realized by providing adjuncts for the sensory organs. This is achieved to a reasonable degree by science and technology in many areas, in particular by the provision of *instruments*. (b) can be realized by fine tuning one's mind to surpass normal ability and with the sharpened mind

---

[61] Where better readability warrants, occasionally the word *see* is used here and elsewhere in a conventional sense to imply *perceive* (with any of the six senses and not just the eyes). This will be apparent from the context

observe the unfolding of natural events as they occur, that is, to see things as they really are, while the sensory mechanisms remain unaided. This is *meditation*, which was the means adopted by the Buddha to achieve Full Enlightenment with a mind that was optimally fine-tuned. In this chapter and the next we focus our attention mostly on (a), specifically, the means that science and technology has provided for us to more closely perceive reality, than is possible with the bare senses.

Now, onto a little bit of science. First, we will examine the electromagnetic (EM) spectrum, which the reader will recall we referred to briefly in Chapter 7. It provides a meaningful way to understand what our sensory mechanisms are capable (and incapable) of doing, in enlightening us about reality.

The EM spectrum is the science's representation, in the form of a chart, of the complete range of radiation energy present in the universe. This energy is related to the behavior of electricity and magnetism which are fundamental attributes of our universe and which affect our lives and the lives of other beings each moment of existence. For example, a part of the sun's radiation energy arriving on the earth gives us every calorie of energy needed for our existence – for an endless list of actions such as breathing, eating, thinking and feeling. Therefore, an understanding of the EM spectrum should provide us with one of the important keys to understanding our existence in the universe (the cosmos and the micro-cosmos).

The EM spectrum contains radio, TV, microwave, infrared, *visible light*, ultraviolet (UV), X-ray, Gamma and Cosmic rays. Of these different kinds of radiation energy, we are sensitive to *only* visible light. This is because the human body has an organ that can only detect visible light and no other. That organ is our eye, which we may refer to as a 'biological instrument'. Together, visible light (the communication medium) and the sensory mechanism (eye/mind) enable us to see. If we have visible light but no eye mechanism - as in blindness - we cannot see. If we have the eye mechanism but no visible light - as in darkness - again we cannot see. Through the entity of visible light, we have our obvious and *direct* dependence on the EM spectrum. To perceive the universe further, we have also an invisible and *indirect* dependence on the other components of the EM spectrum via human-made adjuncts, as we shall see later.

Up until the 18th century, humans had no idea at all about the existence of forms of radiation besides visible light. Then, gradually, scientists began to acquire more and more information about different forms of radiation besides light. Although a fair bit is known about the EM spectrum now, there is more that is unknown (including where it begins and ends). So the scientific exploration of the EM spectrum continues.

The spectrum is very long. Visible light (radiation, which the eye is sensitive to,) occupies an extremely tiny slot: <u>less than one-millionth</u>[62], of the EM spectrum. *What we can observe with our eyes is therefore less than a millionth of the reality 'out there'*, and that too, assuming our eyesight and associated mental/physical support systems are in peak health and do not introduce any distortion to what is seen. For example, if I am color-blind, the reality that I can perceive will be reduced even below the 'less-than-one-millionth' mentioned above. The window of the EM spectrum occupied by visible light may be compared to the "peep-hole" in the entry door of a house. We can just see enough to assist in deciding whether or not to open the door. But the vast remainder of the world beyond the door remains unseen by us.

As far as our unaided sensory perception of the world around us is concerned, we are living in almost total 'darkness'. In that sense, all of us are near-totally blind – enough of a reason for us, tiny specs in an immense and complex universe, to feel utterly humbled. Therefore, we are not knowers of what is around us; not even a millionth of it. If we think otherwise, it's nothing but a reflection of our delusion and indulgence in vainglory. The situation improves somewhat as we supplement our sensory mechanisms with adjuncts. In that improved environment of science and technology we have been able to achieve what may appear to us sometimes as almost miraculous progress (such as space travel and heart transplants). Yet, in terms of the total reality of the universe and our own existence in the universe, we have to humbly admit that we still remain almost totally blind – our knowledge is but a drop in the ocean. The sudden appearance of a new disease such as AIDS and our inability to have total control over it (including a cure) amply demonstrate that fact.

To gain some insight into the nature of our perception of reality let's look at four examples from a list that is endless, the first two relate to the EM spectrum.

Example 1. It was Grandma's 85th birthday. The night was clear so the party was held in the garden of her idyllic country residence. Grandma is

---

[62] Just to give a pictorial idea, if we draw the full EM spectrum as a straight-line 20 miles long, the portion of that line occupied by visible light is about an inch.

a somewhat accomplished astronomer; so she thought that this would be an ideal opportunity to entertain her guests with a little fun stargazing. She focused her amateur telescope on a star and invited others to view it. As the first stargazer was looking through the telescope, Grandma said, "You are looking at the star Achernar. It is my favorite star this year."

After the amateur stargazers had enjoyed the view of this star (which is one of the ten brightest stars in the night sky), granddaughter Chantay asked why Grandma said Achernar is her favorite star this year. Grandma thought this was a good opportunity to educate her eager audience including Chantay with a few facts. Her micro-lesson in astronomy follows:

"Although I said 'You are looking at Achernar' and for sure you *felt* you were looking at it as it exists now, in reality you were looking at the star as it existed 85 years ago, that is in the year I was born! Now you know why Achernar is my favorite star this year. 85 years is how long the quantum of light that left Achernar has taken to reach our planet Earth. Between the instant the light left the star and today, the star could have even died. Therefore, all we can say with certainty is that the light that left Achernar 85 years ago just entered our eyes.

It takes different times for light from different cosmic bodies to reach the Earth, simply because they are at different distances from the Earth. It takes one second for light to travel 300,000 kilometers. So you can imagine the vastness of the distance the light has traveled from the year I was born. An example of a star even further away than Achernar is Deneb. When we think we are seeing Deneb today, we are really seeing light that left the star 1,830 years ago, that is, a little over 100 years after the death of Christ."

So what is the message of the foregoing discussion? To believe that we are *seeing* Achernar, or Deneb or any other star, is a sensory illusion. In general, to believe that what is perceived as being reality is a sensory illusion.

Example 2. Alan, a North American, brings home a tribesman who he befriended during a trip to a remote corner of the world, where the latter lived like our very early ancestors, untouched by the technological progress of the rest of the world. Much has already amazed the tribesman during his trip to North America, but for a moment let us focus on the details of just one experience. The two men enter a modern supermarket, with Alan walking ahead of the tribesman. The door opens 'on its own' and the tribesman is amazed at what happened. In accordance with accustomed beliefs, the tribesman will most likely think that Alan possesses magical or god-like powers and attribute the opening of the door to those powers. He believes this because he <u>does not know</u> that a thing called science and technology is behind the operation. (To be a bit more specific, to open or close doors use is made of detection devices that sense certain waves bounced off, or emitted by, or reflected by, the person.)

Example 3. With regard to what we presently do not know (i.e., our ignorance) and the kind of thinking and action resulting from that ignorance, we are not much different than our tribesman friend. There is the usual human tendency to attribute a currently unexplainable happening to all types of imagined causes, all of which may be wrong. *When we do not have the knowledge or insight to explain the true cause of something or are helpless at an effective intervention (e.g., save a loved one from a serious health condition), the tendency is often to 'plug in' a supernatural agency. The truth is that that agency exists only within our belief system, that is, in the human mind.* To the believer, the belief often provides temporary mental relief in that a way has been found out of a situation in which one felt totally helpless.

As an example, not too long ago, one would have prayed to the gods for help to cure a loved one suffering from pneumonia. However, today with the cause known (lung inflammation by infectious organisms), prayer to the gods is replaced by antibiotics. Therefore, we may be justified in saying that all things for which we now invoke supernatural intervention will, one by one, be replaced with scientific explanations based on natural processes in due course. The supernatural is supernatural only until we can scientifically explain it. A miracle is a miracle only until we can explain the miracle.

Example 4. Human beings have always passed judgement on other human beings based on truth-distorted perceptions, sometimes with grave consequences. At the societal level, it is deemed that passing judgements is essential to maintain law and order. Whether it be by the individual or society, those who pass judgement must be aware of the possibility that their judgement could be subject to error, even if information used is considered current at the time the judgement is made. Even more importantly, action that follows the judgement should not bypass the fact of possibility of error.

A case in point is capital punishment. People in many countries are put to death at the whim of the executioner or with 'justification', after summary trials, on grounds far shifted from the truth. Even in the democratic Western world, seemingly reliable judicial systems have convicted some people based on what was perceived to be the truth. Later, with the availability of new techniques, such as DNA testing, the truth revealed that the 'convicted' were innocent. Unfortunately, in some cases the truth unfolded only after the persons were executed. Developments such as these recently led certain governing bodies (few though) to reconsider things. For example the State of Illinois, USA, declared a moratorium on executions referred to by the State Governor as, "our state's shameful record of convicting innocent people and putting them on death row."

Before we initiate irreversible actions of significance, especially those that are bound to cause harm to other human beings, we need to give the highest consideration to one fact that is of paramount importance. That is that our sensory mechanisms are truth-distorting and therefore we must exercise extreme caution when making judgements, either as individuals or in groups.

Homo Sapiens, watch thy perceptions!

Chapter Insights and Highlights

1. For us to be aware of anything there must be an object, a communication medium and a sensory mechanism (made up of the senses and the mind). We usually focus all of our attention on the objects ('the world out there') and are indifferent to the sensory mechanisms.

2. While the electromagnetic spectrum is our key to penetrating and understanding the universe, the human sensory mechanism is sensitive to less than one millionth of the spectrum and is therefore utterly inadequate to know reality.

3. Even the less-than-one-millionth of reality that can be seen is seen with some distortion, as our senses are imperfect. **Thus we may rightly refer to our senses as "truth-distorting senses".**

4. While our knowledge of reality of the universe is miniscule, within that capability we have made progress that *seems* astounding.

5.   A basic error of human beings is to think that what is seen is reality and that judgements made on what is seen is true. Then, let's be aware *in daily living, that (1) we can make wrong judgements about others and (2) equally well, others can make erroneous judgements about us.* Such awareness is therapy and contributes significantly to harmony amongst humans.

6.   To be in touch with reality and therefore to develop inner peace, we need to understand our sensory mechanisms and transcend their limitations.

7.   Transcendence is possible at the level of the senses to variable degrees with adjuncts (instruments) and Calming Meditation, and totally possible at the level of the mind with Insight Meditation.

8.   Usually we attribute happenings we do not presently understand to supernatural agencies and discontinue the supernatural factor when scientific explanations become available. To quote the celebrated science-fiction writer and inventor of the communications satellite Arthur C. Clarke, "Any sufficiently advanced technology is indistinguishable from magic".

Practice for Inner Peace

Case 1:

Not a moment of our waking life passes by without our *seeing* something of the world around us (objects). So let's focus our attention on this sensation of *seeing*.

We set about life taking what is seen to be reality and not questioning the sensory (processing) mechanism within us to check if its processing was accurate. In this practice we *will* question our sensory mechanism.

There are numerous occasions when we see another person, form a view about that person and believe that conclusion to be reality. Our subsequent actions relating to that person are influenced by that view. This is particularly so when we meet another person for the first time ("first impression").

Select one such event, pause for a moment and ask yourself a few questions. " How did my eyes, ears and the mind form this view about this person? Is it possible that I may not have seen things properly? Could I have heard things erroneously? (And most importantly of all), is it possible that *my* mind may have processed the information incorrectly and left me with a wrong conclusion or judgment?"

See how you feel after this self-interrogation.

Observe how you think, feel and react when you see this person next or when you see another person?

Try to integrate this self-interrogation into your daily living.

(In later chapters, as part of Insight meditation, we will learn not only how to properly query our views but also to challenge what we perceive to be reality and re-align our thinking for inner peace. For now, when we form views and make judgments, let's make a conscious effort to pause occasionally and interrogate our senses and the mind as in the above example and observe how we feel as a result. Let's pay particular attention when we make a 'big issue' about any thing or any person as we live our daily lives).

Case 2:

When someone says something about you – good or bad, praise or blame – remember it is a reflection of the other person's sensory mechanism, not yours. The same applies to the other person's action. The other person's speech or action carries with them the distortions of the sensory mechanisms, and views, of that person, not your's. So we should not take as truth, and not react to, others' expressions but only use them as raw, unprocessed input for our own processing.

17

Help from Instruments

(Concluding the opening quotation of the last chapter,)

Ninety-nine percent of all that is going to affect our tomorrows is being developed by using **instruments** and working in ranges of reality that are nonhumanly sensible.

Buckminster Fuller

" 'Yes, I have a pair of eyes', replied Sam, 'and that's just it. If't they wos a pair o'patent double million magnifyin' gas microscopes of hextra power, p'raps I might be able to see you through a flight o'stairs and a deal door; but bein' only eyes, you see, my wision's limited' "

Charles Dickens, Pickwick Papers

In the last chapter we briefly mentioned that adjuncts (instruments) help us perceive things a step closer to absolute reality than our bare senses permit. In other words, and to be closer to the subject of this book, we can say that science, armed with information gathered using instruments, can enable us to understand the natural laws of existence (Dhamma) expeditiously. This is a great help, since Dhamma, as written in the scriptural works, is generally difficult for the average person to understand. Therefore, let's examine the role of instruments in some detail.

First, note that as functional units, our sensory mechanisms are 'instruments' (though biological) 'installed' in our body to enable us to see, hear, touch, smell, taste and react to mental images. Therefore, we may call them 'biological instruments' as opposed to human-made physical instruments such as microscopes, telescopes and X-ray machines. These physical instruments *make up for some inherent deficiencies of the biological instruments that prevent us from sensing the objects with the clarity we desire.* That is, they enable us to perceive certain aspects of the universe closer to reality than is possible with our sensory mechanisms alone. Therefore, in usage, a physical instrument becomes an extension of the (primary) biological instrument. Thus, when we look at human tissue under a microscope, we are really using two instruments – the eye (the biological instrument) and its physical extension, the microscope.

Why are we not equipped with *biological* instruments that are sensitive to detect forms of radiation energy other than visible light? The answer is because Nature is 'interested' in providing us with the capability of *only* one thing: the propagation of the species and enough survival means for that purpose. All of our natural capabilities are based on that principle. Nature is not interested in any species (including humans) knowing reality or truth. Thus, as Nature oversaw us evolve from unicellular life to human beings, it did not find it essential for us to have as part of our biology, the capability to detect forms of radiation *outside* visible light.

Of the vast spread of the electromagnetic (EM) spectrum, Mother Nature 'deemed' that making us sensitive to a tiny part – the visible light part – is enough for our survival and procreation. Therefore, if we wish to detect the phenomena outside visible light to better understand and use the world around us, i.e., perceive things closer to reality, we have to develop complementary external instruments. That is exactly what scientists have done in developing instruments such as microwave receivers and X-ray machines. These instruments work with forms of radiation invisible to us (i.e., outside the visible light part of the spectrum) but translate the results into a format our senses, primarily sight, can detect.

It is a somewhat different story with (optical) microscopes and (optical) telescopes. They extend the capability of the optical system *within* the visible light part of the EM spectrum but do not venture into the enormous spread outside the visible light part. The telescope helps us with the cosmos, the world of gigantic things, by enabling us to see close-ups of objects that are at greater distances than the eye can see. The microscope helps us see the microcosmos, the world of tiny things. *Thus, these instruments have helped us to overcome deficiencies in our sensory mechanism of sight.* In doing so, they have enabled us to see a bit more of the world out there than is possible with our senses alone.

Next we examine a physical instrument associated with hearing. We are bombarded with radio waves (along with other types of radiation), originating from man-made devices (radio transmitting stations) as well as celestial bodies, every moment of our existence. Unfortunately, we cannot detect (receive) them because the human body does not have a corresponding biological instrument for radio waves. However, when we bring in an appropriate physical instrument (a radio), which can receive EM radio waves and convert them to sound waves, then we can (indirectly) hear radio transmissions because our ears are sensitive to sound waves. In doing so, we have *effectively* extended the capability of our sensory (auditory) system to cover EM radio transmissions. Here we have slightly widened the 'peep-hole' available to us enabling us to perceive a little bit more than our auditory system allows.

Had Nature 'deemed' it necessary for us to have the capability to detect radio signals directly, all we would have needed was our auditory system to be enhanced (during the course of our evolution) to add, biologically, the functional capability of the radio. However, it didn't happen that way and we go about as we are, forever bombarded by radio waves, yet being totally unaware that they ever exist. *Thus our auditory system is adequate to hearing sound, but inadequate to detect radio waves.* This example brings home the fact that **there are laws and processes in operation that are real but which cannot be detected by human beings with their six senses.** There are no gods or other supernatural powers behind them. It is simply that these things happen outside the grasp of our six senses of sight, hearing, touch, taste, smell and mental action.

Let's look at another example. Had Nature deemed it necessary for us to see beyond the skin of other people, all we would need is the functional capability of machines such as X-ray, CT (also called CAT) and PET scanners to be added biologically to our sensory system. Then we could see what's going on inside others (!) – fractures, tumors, cells, brain activity (and therefore clues to what others are thinking and feeling!) as well as many other processes. What a fascinating capability it would have been (besides providing a gold mine of information for gossip!), but Nature again did not deem it necessary for procreation and survival. As a result, we do not have the functionalities of X-ray, CT Scan and other machines built into our biological systems.

Does the availability of many physical instruments of the types referred to above make us better 'knowers' of the world out there? Only a little bit better. For one thing, all humans cannot have extensions of the sensory mechanisms in the form of physical instruments available to them to carry around. Usually, information is gathered via physical instruments by a limited few (e.g., the astronomer for the telescope and medical scientist for the microscope). This information is made available to the rest of us via communication media such as books, newspapers, radio, television and the Internet. Then, we (the public) access only information of interest to us, adding to our knowledge (and sometimes to our wisdom), which otherwise would not have been possible.

In day-to-day living the vast majority of us depend, most of the time, on our sensory mechanisms just as human beings did before the advent of science. However, there is one difference. We now have the added benefit of useful knowledge, obtained by scientists through the use of instruments, available to us via all forms of educational media, not only for matters that concern procreation and survival, but also for spiritual development.

Here's an interesting example to bring home the essence of this chapter. 2500 years ago the Buddha proclaimed, amongst other profound teachings, that our mind is in constant flux.

A very sick boy named Walton is in a state of deep sleep in a University hospital and is connected to a brain-imaging device. Walton's father, Larry, sits next to Walton. He has heard of the Buddha's teaching that the mind is in constant flux, but had not given any further thought to what that meant. Larry gazes at Walton with the notion of an unchanging mind as the backdrop to his thinking.

In a corner of the room, a neurologist is intently watching a monitoring screen. The neurologist signals to Larry to come closer to him. Then, pointing to the screen he explains to Larry that the lively movements seen on the screen are the incessant activities in his son's brain/mind. This came as a profound revelation to Larry.

Driving back home, Larry reflected on the Buddha's profound insight realized and proclaimed two and a half millennia ago, in relation to the compelling visual confirmation he saw on the screen. Though, with his truth-distorting senses he perceives Walton as the same person from moment to moment, now he fully comprehends the fact that the mind is in constant flux, in other words, the impermanence of the mind. By wisely combining the Buddha's teaching with scientific observation, this man moved one step forward in understanding the way things really are.

<u>Chapter Insights and Highlights</u>

1. Our unaided senses are incapable of perceiving reality. Nature provided us with the sensory capability for procreation and survival, not to perceive reality.

2. There are laws and processes in operation in the universe and around us that are real, but which cannot be detected by us with our senses.

3. Instruments, as adjuncts to our sensory systems, can help us perceive things a step closer to reality than is possible with the unaided senses.

4. Science, armed with information gathered using instruments, can help us understand Dhamma expeditiously.

18

Reality in Perspective

It is in this fathom-long body, with its impressions and ideas that I declare lies the world, and the cause of the world and the cessation of the world, and the cause of action. Thus leads to the cessation of the world.

The Buddha[63]

We dance 'round in a ring and suppose
But the Secret sits in the middle and knows.

Robert Frost
American Poet (1874 – 1963)

In Chapter 16 we saw that our perceptions are a distorted portrayal of reality[64] because of the inherent limitations and deficiencies of our sensory mechanisms. If we think deeply, recalling the profound insight from Chapter 16 that our perceptive mechanisms are open to less than a millionth of the reality of the universe, we might even boldly say that what we ordinarily perceive of the universe is nothing but an *illusion*[65] or dream. A different kind of dream from the dream in sleep, but nevertheless a dream to the extent of not being reality. Ralph Waldo Emerson[66] perhaps was thinking along these lines when he said "We wake from one dream to another dream". Or Shakespeare when he penned the line "The whole universe is but imagination, all in all, but a shadow-show of one's own mind."

In Chapter 17 we saw that science and instruments can help us move a bit closer to reality from the illusion perceived by our sensory mechanisms. A small step for the universe but one giant step for humankind!

In this chapter we will take our discussion of perception and reality a step deeper. In the process we will discover some profound insights that will help us progress further in our quest for inner peace.

---

[63] Source: Samyutta Nikaya, Ch. 2, Item 3, para 6
[64] Recall our statement in a footnote of Chapter 16 that we will use *reality, absolute reality* and *truth* as synonyms.
[65] The Pali term for illusion is *maya*
[66] "Illusions", *The Conduct of Life* (1860)

The 'reality' perceived with our unaided senses, with their imperfections and inadequacies[67], is commonly referred to in most Dhamma writings as *worldly reality* or simply as *the world*. The use of the term *world* carries with it a full recognition of the limitations of our senses and therein lies the important difference between the common meaning of the word and its meaning in Dhamma. Unenlightened beings that haven't seen reality beyond worldly reality, and who therefore live their lives in total accordance with worldly reality, are referred to as *worldly beings.*

When a person dies, the *world* dies with him/her. What continues afterwards is the *universe* of truth, which is independent of human perception and therefore devoid of any distortion. We can then say that, if there are six billion people on our planet today, there are six billion worlds, whereas there is only one universe of truth.

The perceived world is obviously unique to each person because the perceiving mechanisms (senses plus mind) of any two individuals are not the same; therefore entities that constitute his/her world are perceived in unique ways. However perceptions of certain things can be somewhat common by virtue of (genetically transferred) attributes that are common to the species. Thus, two individuals will each perceive a stranger in a unique way, but both will perceive the color of the shirt the stranger is wearing as blue.

To say (and believe) that we see a star ("I can see Deneb clearly") is worldly reality. So is it to say "That is my house", "I will meet John today", "The sun rises" or "I am distressed". All these involve human sensory perceptions. When the senses are transcended, none of them hold any meaning.

As mentioned earlier, these worldly realities are distorted truths, the distortion being produced by the inadequacies and imperfections of our senses and the mechanisms of the mind. These inadequacies and imperfections occur at three cumulative stages:

1)   Only less-than-a-millionth of the EM radiation spectrum (visible light) is involved in the perception,

---

[67] The reader familiar with Plato's writings will recall "The Allegory of the Cave" where the world of appearance (worldly reality) is compared to an underground cave.

Another analogy of the world of appearance is a puppet show, in which the audience of children gets fully absorbed and believes what they see, but the reality behind the puppets is a team of human operators.

2) Data is manipulated by the sensory organs before passing into the brain/mind,

3) Data is manipulated by the mind before a final perception is made (e.g., by stored views in interpretation).

Obviously, to consider *all* worldly realities and remove distortions from them is an impossible task because the number of such realities (and corresponding truths) is infinite. More importantly, such a task is irrelevant to our quest for inner peace. Therefore, in Dhamma, the truths we need to investigate are narrowed down to what applies to our *existential distress* and liberation from that distress. This approach is captured in the scriptures[68] via a story, the essence of which is given below.

One day, the Buddha addressed the possibility that, before deciding to follow his teachings, certain persons may want answers to questions such as "Is the universe finite or infinite?" "Is the universe eternal or temporal?" "Is the life-principle identical with the body, or something different?" etc. The Buddha said that the questioners would die before answers to all such questions can be provided. He further went on to illustrate the point with a beautiful analogy.

'Imagine a man pierced by a poisoned arrow. His friends and relatives decide to immediately send for a surgeon. But the injured man says, "I will not allow this arrow to be pulled out, until I know about the man who wounded me; whether he is a nobleman, tradesman, priest or a servant, what his name is, and to what family he belongs, whether he is tall, or short or of medium height". Truly, the man would die before he could learn all this. Therefore, the man who seeks his own welfare should pull out this arrow – this arrow of lamentation, pain and sorrow.

'For, whether the theory exists or not, that the world is finite or infinite, or eternal or temporal – yet certainly, there exists birth, decay, sorrow, lamentation, pain, grief, despair and death, the extinction of all of which is attainable even in this present life, I make known unto you.'

Given the above, let's focus our investigations on worldly realities and corresponding truths pertaining only to the *existence of beings*. In particular, we need to address existential distress of human beings - which is *our* poisoned arrow - and liberation from that distress. These truths are the Four Noble Truths. Included in the Four Noble Truths are teachings covering causal dependence of things and the three characteristics of existence, namely, impermanence, no-self and existential distress. The fourth Noble Truth effectively becomes the Noble Eightfold Path – the detailed guide for deliverance from existential distress.

---

[68] Majjhima Nikaya, Sutta 63 and Sutta Nipata 592

Buddhist literature sometimes compares the path to enlightenment to a river-crossing, with the sailor as the practitioner and his raft as the aid, the Noble Eightfold Path. Recognizing that crossing the river is an arduous task and few exhibit the required diligence and courage to complete the task, The Dhammapada 85 says: "Few cross the river of time and are able to reach Sublime Peace. Most of them run up and down only on this side of the river."

Dhamma ➡	
Worldly Reality	Absolute Reality Truth Reality
Sensory Perception	Sense-transcended 'Perception'
Self view	No-self view
Distress	Sublime Peace
Worldly Being	Fully Enlightened Being The Buddha Arahant
Analogy: The Raft ➡	
Hither Bank (of River analogy) Bank A	Thither (or Yonder) Bank Bank B

Fig: Some Attributes of Two 'Realities'

A being who is totally ignorant of the truths and whose life is completely based on worldly reality, i.e., a worldly being, is at bank A of the river.

A being who fully understands these truths and who totally integrates them into his/her life, i.e., a Fully Enlightened Being (a Buddha or Arahant) has reached the other bank, B. (In passing, let's note an interesting point made by the Buddha about complete relinquishment of worldly things, i.e., not to cling to anything physical or mental. Just as the person reaching bank B of a river discards the raft, the Buddha has admonished us to discard even his teaching of Dhamma upon reaching the truth).

A person striving towards the goal of realization of truth, but whose life is presently driven partly by Worldly Reality and partly by Truth is somewhere between A and B. No being suddenly transforms from A to B. The passage from A to B is a gradual and arduous path. Individuals are at different points between A and B, depending on the advantages or disadvantages with which the person started life including genetic factors, and what kind of environment influenced the individual during the formative years. An individual practitioner will be at different points on the path at different times of his/her life.

To illustrate what we have discussed so far, let's refer again to the earlier figure and examine it specifically in relation to the principle of no-self, as its integration into one's life is the pivotal determinant of progress towards Sublime Peace. A being who *totally* believes in a self and lives all aspects of his/her life according to that notion will be at point A. At the opposite extreme, point B, is one who *totally* understands, intellectually, the principle of no-self and also has integrated that principle into all practical aspects of his/her life. Such a person is a Fully Enlightened Being (the Buddha or Arahant). Those who are practicing Dhamma and who have integrated the principle partially into their lives will be somewhere on the path between banks A and B so that they operate under a mix of worldly reality and truth.

We have also seen that by transcending the limitations of sensory mechanisms, especially by using information gathered through physical instruments, we can perceive things closer to how they really are. In some cases, we may see something very near what it really is - for example, a cell under an electron microscope. In other cases, it may be an improvement over direct sensory perception, but not enough of an improvement to see the way things really are – for example viewing a very distant star through a telescope. In both cases we have transcended sensory (worldly) reality but not reached truth. In any event, even as we use instruments that aid our senses, we can accept that there is a reality beyond sensory (worldly) reality. Then our next step would be to define that reality without ambiguity? What follows is a simple but powerful way to do this.

Imagine that *all* human beings on earth perish within a short period of time (a few days), due to a global catastrophe[69] such as biochemical warfare. The aftermath of such an event on planet earth is too baffling for the human mind to visualize or describe, primarily because we are conditioned to think of our familiar world. However, for the purpose of the present discussion, we need only to ponder over a few easy questions.

Consider what was called a peach tree before the catastrophe. When we are all gone, is it a *peach tree?* No! Why? Because *peach* is a term human beings created. It is not even a *tree* - for the same reason. But does it exist? Yes, but not in the human-created terms or concepts like *exist,* but only in the 'sense' of a universe without human beings. It is a universe like the one that existed before humans appeared on earth and began to assign names, labels, conventions and the like. Now *that* existence, which has nothing to do with human sensory mechanisms and perception, is **truth.** Truth (Nature, the Universe) operates independent of human perception. This is the closest we can get to explain in human-created terms what is ineffable. It is a reality as the Universe 'knows', but not as we humans know.

In truth, a peach tree ceases to be a peach tree and it ceases to be an entity ('self', if we are to compare it with the human being) separate from the rest of the universe. The peach tree is merged with the universe and all is one. All this happens with total indifference to sensory reality of the human species including our description in this paragraph and the human-created terms used therein. It is subject to impermanence as everything else in the universe is (and was, for billions of years and will be, for billions of years more), and of course with total indifference to our word *impermanence.* Thus it will be seen that we have to stretch our imagination and contemplate deeply to get even a glimpse of that truth. However, if we are pressed for a concise yet simple definition, we could say that *truth is that which is beyond sensory perception of beings.*

---

[69] In fact, before the human species appeared on earth the universe was exactly as we imagined here (and continues to be so except for human sensation and imagination) – a universe in totality without separation or isolation of constituent parts, without a thing called sensory reality, labels, conventions, "me", "mine", "you" and so on. Even when humans first appeared on earth, there were no conventions, names, labels etc. These things began to appear only as our brains began to evolve and we began to think.

Regarding the idea of all of us perishing in an instant, it does happen on earth in a slightly different way. **All** of us living today, from today's newborn to the oldest amongst us, will for sure cease to exist within the next 120 years (the maximum lifespan of the human being). In cosmic terms, 120 years is nothing but an *instant.* But in this case, sensory reality including the self-notion, names, labels etc. do not perish with us because we pass on these human-created entities to our offspring, who will pass them to their offspring and so on.

Now, reverting back to our familiar world (and finding that we haven't perished!), it would be obvious that what we discovered about the peach tree applies equally well to human beings in truth. Most importantly, that there is no identity (no-self). We are, therefore, one with the universe and that we are all impermanent in a universe that is in unrelenting flux. Self (and all that follows from it such as "me", "mine", "you" and other conventions) and beliefs based on permanency are just our creations existing only within the boundary of our sensory world.

A prisoner who wants to escape from prison has to plan the escape and launch it from within the prison. Likewise, we have to 'plan and launch' our path to Full Enlightenment or freedom, which is in the realm of Absolute Reality, from within (the prison of) the sensory world. Later chapters will explore that mission in detail.

Chapter Insights and Highlights

1. The world that is perceived by each one of us is *worldly reality*. It is a reality in relation to, and perceived through, our truth-distorting senses. Because it is inherently a distortion of truth, worldly reality in which we conduct our 'business of living' is described as an *illusion* (Pali: *maya*). We who live under that reality are *worldly beings*.

2. The world perceived by each one of the billions of human beings on this earth is unique to that person. If there are six billion people living today, there are six billion worlds, but one universe of truth.

3. With the death of a person, his/her world dies.

4. To search for truths pertaining to all things in this universe is an impossible task and unnecessary. Therefore, Dhamma focuses on truths that pertain to our existential distress and the liberation from that distress. (Note the Buddha's analogy of the man pierced by a poisoned arrow).

5. The most important reality is that there is no abiding self, but our truth-distorting senses make us believe there is one.

6.   Our path from worldly reality to truth can be compared to a crossing of a river in a raft. The bank *here* is the world, the bank *there* is truth (therefore, *Nirvana* – Sublime Peace). The raft is the Noble Eightfold Path.

7.   Since truth operates independently of human perception, it is prudent on our part to use perception only to help us harmoniously carry out the business of daily living but not to take that perception as truth, i.e., not to take that perception too seriously. It is when we take our perceptions too seriously that we create problems for ourselves and others.

Practice for Inner Peace

Let's revisit the story of the peach tree.

Then, let's think of any familiar entity in our life (for example, a pet) the way we are accustomed to thinking of this entity (for example the way the pet has grown over the years, the love we have for the pet etc.).

Now try to compare its existence under truth, as in the case of the peach tree and contemplate deeply on these thoughts.

19

A Walk in Serengeti

We must, however, acknowledge, as it seems to me that man with all his noble qualities
... still bears in his body frame the indelible stamp of his lowly origins.

Charles Darwin
English Naturalist (1809 – 1882)

When all is said and done, what we want in our lives is inner peace. As implied in the Dhammapada verse quoted in Chapter 1, if our life is to be one of inner peace, then there must be a particular way of thinking that brings peace as opposed to distress. We have some inkling of what that entails from our discussions so far. One conclusion is that the way we choose to view things and happenings in our lives, our *attitude,* makes the difference between a life of inner peace and one of distress. Stated differently, we may say that if our thinking is in touch with reality, our lives will be peaceful, otherwise, distressful. Thus, if the starting point of our equation is right thinking, the end point is inner peace. But what happens in between? The pursuit of the answer to that question is the task of this chapter and the five chapters that follow.

First let's discuss a subject of relevance – *stress*[70]. Stress is an extensively used modern term for a condition that has existed since earliest times when our ancestors (and other animals) faced threatening (fearful) situations. More generally, stress can be thought of as the response of the body and the mind to changes in one's environment. Once the word stress became popular, people began to use the term as a catchall to refer to all types of common distresses such as worry, fear, depression and anxiety. Thus, in common usage, stress has become a term that is almost synonymous with distress or suffering.

---

[70] The term *stress*, meaning a physiological condition as implied here, was first used by the noted Canadian physiologist Dr. Hans Selye in 1956. Selye's formal definition of the term is: "the nonspecific response of the body to any demand made upon it".

More importantly, the mental-physiological basis underlying stress is now known to be similar to mental-physiological underpinnings of distress (suffering) in general, thus giving credence to the current catchall usage of the term. Therefore, a study of the stress response mechanism – in practical terms, the mental-physiological response to threatening (fearful) situations – will be invaluable in our study of distress in general and the means to overcome it.

It is known that the body and the mind are designed to have a certain natural hardiness to handle and cope with stress up to a point. In fact a certain degree of stress is considered good to the extent that it results in vitality. Once that threshold has been exceeded, and exceeded frequently, stress begins to cause harm to both body and mind, leading to potentially debilitating or life-threatening consequences. As a result, today's health-care professionals urge us to get our stress under control. Unmanaged stress could result in various physiological conditions that include high blood pressure and cardiovascular disorders, diabetes, stomach disorders including ulcers, immune system disorders and backache. Possible mental health conditions include insomnia, anxiety, anger, cognitive impairment, depression and suicidal thoughts.

If something as intangible as *thinking* can trigger or contribute to such an array of tangible and intangible illnesses, creating mild discomfort to havoc in our lives, surely we would be interested to know how thinking could bring on these undesirable results. In other words, it would benefit us to be able to trace the sequence of events from the act of thinking to, for example, the physiological condition of high blood pressure or the mental condition of anxiety.

In Chapter 16, we briefly mentioned that, to be aware of anything, we need three things: an object, a communication medium and a sensory mechanism. The sensory process was also covered at an introductory level in Part A (Chapter 7).

We will now examine this whole process of perception and beyond in greater detail until we uncover and understand the complete pathway of thinking-caused illness. For that purpose, we will use the following scenario.

Bertram and his family have been spending a month-long holiday in the Serengeti National Park in Africa and today is the last day of the holiday before they head back home to Canada. Bertram had just finished an early dinner with the family. On a whim, disregarding advice to the contrary, he decides to go out for a solitary walk. He is about a quarter mile from his camp when he sees a large object not too far away. His mind instantly shifts into rapid thinking.

Though things are happening in Bertram's mind at lightning speed, we will go through these mental events *in very slow motion* so we can get some reasonable insight into his thinking process. We will trace the significant events of perception, cognition, reaction etc., step by step, all the way from the object as far into the body and mind of the perceiver (Bertram) as we need to go. That is, until we understand all the important mental and physiological reactions that take place within the perceiver.

Once we understand the process applicable to this example (over the next few chapters) we can apply the same ideas to our own situations in daily living, and take well-informed action for our benefit. In other words, we will use this case as a model to trace and study the course of the whole process of human experience in general from beginning to end. This experience can cover a whole spectrum ranging from unpleasant encounters (like the meeting with the boss when he announced impending layoffs in the company) through pleasant experiences (like meeting one's child at the airport after a trip abroad), to those of perfect tranquility (achieved through meditation).

Let's begin by stepping back to the instant *just before* Bertram saw the large object. The events leading to the current perception in Bertram, in very slow motion, are as follows:

1. Light bounces off an object.

2. The reflected light enters Bertram's eye; a bare image is formed on the retina (at the rear of the eye).

3. The receptors in the retina convert the image into electrical impulses.

4. The electrical impulses travel along the optic nerves to the brain. The first brain structure the impulses encounter is the *thalamus* (more accurately, the part of the thalamus called the *visual thalamus* that handles visual information).

5. The visual thalamus transmits the information along two routes, both leading to two other brain structures, first the *amygdala* and then the *hypothalamus*. The amygdala is the brain's emotional core with a primary role of key player in the stress response

mechanism. The hypothalamus interfaces between the amygdala and the body organs associated with the stress response.

6. The first route goes directly to the amygdala and thence to the hypothalamus, bypassing the higher processing centers and therefore quickly transferring crude data onwards. The intent behind this quick route is to initiate time-critical action by the amygdala in the form of communication to the hypothalamus – action that cannot await validation of data for accuracy. Effectively, the hypothalamus is told, "Assume there is danger and prepare the body to fight or flee.[71]" The hypothalamus acts accordingly.

7. The second route (which produces accurate information slowly) involves higher-level processing by a brain structure called the *visual cortex* (being that part of the sensory cortex which specifically handles visual data). The highest level of processing of sensory data in the brain takes place in the sensory cortex. Then, as in the previous step, the result of the processing is passed onto the amygdala. The amygdala in turn, after examination of the data, issues a command once again to the hypothalamus. The information will effectively tell the hypothalamus either that the earlier raw warning of danger is confirmed (and provide additional data for action) or ask the hypothalamus to ignore the earlier warning because detailed investigation showed that there is really no danger.

8. The higher-level processing referred to in the previous step effectively involves the sifting, analysis and interpretation of the new information in relation to existing data. The outcome of this complex processing is a 'meaningful' conclusion to the new information received and is referred to as *perception*. In this example, what Bertram's mind perceives (the 'meaningful' conclusion) happens to be a message to the effect "It is a tiger!" or simply, "Tiger!"

Replacing the bird in the figure of Chapter 16 with the tiger, we have the following diagram to represent our present scenario.

---

[71] This response mechanism, an involuntary defense mechanism, was discovered by the prominent physiologist Walter B. Cannon in the 1920s and termed the fight-or-flight response.

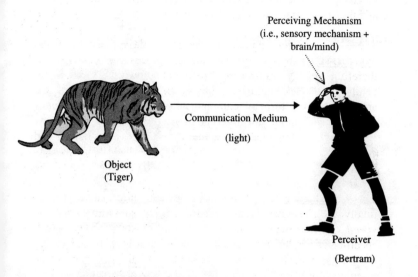

The perceiving mechanism (steps 2-8) in magnified form is shown in the next diagram.

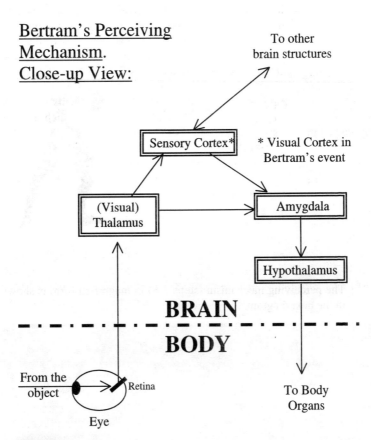

Bertram's Perceiving Mechanism.
Close-up View:

To other brain structures

Sensory Cortex*

* Visual Cortex in Bertram's event

(Visual) Thalamus

Amygdala

Hypothalamus

BRAIN
- - - - - - - - - - - - - - -
BODY

From the object

Retina

Eye

To Body Organs

BRAIN STRUCTURES

(Visual) Thalamus
Sensory data is first received here.

Sensory Cortex
Data received from the thalamus undergoes sensory processing in 'consultation' with other cerebral structures

Amygdala
Brain's key player in the stress response mechanism; determines if there's threat of danger and if so, orders hypothalamus to request appropriate action from the body systems.

Hypothalamus
Requests bodily actions.

9. The meaningful conclusion of the perceiving process ("Tiger!") now becomes the trigger for a series of additional mental processes some of which will involve higher cortical structures of the brain. This complex process determines Bertram's eventual reactions, including his physical and verbal actions.

(To reiterate an important point made earlier, the above events 1-9 happen *in a mere flash of time* in contrast to our analysis which is being conducted in very slow motion, step by step.)

The above sequence of events would apply to the visual perception of anything, even a picture we see in the daily newspaper. Furthermore, similar sequences apply to other senses, i.e., hearing, tasting, smelling and contacting (touching).

It should be noted that the essence of the stress response mechanism we have just discussed applies to other animals as well. In fact, we can say the indelible stamp of our lowly origins referred to by Charles Darwin[72], is this inherited stress response mechanism. It is primarily in the form of a hard-wired mechanism in us and is responsible for all our fear-based responses - some unwholesome behaviors such as anger and hatred and some beneficial behaviors such as ducking a rock approaching one's head.

Steps 1-8 are fairly standard in the study of sensation and perception and neuroscience. Of critical importance to us in the context of this book is step 9. We need to know how the current perception ("Tiger!"), and all other perceptions made during a lifetime and now stored in memory, lead to reactions (mental, physiological, vocal and physical) in Bertram and therefore in you and me. What are these reactions? What determines the nature of these reactions? What bearing do these reactions have on one's health in the short and long term? If they contribute to ill-health, can anything be done to change the course of events so that the end results are wellbeing and inner peace instead of ill-health? Analysis of step 9, thereby answering these questions, will be the task of the next few chapters.

Chapter Insights and Highlights

1. Whether we have distress or inner peace will be determined by the way we think about the world around us.

---

[72] Quoted at the beginning of this chapter.

2. The condition implied by the modern term *stress*, which is the reaction of our body and mind to threatening or fearful external stimuli, underlies virtually all distress.   That is, unmanaged stress triggers, or contributes to, physiological and mental illness.

3. If we can trace human experience from sensory triggers through the thinking process to the end results of physiological or mental illness, then we should be able to devise a means to deal with these thinking-caused illnesses.

20

Brain or Mind?

The flesh endures the storms of the present alone,
The mind those of the past and future as well as the present.

Epicurus
(4th Century B.C.)

What is mind?
It doesn't matter.
What is matter?
Oh, never mind!"

Thomas Hewitt Key
19th Century English scholar

In the last chapter, we were able to trace the stress mechanism from the body, through the brain and back into the body where the final outcome is manifested, thanks to the remarkable progress neuroscience has made in the last two or three decades to unravel the brain. Does it then follow that we can portray the more intricate mental phenomena such as thinking, reasoning, intuition, will, sadness and joy in terms of the brain and not in terms of the more elusive entity called the mind? Not yet.

We are living at a time (early 21st century) when neuroscience is progressing well, in some areas exponentially, in mapping the brain. No doubt, given this speed of progress, the day will come when human beings will be able to explain all mental functions clearly and explicitly in terms of the brain. When that happens (likely a few generations from now), one of the terms – mind or brain – will become redundant. Then we will no longer be able to take cover under humor about a mind that is mysterious, as did Thomas Hewitt Key in the quotation above.

Until the time comes that the mind can be fully explained in terms of the brain, we need to utilize the familiar concepts of the *mind* and *mental processes (functions)*. Given the knowledge available at the time, the Buddha formulated the profound Dhamma using exclusively the concepts of the mind and mental processes. However, as we have seen so far, and as we will find in the rest of this book, scientific knowledge and facts facilitate our understanding and appreciation of Dhamma greatly. Therefore, with regard to the brain-mind issue, the most meaningful position for us to adopt is to make the utmost use of the available scientific knowledge regarding the brain but continue to use the concepts of mind and mental processes.

Then, let's get our bearings with regards to the Bertram-tiger event. In terms of the concept of brain, we have been able to go as far as the visual cortex. Beyond that is territory that neuroscientists are currently working in but at this time are unable to offer us concrete information to use in our study of Dhamma. So, we will revert to the concepts of *mind* and *mental processes* to continue our exploration.

What are the mental processes encountered in day-to-day living? The most important that we need to consider are the following five:

1. We *perceive*. (Example: "It's a tiger!" or "I smell smoke!")
2. We *think*. (Example: "It's cloudy. It might rain. I had better take the umbrella.")
3. We form and use *memories*. (Example: "13th October – Mary's birthday.")
4. We have *emotions (mental feelings)*. (Example: "I feel so upset since the accident")
5. We have a *will* (volition). (Example: "I'll breath deeply now.")

We lump together all these processes of which we are ordinarily aware and assign the label *mind* to that collection of processes. We do not need to go beyond this elementary view of the mind, to proceed to the next step in tracing the events taking place within Bertram. In fact, for the purpose of understanding the really important principles of Dhamma, this elementary view of the mind is completely adequate.

In the following diagrams, we will use the oval-shaped figure to symbolically represent the *mind* and also the five distinct processes within it, i.e., *perception, thinking, memory, emotion* and *will*. Thus, our symbols for the five mental processes are:

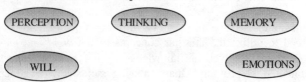

It is very important to note that these are representations of *processes* of the *mind* and not necessarily identifiable physiological structures of the *brain*. For the purpose of our discussion, there is no implied one-to-one correspondence between each of these mental processes and any demarcated and named area of the brain, although for some processes there may be a scientifically established *partial* correspondence.

The following diagram represents what we have discussed so far regarding Bertram's encounter with the tiger and will be used in future chapters to generate further simplified explanations.

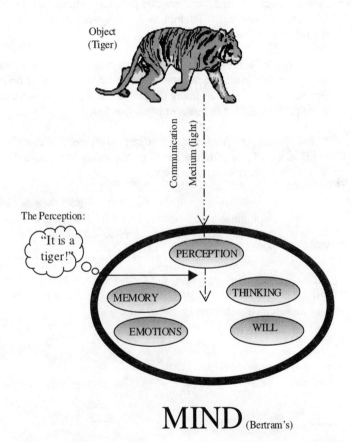

Up to this point in our voyage of the mind, nothing much has happened beyond Bertram's mind perceiving[73] a tiger. What happens next in his mind? That will be explored in the next chapter.

Chapter Insights and Highlights

1. Neuroscience has made tremendous progress, particularly in the last few decades, in its attempt to unravel what goes on inside the brain.

2. As a result, some mental phenomena that were considered unexplainable, such as fear, are now explained in terms of brain functionality. However, many (higher) mental processes remain to be fully explained in terms of brain function.

3. Given the current rate of progress in neuroscience, a complete explanation of the mind in terms of the brain is a possibility, likely a few generations from now.

4. In the meantime we can 'make the best of both worlds' by utilizing a combination of current scientific knowledge of the *brain* and the processes (primarily perception, thinking, memory, emotions and will) of the *mind*.

5. Mental processes (perception, thinking, memory, emotions and will) do not necessarily have a one-to-one correspondence with any demarcated and named areas of the brain.

---

[73] Besides *form* recognition, in reality the visual mechanics will perceive movement (that the tiger is moving towards Bertram) and colors (of the tiger and the surroundings). However, we will stay focused only on form recognition, to keep our analysis uncomplicated.

21

The Mind at the Controls

A man is what he thinks all day long.

Ralph Waldo Emerson

In chapter 19 we saw how Bertram perceived a tiger during a walk in the Serengeti Park. In this chapter, we will see what happens next, specifically how the processes of *perception, memory* and *thinking* produce the next event in Bertram's mind using the result of perception ("It's a tiger!") as the stimulus. Note that earlier, *light* reflected off the object was the initial starting stimulus and now, the *perception* that resulted from the earlier process becomes the new starting stimulus.

First let's discuss what we mean by the terms *memory* and *thinking* within the context of this book. (The process of *perception* was already covered in much detail in the previous chapters.)

MEMORY

Memory is made up of two main components:
(a) experiential memory, and
(b) memory resulting from evolutionary/genetic processes

(a) is the memory that each one of us accumulates during his or her lifetime, as a result of our cumulative sensory interaction with the world around us. This memory component affects our every living moment, but selected contents can be *willfully* modified to our benefit, via Insight Meditation. To make it more meaningful, this memory can be broken down into categories, even though some may be related or overlapping. Included are:

   ♦ Records of life events (e.g., "For my 14th birthday my parents surprised me with a present of a racing bike.")
   ♦ Beliefs and views. (e.g., "My religion is the true religion and all others are fake.")

◆ Biases and prejudices (e.g., "People from the South cannot be trusted.")

◆ Concepts and ideas (e.g., "Rising air currents within thunderstorms create tornadoes.")

◆ Acquired knowledge (e.g., "Excess LDL cholesterol can contribute to cardiovascular disease.")

◆ Motor-skill memory (e.g., Organism's memorized skills needed to ride a bicycle.)

◆ Data (e.g., one's home telephone number.)

(b) is the result of the slow and gradual natural process of evolution, that has been in operation from the time of the earliest living organisms millions of years ago to today's life forms of plants and animals, including human beings. This memory includes what we usually refer to as 'instinctual behavior'. As in (a), this component affects our every living moment. However, it is hard-coded into us, which means that, setting aside results of artificially isolated efforts made via current gene technology, this component is something we need to accept as is.

(It may be of interest to note that even evolutionary/genetic memory can be thought of as a different kind of experiential memory. That is, it is not memory resulting from the experiences of the individual under consideration but relates to the essence of cumulative experience of our ancestors from the first single-celled life form all the way to us. Having made that point, we will keep the two components distinct for the balance of our discussion.)

THINKING

In neuroscience, a thought would be made up of millions of extremely rapid firing patterns in the neural networks. Also, in the Buddhist classical work *Abhidhamma,* extremely small thought units are used to explain the human thought process. However, such microscopic analysis, while certainly profound in endeavor for scholars and academics, does not get us - those looking for practical applications in daily life - beyond abstruse discussion. Our purpose will be well served if we select our *elemental thought* (the basic "building block" of thinking) at a somewhat higher functional level. That is, the mental processing that corresponds to a simple discrete thought that can be written on paper. For example, the thought in Bertram's mind "The tiger might kill me" is a practical statement of an elemental thought with which we can meaningfully operate. A string of logically connected elemental thoughts will form a *thought process*, which covers a meaningful sequence starting with a triggering thought and ending in a conclusion.

One of the most important characteristics, or principles, of the human thinking process is this: *only one elemental thought operates in a single thought moment.* For example, in the *instant* in time when Bertram's mind is focusing on the thought "The tiger might kill me", it cannot also focus on another elemental thought, for example "What will happen to my kids and wife?" The second elemental thought can take place *after,* but not at the same time as the first elemental thought. This principle of the mind is a key factor around which human behavior modification and healing techniques are based and which we will discuss later in the book.

Since the above principle is important for our investigations, let's solidify our understanding with two analogies:
(1) The Central Processing Unit (CPU) of a computer can handle only one program *instruction* at a time. Only after that instruction has been dispensed with will it take another. The elemental thought is comparable to the program instruction in the CPU.
(2) This is a simpler analogy. A ballpoint pen accommodates only one refill at a time. If it has a blue refill, you cannot write red until a red refill replaces the blue.

Because thinking happens at lightning speed and our cognitive mechanisms are not designed to see things in slow motion, a whole string of elemental thoughts *appears* as though happening at the same time. For example, Bertram might one day describe the tiger incident saying, "My thought was the tiger will kill me. *At the same time,* I thought what will life be like for my kids and wife without me." What is incorrect here is '*at the same time*'. Elemental thoughts do not happen at the same time, but in sequence. As we shall see later, thinking happens in a linked sequence.

Having completed the above clarifications about the *thinking* and *memory* processes, we can now resume our tracking of the next events in Bertram's mind. The relevant diagram needed for our discussion appears next.

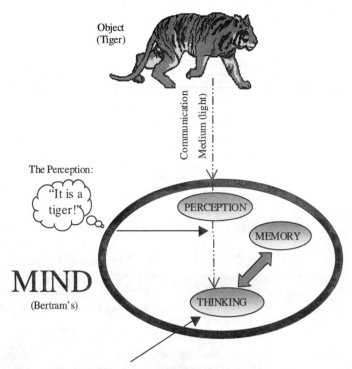

Object
(Tiger)

Communication
Medium (light)

The Perception:

"It is a
tiger!"

PERCEPTION

MEMORY

MIND
(Bertram's)

THINKING

The perception "It is a tiger!" is passed
from the PERCEPTION process to the
THINKING process and becomes the
trigger for a complete thought process,
with ongoing input from the MEMORY
and PERCEPTION processes.

What is happening in the human mind is extremely complex. However,
the following simplified view (of what's going on in Bertram's mind) is
adequate to help us progress with our present analysis:

I.   The *perception* process passes on its conclusion "It's a tiger!" to the
        thinking process.

II.   The *thinking* process uses the input "It's a tiger!" as the trigger for a
        series of escalating elemental thoughts, with input from the

perception and *memory* processes. The general idea is illustrated by the following sequence of cognitive events.

EVENT SEQUENCE	ACTIVE PROCESS	SPECIFICS
1	PERCEPTION Serves as initial stimulus for *Thinking* process)	"It's a tiger!"
2	THINKING Initial stimulus received from *Perception* process	"It's a tiger!"
3	MEMORY	Tigers are dangerous
4	THINKING	I am facing danger
5	MEMORY	I saw a TV show about how they kill
6	PERCEPTION New perception (of depth and movement)	The tiger is fairly far away. It's moving slowly.
7	MEMORY	The outhouse is close by.
8	THINKING Conclusion of process	There is enough time to run to the outhouse for safety.

Note that the whole thought process is made up of progressive elemental thoughts. Each new elemental thought is the result of blending of the last thought with either a fresh sensory input (presented as a *perception* after due processing) or a new element of *memory*.

While in this incident the data fed by the memory process is sensible, in other situations the data can be erroneous and dangerous, resulting in erroneous and dangerous conclusions. In humans, *these erroneous and dangerous conclusions are what drive people to dangerous (harmful) actions* such as the utterance of words of anger and hatred all the way to murder. For those situations, if the erroneous data held in the memory can somehow be modified to be in touch with reality, then the end result will be realistic and beneficial. Insight Meditation achieves just that and therefore we can see the tremendous benefit the practice can bring not only to the individual but also to society.

III.   Back to our case of Bertram and the tiger. Any steps shown in the table above that signify danger result in the hypothalamus being informed by the amygdala, as we saw in the last chapter when Bertram perceived "Tiger!" What happens thereafter is explained in the following steps.

IV.   Since the body cannot wait for perfect conditions to act in emergencies, Mother Nature got around the problem smartly by using two distinct pathways to transmit the message of danger via the hypothalamus to organs of the body. (It's a bit like light and sound pathways carrying the 'message' of a lightning discharge). One, the *Sympathetic Nervous System,* is a neural pathway that enables *rapid* communication with the organs to cover essential preparation. The other, a *slower* but more well-rounded communication mechanism, uses a hormone-releasing pathway called the <u>H</u>ypothalamus-<u>P</u>ituitary-<u>A</u>drenal *Cortex Axis* (or *HPA Axis* for short). It's like sending a quick Email first regarding an important matter and then following up with a comprehensive package via the postal system.

Now, a bit more about these two pathways.

V.   The *Sympathetic Nervous System* (SNS) is a network of neurons that speedily readies the organs of the body for vigorous activity ("fight or flight") by causing changes to body functions.

VI.   Next the *HPA Axis.* The hypothalamus releases a hormone which activates the "master endocrine gland" the pituitary gland (located at the base of the hypothalamus). The pituitary gland, in turn releases a hormone that stimulates the next gland down the line. This is the adrenal cortex (adjoining the kidneys). The adrenal cortex releases the "stress hormone" *cortisol* into the blood stream[74]. Carried into the various body organs by the blood, cortisol helps mobilize the

---

[74] The complete line-up of organs and hormones released are, in sequence: Hypothalamus – Corticone Releasing Factor (CRF), Pituitary – Adrenocorticotropic hormone (ACTH) and Adrenal Cortex – Cortisol.

body's energies[75] to fight or flee the difficult situation (the encounter with the tiger in the present example.). In a sense all this happens like a relay race, the 'runners' being the body organs.

VII. A number of bodily changes occur in Bertram to prepare him to fight or flee. These include *rise in blood pressure and heart rate, tightening of muscles, dilation of pupils and increase of blood sugar and metabolism.* Bertram is now ready to fight or flee. In the present situation Bertram flees to the outhouse and locks the door.

VIII. The body is designed (by virtue of evolution) to handle a reasonable number of emergency (stressful) situations. Within that threshold no harm is caused to the body. In fact, it is essential for one's safety and wellbeing, as the incident involving Bertram demonstrates. However, *when the demands are excessive and too frequent, one's body organs and systems, and consequently the mind and emotions are affected taking a toll on one's health, sometimes critically.* This is a major component of the existential distress that we face. Hence, the understanding that we now have of how stress is caused in our lives will enable us to appreciate, and effectively apply, the means available for overcoming emotional distress. This will be covered in forthcoming chapters.

In the example, the ferocious tiger was the stimulus for Bertram's response system. In today's world, tigers would be a most unlikely threat. Instead there are other forms of fears and threats, imagined and real, that we have to consider. But the stress response mechanism we outlined above remains exactly the same as it was for our ancestors. It works the same whether confronted by a boss with a pink slip, an out of control car coming towards you or having your boat capsize in Lake Huron in a dream. Thus, all we have to do to relate the diagrams and description to us, is to replace the tiger with any other dangerous or threatening object or situation encountered in daily living in today's world. The response mechanism and the resulting harm to the body and mind are similar.

In all the above cases, it is important to note that these are triggers and *not the causes* of stressful developments in the perceiver. In fact, all daily events that are of a disagreeable nature, from the mildest nuisance to the

---

[75] E.g., The liver, when stimulated by cortisol, elevates blood sugar and increases metabolism of fats and proteins, thereby providing the needed gush of energy.

Although the effect of hormones on *body* functions is the focus here, note that they influence also *emotional* states such as anger, love, joy and depression.

most traumatic event, trigger the activation of the above processes to some degree *dependent on the perceiver's assessment (view)* of the severity of the disagreeable event.

The stress response mechanism we discussed above (which is sometimes labeled the-flight-or-fight mechanism), may also be referred to as the fear-response mechanism with good reason. A basic element of fear is built into us genetically, for reasons of survival in the face of danger – that's what makes us, for example, run away from a house on fire. That is the element of fear that helps us, so we do not want to eliminate it. But the fear we superimpose on the genetically downloaded element is a learned one and involves our erroneous sense of self (ego). Unfortunately, the erroneous fear uses the same mechanism and the overuse causes great harm.

The typical human being lives with a perpetual subconscious feeling of fear, believing that he or she (the self) is under some form of threat. This fear causes a person to do all kinds of things to protect that self and results in unnecessary distress. An example is the wealthy head of a company who falsifies company financial records, in order to make a few million dollars quickly. His greed (overprotection of the self) lands him in prison for ten years. Or the person who kills his/her ex-spouse (and, in some cases even his/her children) because of a feeling he/she has been wronged. The root cause of this feeling is a paranoid obsession with the one's ego (that in reality does not exist, after all). Eliminating irrational learned fears (but not the genetically hard-wired survival-based fears) and the associated layer of distress is the essence of what Dhamma achieves through Insight Meditation.

The next diagram summarizes the path thus far:

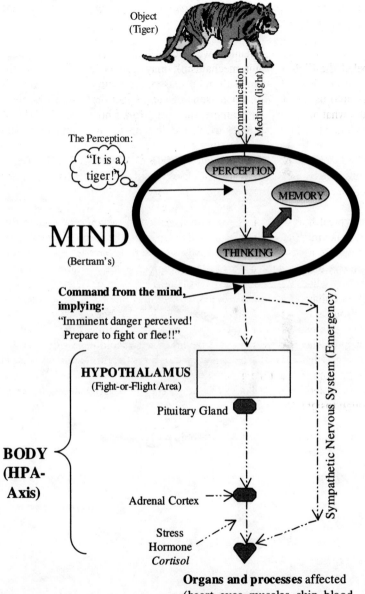

Object
(Tiger)

Communication
Medium (light)

The Perception:
"It is a tiger!"

PERCEPTION

MEMORY

MIND
(Bertram's)

THINKING

Command from the mind, implying:
"Imminent danger perceived! Prepare to fight or flee!!"

Sympathetic Nervous System (Emergency)

HYPOTHALAMUS
(Fight-or-Flight Area)

Pituitary Gland

BODY
(HPA-Axis)

Adrenal Cortex

Stress Hormone
Cortisol

Organs and processes affected (heart, eyes, muscles, skin, blood vessels, sweat glands, blood sugar, metabolism etc.)

In the above discussion, the response mechanism was described for the sense of vision. For other senses (auditory, taste, smell and touch), the mechanism works similarly, the only difference being the activation of sense-specific processing for each sense, e.g., ear and auditory cortex for sound. Then, expanding the last diagram to cover the other four senses too and keeping only the most important information, we have:

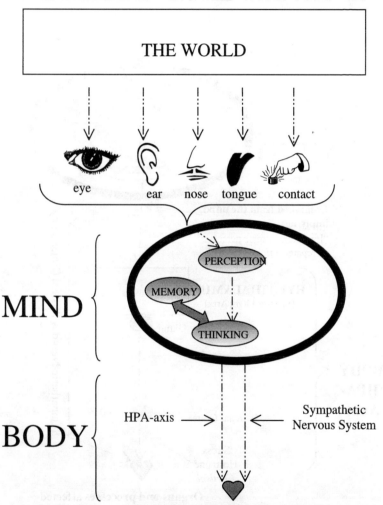

Or, combining all five senses, we have the following simplified general diagram.

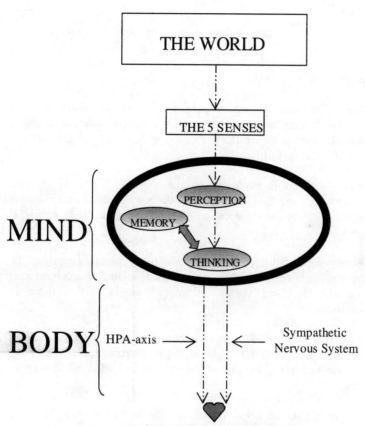

Organs and processes affected
(heart, eyes, muscles, skin, blood
vessels, sweat glands, blood sugar,
metabolism etc.)

Chapter Insights and Highlights

1. Memory is made up of two components, (a) experiential memory and (b) memory resulting from evolutionary/genetic processes. Experiential memory is that accumulated through sensory interaction with the world from birth to death.

2. An elemental thought is a discrete building block of cognition.

3. Thinking happens in a linked sequence to deliver a meaningful conclusion.

4. One of the most important characteristics of the human thought process is that *only one elemental thought operates in a single thought moment.* Breathing meditation (used to develop a calm mind) pivots on this fact.

5. When a threat is perceived by the mind, it sends signals (via intermediary agents) to the organs of the body to prepare for vigorous action to meet the emergency. This is called the 'fight or flight' response.

6. Bodily changes that occur in response to the mind's request to the body to 'fight or flee' include rise in blood pressure, rise in heart rate, increase of blood sugar, dilation of pupils and increase in metabolism.

7. By design, our bodies (organs/systems) can only cope with a certain number of requests for 'fight or flight' preparedness. When that threshold is exceeded, the organs/systems are affected leading to sickness.

8. Insight Meditation helps to maintain the activation of the 'fight or flight' mechanism within healthy limits.

22

The Cubic Six-Inch Universe

In the human head there are forces within forces within forces, as in no other cubic half-foot of the universe that we know.

Roger Sperry
Neurosurgeon and
Nobel Prize Winner

It is two days after the tiger incident and Bertram is back home (all in one piece!). He is alone in his backyard, seated on a rocking chair under a shady tree, enjoying a drink of orange juice. No tigers here, only squirrels jumping from tree to tree and some birds chirping. Bertram bathes in the tranquility and feels happy.

In a short while, the tranquility lulls Bertram into daydreaming. His mind wanders from one thing to another. Presently, and suddenly, a thought pops in about the tiger; in a few seconds his mind becomes deeply entrenched in that subject and totally oblivious to his present surroundings. Soon his heart begins to beat faster, muscles tighten, breathing becomes rapid and many other changes that normally accompany perception of a threatening or dangerous situation occur. In fact, what happened to his body is identical to what happened two days ago when he saw the real tiger. But now there is no tiger – he is in the safety and comfort of his own backyard. Then, why all these bodily changes? Why the fear? What made his tranquility suddenly change into distress?

What has just happened to Bertram is the manifestation of a basic built-in characteristic present in all of us. It is that *our stress response mechanism cannot differentiate between a real threat (such as a ferocious tiger) and an imaginary threat (like deeply re-living the tiger event in one's imagination).* The initial thought that pops out of memory (such as, "Tiger!", in Bertram's mind as he sat in his backyard) is the *sixth sense.* Why call it a *sense?*

Seen from the vantage point of the stress response mechanism, it is a stimulus that jolts the stress mechanism into action exactly *like* any one of the senses with biological organs, that is vision, hearing, taste, smell and touch. The only difference is that the stimulus originates not from the outside world, but from within our own 'inner world', the cubic six-inch (or three-pound) universe - the brain/mind. Hence, quite rightly, it is called a *sense*, the sixth sense. The next diagram captures the essence of this situation.

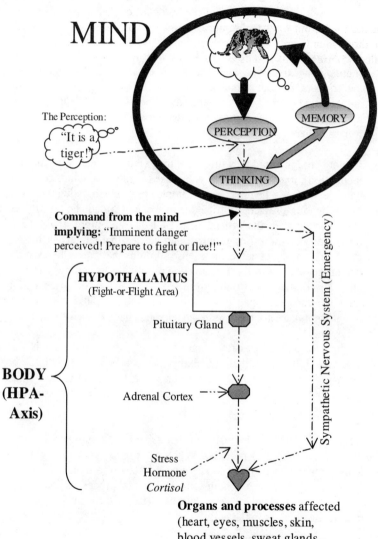

MIND

The Perception:
"It is a tiger!"

PERCEPTION

MEMORY

THINKING

Command from the mind implying: "Imminent danger perceived! Prepare to fight or flee!!"

HYPOTHALAMUS
(Fight-or-Flight Area)

Pituitary Gland

Adrenal Cortex

Stress Hormone *Cortisol*

BODY (HPA-Axis)

Sympathetic Nervous System (Emergency)

Organs and processes affected (heart, eyes, muscles, skin, blood vessels, sweat glands, blood sugar, metabolism etc.)

The sixth sense has the following important characteristics under normal (involuntary) functioning:

1) It is the most active of the six senses.

2) It is working all the time, 24 hours a day. Unlike the other five senses, it is active even when the person is asleep. In fact, it provides the triggers for our dreams, when the five biological senses are quiescent. Often, it has a 'field day' when we are asleep, creating nightmares and other disturbances that, upon waking, we would wish were not there.

3) If not brought under willful control (most effectively through meditation), it is the sense that can cause the most mental distress and damage to one's health. For example, the only breadwinner of a family who is stressed at office due to work overload can be stressed even when not in the office, in fact all day and night, if he/she is obsessed with the office problem and carries that subject in his/her mind. The problem is the sixth sense stimulus that goes wherever the person goes, even to the Bahamas on a holiday 'to get away from it all'. In contrast the stimuli from the other senses (such as *seeing* piles of unattended paper or *hearing* the ruthless boss outline new assignments) are not there until the person is back in the office.

4) In contrast to the stressful situations of (3), the good news is that when willfully controlled, the sixth sense can be used to help us be creative without external stimuli or to realize unsurpassed inner peace through meditation. This aspect will be fully addressed in a later chapter.

It is very important to distinguish between a mental stimulus (sixth sense) and the mental (thought) process. A mental *stimulus* is a thought that suddenly pops out of memory to serve as the start of a mental (thought) *process* that ends in a clear conclusion. The mental process is *common* to all six senses, in that all sensory data have to go through that process before causing changes in the body.

Adding the sixth sense (mind-generated stimuli) to our diagram of the last chapter, we have a comprehensive diagram that essentially summarizes what we have discussed so far about the human mind and body in relation to existential stress.

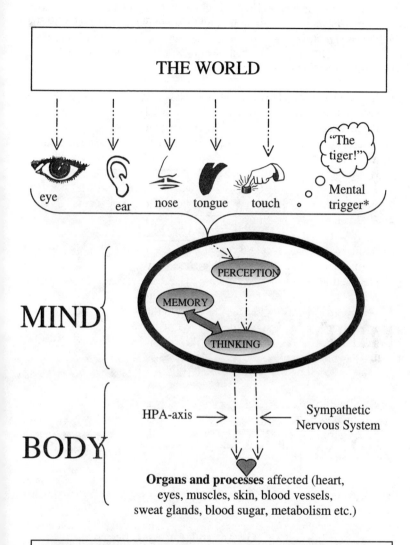

* This is a stimulus generated purely within the mind - a stored thought suddenly popping out from memory. For all practical purposes it can be positioned side by side with the other senses, because the mind-body response to it is the same.

The next diagram is a simplified version of the previous diagram. These two diagrams capture the important highlights of the current and previous chapters and are therefore important. They will be used in future chapters in which we will develop and discuss practical applications, especially meditation.

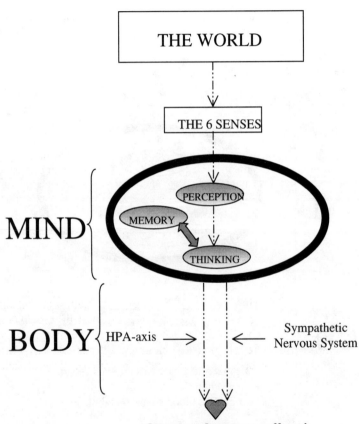

▶ *Digression*

DREAM WORLDS

Now that we covered all six senses, an interesting topic to explore is our dream worlds from a sensory perspective.

Dream World 1. What we normally refer to as a dream (dream in sleep) is a state of mind when only the sixth sense (mental trigger) is active and the other five senses are in a dormant state.

Dream World 2. What we normally refer to as an awake state is one where the five dormant senses also have become active, that is, all six senses are active. If by 'awake' we mean 'in touch with reality', it certainly is not, because we are still perceiving the world through the senses – now simply six instead of one. So it is still a dream world.

It is only when we transcend the six senses that we are 'in touch with reality'. It is only then that we can truly say we are *awake*, that is awake from both dreams described above. It is this wakefulness that is being implied when Buddha proclaimed that he is awake and when we refer to The Buddha as the Awakened One.

Chapter Insights and Highlights

1) Triggers originating from within the mind itself, i.e., thoughts suddenly popping up from memory, are received by the response mechanism as though they are from any one of the five biological senses. Therefore, for practical purposes, we can consider mental triggers to be occupying a position equal to a biological sense such as vision. Hence it is called the *sixth sense.*

2) Of all the six senses, the most active is the sixth sense. In fact, it works 24 hours a day.

3) If not brought under willful control, the sixth sense can cause anything from mild mental discomfort to havoc in our minds. In contrast, if brought under control (through Insight Meditation), it can facilitate realization of peace.

<u>Practice for Inner Peace</u>

As a review of the principles discussed in this chapter, recall some events in your life when imaginary situations caused some mental discomfort.

23

Sunset Over Georgian Bay

A sound mind in a sound body, is a short but full description of a happy state in this world.

John Locke
English Philosopher (1632 - 1704)

What we have discussed so far is the body's response to a situation that the perceiver perceives as unwelcome as illustrated by Bertram's encounter with the tiger. In contrast, what happens if Bertram comes upon something that he perceives as pleasing, tranquil or neutral, for example a breathtaking sunset over Georgian Bay? The path is the same for the most part, except for the following differences:

(1) The sympathetic nervous system (SNS) discussed in Chapter 21 takes a back seat, relatively speaking. Now, the functionally opposite[76] system to the SNS called the ***para**sympathetic nervous system* (PNS)[77] steps into dominant action. The PNS facilitates non-emergency (normal) responses by the various organs and body systems, thereby promoting health. (Only as an aid to remembering, think of S̲NS as S̲tress Nervous System and P̲NS as P̲eace Nervous System).

(2) The hormonal correlative of the nerve-based SNS, that is the HPA-Axis, too takes a back seat.

The relevant diagram depicting the (PNS dominant) response pathway of calmness (peacefulness) appears next:

---

[76] Although, as seen from the subject of stress, SNS and PNS cater to opposite functions (i.e., SNS facilitates emergency responses and PNS non-emergency), on a broader scale, they work as a team. The operations of the SNS and PNS are always inter-related, like a seesaw, because their joint goal is to maintain internal equilibrium of body systems, that is, homeostasis.

[77] The *sympathetic* and *parasympathetic* nervous systems together make up what's called the *autonomic* nervous system.

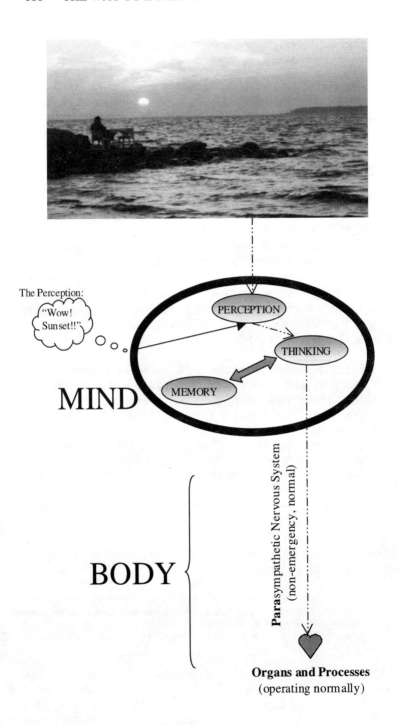

The mental processes are similar to that of the tiger-incident, with *perception* and *memory* processes feeding the *thinking* process. However, the conclusion of the thinking process would be something like "The sunset over Georgian Bay is breathtakingly beautiful. I feel at peace." *It is the mental acknowledgement of a process that contributes to wellbeing rather than illness.* It is the opposite of activating the fight-or-flight mechanism (associated with SNS). Therefore, for the most part, one needs to help the mind keep the PNS, and not the SNS (and HPA-axis), in dominant control of the body organs. In fact this principle should be the backbone of any worthwhile stress management program.

The important question that follows from the above discussion is: "How does one help the mind keep the PNS in dominant control most of the time?" While the view of the sun setting over Georgian Bay or a field of lilies or the sound of the waves promotes mental wellbeing, one cannot order them because they are externals not under our control. So we look for the answer within. The answer is to use the mind with right views to create the health-promoting environment. More on this when we further investigate Meditation.

As we have already seen, the stress response mechanism (including the SNS) evolved to enable beings to fight with, or flee from, threats to their physical existence. However, in today's world for most human beings, most of the time, there are no threats to our physical existence. So one could expect the stress response mechanism to be underutilized (which is good for health). In reality, the opposite is true. We humans, as a species, are overworking the mechanism as though we are facing a continuous, lifelong, emergency. This is due to a never-ending line-up of *perceived* threats, all mind-made. These threats are predominantly in the form of worry about things that have happened in the past (e.g., not doing well in college) and anxiety about certain things that may happen in the future (e.g., being lonely and sick in old age). The result is overworked body organs and systems, leading to physical and/or mental illness.

The last two diagrams in the previous chapter captured the body's response to stimuli from perceived *disagreeable* objects/situations, covering all six senses. The next two diagrams cover the opposite situation, i.e., the body's response to stimuli from perceived *agreeable* objects/situations. The four diagrams together provide us with a rational basis for discussion and development of effective methods for the management of distress.

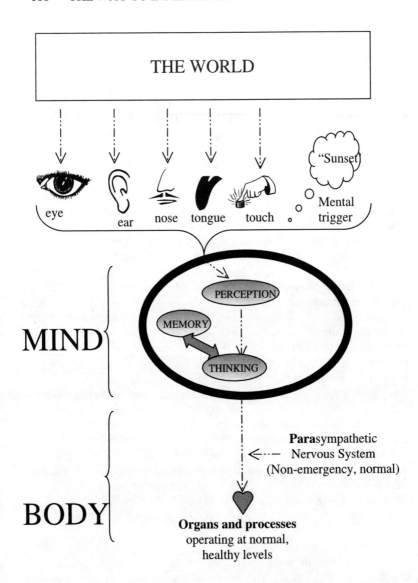

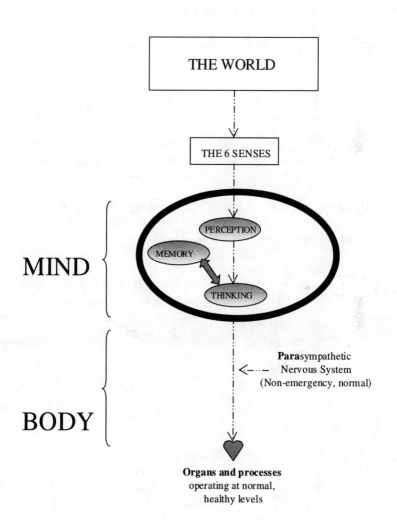

Chapter Insights and Highlights

1) While the sympathetic nervous system (SNS) steps into dominant action when a situation threatening our physical existence (emergency) is encountered, the parasympathetic nervous system (PNS) is in dominant control when the body is at rest or facing calm situations.

2) However, at all times, both systems carry signals and the net outcome of the two opposing signals is what determines the state of the organs and systems of the body.   Thus, for example, when the SNS dominates, the heart beats faster and blood pressure is high.   When the PNS dominates, the heartbeat and blood pressure return to resting levels.

3) We humans, as a species, overload the stress response mechanism not because of actual threats to our physical existence, but with our mental preoccupations of worry, anxiety and the like.

4) For promotion of wellbeing, it is necessary to help the mind keep the PNS in dominant control most of the time. This goal is realized in an optimal manner with meditation.

24

Will (Volition)

It is volition (will) that I call 'karma'.
Having willed, one acts by body, speech and the mind.

The Buddha[78]

The good or ill of man lies within his own will.

Epictetus

There is one thing common about the mind and body processes that we discussed in the last few chapters. That is that they are all *involuntary*. These involuntary actions, taking place at lightning speed, are supported by mechanisms that have been firmly established in us as a result of evolution and life experiences. The main involuntary actions discussed so far are (in sequence): an object is sensed, then it is perceived, the perception triggers a thinking process fed by memory and finally, the conclusion of the thinking process initiates other processes leading to changes in emotional make-up and body functions. Included in the body functions are the resultant physical and verbal actions.

If we were equipped only with involuntary mechanisms, then our destinies would be cast in concrete. In the existential sense, humans would be no different than rabbits – being born, existing, procreating and dying. Fortunately, this is not so, because we have the mental process within us called *volition* (or *will*). It is this one mental process that gives us the 'tool' to be different from other animals, creatures of mere habit.

Used in conjunction with wisdom, the tool of *will* has enabled human beings to create the phenomenal advances that we see around us today, thereby surpassing capabilities of other animals. Even more important than technology-based advancement, it has provided us with the adjuncts needed to overcome our existential stress. On the other hand – and unfortunately – used in conjunction with ignorance, craving and hatred, *will* is also the tool that enables human beings to perform acts of

---

[78] Anguttara nikaya part 6 sutta 63

destruction such as genocide, to name one from an endless list. The role of the *will,* as a mechanism for overcoming existential stress, is the subject of further study in this chapter. By now, it should be apparent to us that the *karma* referred to in Dhamma is the same as the *will* (volition) we are discussing in this chapter.

The prime example of a change from a prevailing unsatisfactory status quo to one of welcome contentment, using one's sheer *will*power, is none other than that of the Buddha himself in his 6-year long struggle to overcome existential suffering. He commenced that task with the following declaration:

> "Though my skin, my nerves and my bones should waste away and my life-blood dry, I will not leave this seat until I have attained Supreme Enlightenment."

And what was his reward for that exercise of *will*power? Supreme Enlightenment for the Buddha and the way to get there ('The Noble Eightfold Path') for the rest of us.

And here's another good example, though the result is not quite spiritual in nature. Yet it is an illustrious case of victory for the human will over adversity and realization of a worthy goal.

A child was born to poor parents who lived in a log cabin. The year was 1809. When the little boy was only 9 years old, his mother passed away. He tried his hand at business a number of times but failed notably when he was in his twenties. His sweetheart (fiancee) died when he was 26. But he fought the adversities with his utmost will. He tried politics – he was often defeated in his attempts at positions in the legislature, U.S. Congress, Senate and Vice-Presidency. He had some successes, like his career in law, but a preponderance of failures. He had two nervous breakdowns, one in his late twenties and the other in his early thirties. But he kept marching on. Eventually, in 1860, at the age of 51 he was elected the 16th President of the United States of America. His name was Abraham Lincoln, best known as the man who abolished slavery in the United States.

We have used the lives of two pre-eminent human beings for the above illustrations to convey the message of willpower. However, it is not difficult to find many not-so-famous amongst our immediate social group whose exercise of will and realization of goals can serve as guides for the rest of us.

We need to invoke the process of *will* only when it becomes necessary to think and act differently from involuntary thinking and action. This situation often arises when we realize that some aspect of our present involuntary behavior is unsatisfactory and we desire to change it. When we have carried out the chosen voluntary (*will*ed) thinking and action long enough, it now becomes our involuntary thinking and action, that is, a *habit* or part of one's personality.

As an example, take the case of a man who only knows how to drive automobiles with automatic transmissions and who has just started taking lessons in driving a manual-gear (standard) car. The first day he needs to willfully think through the steps of driving a standard, such as pressing the clutch to change gears. As he progresses with his training, the voluntary nature of the activity becomes less while the involuntary nature picks up by an equal amount. After much practice driving the standard, there will come a time when the *will-* factor is not involved at all. The moment he gets in the car, with no voluntary thinking and no voluntary action, he drives away fully under involuntary control. The mental action of driving a standard is now added to the vast repertoire of involuntary mental actions already stored in his mind.

The principles brought forth by the above example apply also to management of our existential distress. Certain thinking patterns within us, which are not in touch with reality, happen involuntarily, causing us and others distress and harm. If that is the case, then, obviously, we need to change our involuntary thinking by the use of our *will*, to think thoughts that are orientated to wellbeing and thereby overcome the distress. If we can identify the distress-producing involuntary thoughts and *will*fully (voluntarily) substitute corresponding thoughts that are in touch with reality, we will be on the path to managing our distress. After adequate practice in the new ways of thinking (and associated behavior), the voluntary new ways gradually become involuntary. Thus, the crucial point about *will*ed thinking is not the use of memory (views) but the reverse process, i.e., modification of memory (views). The next diagram shows the position of the *will* factor, in the mind.

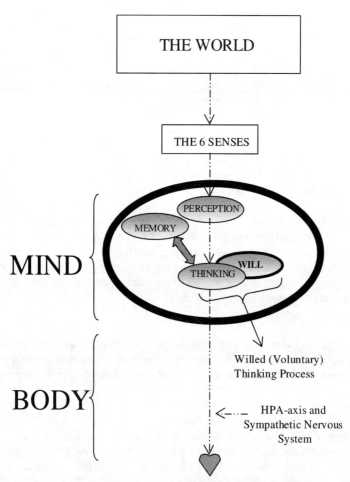

THE WORLD

THE 6 SENSES

PERCEPTION

MEMORY

THINKING   WILL

MIND

BODY

Willed (Voluntary)
Thinking Process

HPA-axis and
Sympathetic Nervous
System

Organs and processes affected
(heart, eyes, muscles, skin, blood
vessels, sweat glands, blood sugar,
metabolism etc.)

The health-promoting involuntary thinking and actions, which replace the old distress-promoting thinking and actions, become part of the personality. Insight Meditation uses this principle.

For behavior modification, three conditions must always be satisfied:
> (1) willed *thinking*, followed by
> (2) *action* (bodily or mental), and
> (3) adequate *repetition* of the thinking and action.

Thinking followed by bodily action is easy to understand. For example, one thinks, "Now I will raise my hand" and then raises the hand. How about thinking followed by *mental* action? To illustrate, let's take the concept of no-self. (1) We study and rationalize the concept untill we are convinced – this is the thinking part. (2) Upon seeing an object we *contemplate* on its no-self nature – this is the mental *action* part. (3) We repeat the mental action on other objects seen until no-self-based thinking and living become involuntary, i.e., habitual.

Before we close this chapter, let's discuss a few important points about the topic of bodily action.

1. Although bodily action should include action by any organ or part of the body, it is customary to refer to speech as being separate from other bodily actions. Thus in Dhamma literature one often comes across the reference 'bodily action or speech'.

2. What causes us to take bodily action or speak? It is *thinking* which eventually leads to muscular movement of the vocal chords and tongue for speech, and primarily muscles of relevant body parts for bodily action. (The exception is direct sensory-motor action).

3. As we have seen earlier, the conclusion from the thinking process is crucially dependent on one's views. Therefore, our bodily actions and speech will be wholesome or unwholesome dependent on whether our views are in touch with reality or not.

4. Bodily actions and speech will be involuntary or voluntary dependent on whether the thinking is involuntary or voluntary.

Chapter Insights and Highlights

1. Normally our thinking and actions (i.e., our behavior) are involuntary.

2. Yet, using the *will* factor, humans have the capability to think and act voluntarily.

3. When we identify any aspect of our behavior as unsatisfactory, we need to invoke our *will* and use it with wisdom to change the behavior for the better.

4. When used with ignorance, craving and hatred, the *will* can lead to unwholesome and evil behavior.

5. *Will*ed (voluntary) thinking and action applied long enough becomes involuntary, i.e., part of one's personality.

6. To change behavior we need to satisfy three conditions. They are: (1) *will*ed thinking, (2) related action and (3) adequate repetition.

7. In the final analysis, having views that are in touch with reality will be the means to overcoming existential distress. In practice this can be realized by implanting right views in one's mind by persistently thinking thoughts which are in touch with reality.

25

Dhamma at the Synapse

" 'You,' your joys and your sorrows, your memories and your ambitions, your sense of personal identity and free will, are in fact no more than the behavior of a vast assembly of nerve cells and their associated molecules."

Francis Crick
Co-discoverer of DNA
Nobel Laureate (1962)

No emotion, any more than a wave, can long retain its own individual form.
Henry Ward Beecher (1887)

We have so far seen how our perceptions of the world and the resulting thoughts affect our physical organs and body systems. But what about our emotions? When an erratic driver almost runs over us, we get *angry*. When a loved one falls sick we feel *sad*. When we are in financial straits, we *worry* how we will pay the mortgage and provide for our dependents. When we hear of impending layoffs during a time of severe recession, we feel *anxious* and so on. Anger, sadness, worry, anxiety and similar conditions are all states of the mind. How do these happen? How do they affect our wellbeing? What can we do to soften the impact of, or eliminate, these conditions?

To start our investigation, we need to digress for a moment from the mind to its physiological platform, the brain. The building block (the basic functional unit) of the brain is a special cell called the *neuron*. The real actors behind all our mental processes, including emotions, are the neurons. The human brain has an enormous number – about 100 billion – of these living cells.

Neurons vary in size and shape. Given that about 100 billion neurons are packed into a mere 6-inch cube head, we can appreciate that the typical neuron is a microscopic entity. The next diagram depicts a typical neuron, magnified about 10,000 times, showing the features that are important for our discussion.

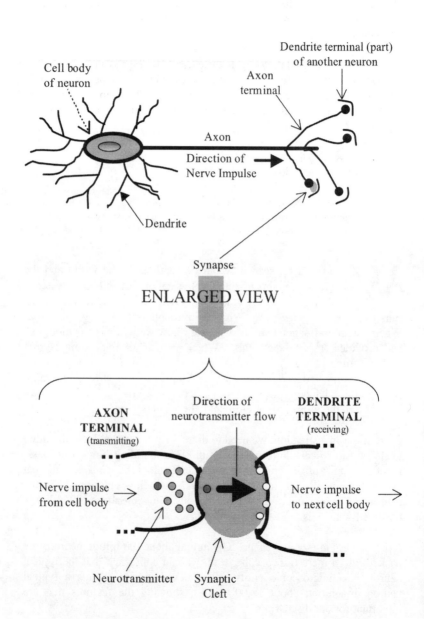

As the center of its operations and intelligence, the neuron has a *cell body* from which emanate branches. These branches are of two types: (a) one long branch called the *axon*, its function being to transmit signals *away* from the cell body and (b) many *dendrites* to bring signals *towards and into* the cell body.

Now, what is the relationship between the 100 billion neurons and our amazing cognitive functions such as thinking and memory?   What relationship do these diminutive living entities have to our emotions? Before we can answer these questions, we need to look at how just one neuron 'talks' to another.

As shown in the top part of the last diagram, the terminals of the (transmitting) axon do not make physical contact with the terminals of (receiving) dendrites. Instead there is a gap between the two. The area that comprises the end of the axon terminal, the gap and the end of the dendrite terminal is collectively called the *synapse* (see the enlarged view at the lower part of the diagram). The gap itself is given the term *synaptic cleft*.

From the 100 billion neurons, arbitrarily picking any two in communication, here's what happens at a synapse when a neuron *fires*[79]:

> ➤ A nerve impulse[80] (electro-chemical wave) travels from the cell body, down the axon, to the axon terminal at the synapse.
> ➤   At the terminal, the impulse causes the release of a quantity of a chemical, called a *neurotransmitter,* into the synaptic cleft.
> ➤ The neurotransmitters diffuse ('swim') across to the bank of the dendrite terminal of the next neuron.
> ➤ Having reached the next bank, the neurotransmitters trigger a nerve impulse (like the one that traveled down the previous axon).
> ➤ The new nerve impulse travels down the dendrite to the next cell body and the whole cycle repeats from neuron to neuron, thereby transmitting the signal from wherever it started in the neural maze, to wherever it has to end, to serve a meaningful mental process.

It is difficult to find an analogy of impact to fully illustrate the neural activity described above because of the complexity of the neural brain. However, for a highly simplified analogy, imagine the brain to be a

---

[79] In neuroscience jargon, a neuron is said to be firing when it becomes active.
[80] Also called an *action potential.*

microscopic model of a forest as complex as the Amazon, the world's largest rain forest. Assume that any two facing branch-ends (of different trees) have a gap between them and no branch-ends touch.

To send a signal (or communicate a message) from one point to another in the forest, this is what happens. Upon activation of an initial trigger (say, the roar of a lion), squirrels jump from a branch end to the facing branch end (of another tree), causing the latter branch to shake. Squirrels at the next point (another branch end of the same tree) feel the vibration of the branch. Upon feeling the vibration, these squirrels jump from branch end to the facing branch end (of another tree) repeating the cycle. In this manner, messages are conveyed from any point in the Amazon to any other point, whether it is from one tree to an adjacent tree or a tree at one end of the Amazon to one at the opposite end.   The squirrels represent neurotransmitters, the branches the axons and dendrites and the vibrations the nerve impulse.

Coming back from the analogy to the real thing – the complex microscopic world of neurons – a few worthwhile points to note are:

◆   To enable functionality, neurons form networks in a hierarchical manner, the lowest and simplest network being called the *local circuit*[81].

◆   Thus, while the neuron is the building block of the brain /mind, the real activity and state of the brain/mind depends on the firing patterns of many neural circuits.

◆   Whether the next neuron in a path will fire or not depends not just on receipt of a signal via a dendrite but on other conditions such as influences from nearby neurons and arriving hormones (transported by the blood).

◆   A neural firing happens with extreme rapidity – in a few milliseconds. Therefore in one second of the life of a person, millions of firing patterns are produced in the brain. Thus, even if a person is outwardly still, there is incessant activity within, at the microscopic level.

---

[81] Next in increasing order of complexity are networks named *subcortical nuclei, cortical regions, systems and systems of systems.*

▶ *Digression*

IMPERMANENCE OF THE MIND (EMOTIONS)

This would be an appropriate place to slightly digress from the general discussion and make a few important observations about our mind. Many times the Buddha, with his extraordinary contemplative and penetrative power gained insight into the undercurrent of incessant activity that exists within the human mind. For example, at one point he proclaimed[82] " ...... that which is called thought, or mind, or consciousness arises continuously during day and night ......". On such basis he proceeded to formulate the Noble Truths about distress and the means to overcome the distress, i.e., realize peace and eventually Sublime Peace (Nirvana). From the discussions in this chapter on the neuroscientific perspective, we know that the key action center for all emotions (mental conditions) is the synapse. Distress and peace and even Sublime Peace are all states of the mind, and are therefore synaptic states. Thus, celebrating the convergence of Buddhism and neuroscience we can say that *Dhamma happens at the synapse*. (Incidentally, scientists have named one of the neurotransmitters associated with mood *anandamide*, *ananda* in Sanskrit meaning "bliss".)

The therapeutic implication of this convergence of Buddhism and neuroscience is very significant. When we are mired in negative emotions such as worry, sadness, anxiety and depression, we often tend to think that the mental state will never pass away. However, the truth is that neural changes are taking place incessantly and the emotion will change, given time. In fact the change will be hastened if we replace our irrational thought "This will never pass" with the thought in touch with reality, i.e., "Given time, this too will pass."

In chapter 4: Living Through Change, we retold an ancient story of a king whose distressful emotional life changed profoundly upon realization that "This too will pass". It's a truth not just for kings but for all of us to embrace. So, not surprisingly, many readers of the first edition of this book have reported benefiting profoundly upon reading that little gem of a story and deeply absorbing its meaning. Now, thanks to modern neuroscience, we know also *why* "This too will pass". Knowing *why* should make the passage from distress to peace even easier for our minds, because the mind is always more comfortable when the *why* is answered.

---

[82] Ref. Samyutta Nikaya, Division XII, Sutta 62.

It has been estimated that the typical neuron gives rise to an average 1000 synapses, so that a human brain has about 100 *trillion*[83] synapses. Try to imagine 100 billion, the total human population of the world today being about 6 billion. Then try to imagine a thousand times that, i.e., 100 trillion! No doubt we agree those are incredibly enormous numbers, defying our imagination of meaningfulness. Yet they are all real entities right inside our head.

Transmission of signals from neuron to neuron to neuron through these synapses in complex linkages (networks) produces meaningful, harmonious end results, which make possible all our amazing mental processes such as perception, thinking, memory and emotions. While the physical collection of 100 billion neurons and their 100 trillion synapses may appear as an enormous tangled mess, in functionality not a single neuron or synapse is out of place in Mother Nature's most prized design called the human brain – that is, in the healthy human brain.

In an earlier chapter we saw that hormonal and autonomic nervous system activities determine the state of the physical organs (e.g., the heart) and systems of the body (e.g., metabolism). The activities taking place at the same time in the neural pathways, most significantly the neurotransmitter action at the synapse, primarily determine our mental state, in particular, our emotions (anger, joy, depression etc.), being the subject of this chapter. For example depression is associated with changes in concentration of certain neurotransmitters such as *serotinin*. (More on depression in a later chapter.)

We started the discussion of the functional compartments of the mind by listing in Chapter 20 the following five processes:

In the chapters that followed 20, we covered details of these processes ending with *Emotions* (covered in this chapter). Hence, this will be an appropriate place to collect the essentials of the last six chapters in one

---

[83] 1000 synapses per neuron x 100 billion neurons = 100 trillion synapses

diagram - the next. This diagram depicts the essence of the biological
interaction of a human being with his/her world.

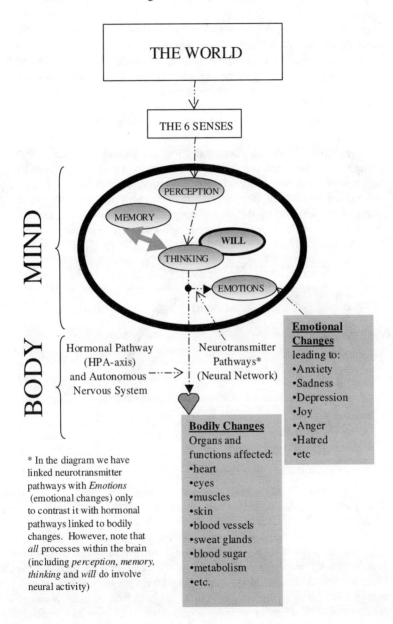

THE WORLD

THE 6 SENSES

MIND

PERCEPTION

MEMORY

WILL

THINKING

EMOTIONS

BODY

Hormonal Pathway
(HPA-axis)
and Autonomous
Nervous System

Neurotransmitter
Pathways*
(Neural Network)

**Emotional
Changes**
leading to:
•Anxiety
•Sadness
•Depression
•Joy
•Anger
•Hatred
•etc

Bodily Changes
Organs and
functions affected:
•heart
•eyes
•muscles
•skin
•blood vessels
•sweat glands
•blood sugar
•metabolism
•etc.

* In the diagram we have
linked neurotransmitter
pathways with *Emotions*
(emotional changes) only
to contrast it with hormonal
pathways linked to bodily
changes. However, note that
all processes within the brain
(including *perception, memory,
thinking* and *will* do involve
neural activity)

A stimulus from an object or event arrives at the brain/mind through any one of the six senses and is processed by the brain/mind. Involved are many processes, but of particular interest to us are *perception, thinking, memory, will* and *emotion*. The end results are:

    (a)   changes to emotions via neurotransmitter pathways and

    (b)   changes to body organs/systems via hormonal pathways and the autonomous nervous system.

Although we have discussed changes to the states of bodily organs and emotions as though they were independent, in reality they affect one another through internal communication mechanisms. One's bodily changes are monitored and detected by the senses continuously. What's detected become fresh stimuli for activation of the body's response mechanism, which in turn affects the emotions and organs. These changes are detected by the senses starting the next cycle. To illustrate, take the case of the heart as the organ and anxiety (about potential heart attack) as the emotion.

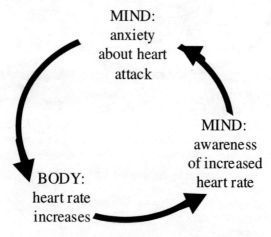

The possibility of a heart attack pops into Ivan's mind (6th sense stimulus), he becomes anxious and the heart rate increases. Through sensory detection the mind becomes aware of the increased heart rate. This awareness acts as a sensory stimulus for the response mechanism. Ivan's anxiety increases, which causes the heart rate to increase even more and the cycle continues. In people who do not have the skills to nip this vicious cycle in the bud, the build-up could lead to what is called a *panic attack*. Meditation provides a definitive method to take control of this situation.

The above example shows that the mind and body are not operating as stand-alone entities but are interactive through complex mechanisms. In other words, changes in the functionality of the mind cause changes in the functionality of the body and vice versa. The mind-body phenomenon is very complex; there is more interaction between mind and body than we tend to imagine.

Chapter Insights and Highlights

1) The building block of the brain is the special cell called the *neuron*. There are about 100 billion of these cells in the average human brain.

2) Signals are passed from one neuron to another in a sophisticated process involving (a) electro-chemical impulses and (b) chemicals called *neurotransmitters* that diffuse ("swim") across gaps that exist between branches of communicating neurons. Messages are sent from any one point in the brain to any other point, near or far, by repetition of this process.

3) The functional area around the gap is called a *synapse*. The average human brain has about 100 trillion synapses.

4) Our mental states are determined, not by individual neurons, but by complex networks of neurons and their interactions.

5) In every millisecond in the life of a person millions of firing patterns are produced in the brain. Thus the human brain is very much an active entity during each moment. 2500 years ago the Buddha highlighted this fact, though in terms of the mind.

6) Recognition of the volatile nature of our brain/mind can bring significant therapeutic benefits.

7) Within the complex mind-body phenomenon, the mind and body work as inter-dependent partners.

8) The convergence of Dhamma and modern neuroscience can be aptly summarized in the statement: *Dhamma happens at the synapse.*

9) The incessant synaptic changes explain *why* our thoughts and emotions are subject to continuous change.

26

How We Got Wired

In previous chapters, we saw that the essence of our brain is a mass of neural connectivity or *wiring*[84] that reflects genetic and environmental influences. The underlying mechanisms of all our mental processes – thinking, perception, emotions, memory, will (volition) and any other – are neural networks. Therefore, it is this neural networking that is responsible for our unique personalities. How did this assemblage of neural wiring get inside the brain of each of us? What is the nature of this wiring? Of special interest at this stage is how our enormous memory (of values, beliefs, views, biases and prejudices) was formed? Answers to these and other related questions will be explored in this chapter.

We will follow the important milestones of development of the embryo/fetus, with the main focus on the brain (the neural formations) and senses, from conception to adulthood.

Inside the Womb

Day one: fertilization occurs and soon thereafter, the embryo is formed. The development of the embryo will be governed by two factors: (a) nature - *genes* inherited from the parents and (b) nurture - *environmental factors*, the most influential environment for an embryo being the interior of the mother. Regarding the latter, some conditions that can have an impact on the embryo include the mother's emotional state, her nutritional intake, the type of drugs whether prescribed or not (including alcohol and smoking) that she is taking and any viral infections. During prenatal development, the predominant factor is nature while nurture plays a secondary role. Thus starts the 'nature and nurture' team effort that will prevail right through the life span of the new life.

---

[84] Neuroscience has borrowed the word *wiring* (note the familiar "electrical *wiring*") from electrical science/trade. However, note one significant difference: there is no hard wiring continuity in the brain, in that the 'wires' (the axons and dendrites) do not physically connect at the synapse, but simulate connectivity with neurotransmitter flow from a tip of one 'wire' (axon) to the tip of the other 'wire' (dendrite). The formal term for the colloquial term *wiring* is *neurobiochemistry*.

Brain development does not start until the beginning of the 3rd week, when a layer of a small number of neurons folds into a tube-like structure called the *neural tube*, being the precursor of the central nervous system (brain and spine). Starting slowly, the neuron production in the tube soon proliferates at the amazing rate of about 4,000 neurons per second (360 million per day!). The work on the formation of the universe's 'super computer par excellence' has begun.

Over the period of some weeks more neurons than necessary will be produced and later, those that are not serving the purpose of neural connections are eliminated.

In week 4, the neural tube shows a distinct growth at its upper end, being the rudimentary brain. At this point, eyes and ears in their earliest stages of development also appear. However, it will be a long time before these organs acquire functionality.

By week 8, nervous system development begins. So does motor activity.

About week 10, the neural activity in the *fetus* (the embryo being referred to as the fetus from week 9) intensifies. Bursts of electrical activity busily carve out neuron-to-neuron connections via synapses, reminiscent of wiring of computer parts in a giant assembly plant. Small circuits are combined to form even more complex circuits resulting in purposeful patterns.

During the period of weeks 16 to 20, the fetus begins reacting to sound.

Week 24 – eyes begin to sense light. The sense of hearing is now near perfect and loud noises may startle the fetus.

(Since neural pathways, synapses and circuits are physical entities, all these developments change the physical shape of the brain as well. After birth, these neural patterns will enable the newborn to recognize sensory stimuli such as the mother's voice.)

By about the 28th week of gestation, practically all the neurons needed for a whole lifetime (about 100 billion) are in place. It is thought that at about this time the sense of taste also begins to be established.

Two more months of overall growth and the new life is ready to leave the mother's womb.

Birth

The newborn can respond to sensory stimuli, but very dimly. At this stage, the only completely wired brain structure is the *brain stem*, which controls vital functions such as heartbeat, blood pressure, breathing and temperature. The neural wiring of any other part of the brain is faint.

The brain at birth is a rough mold of the future adult brain and awaits refinement in the days, months and years to follow.

From Birth to Adulthood

While neuron production was virtually completed inside the mother's womb and some circuitry wired, laying the bulk of the neural pathways happens after birth. This most important brain development occurs in response to stimuli from the myriad of new situations that the newborn will experience. *The neurons of the newborn await experiential stimulation to sprout connections and spread out networks* as a dry sponge awaits water to expand.

In response to each new experience, such as a smile from the mother, some or all of the following will occur in the appropriate regions of the brain:

- Axons, dendrites and synapses will form pathways and store a chemical signal. This process is referred to as *wiring.*
- *When the experience is repeated or re-lived, the strength of the chemical signal increases.*
- When the strength of the signal reaches a certain predetermined threshold, the pathway is selected for retention over the years to come.
- If the signal does not reach the threshold by a certain time, the pathway is pruned.

All cognitive processes involve the building or use of pathways in the above manner. In particular, our enormous memory (of values, beliefs, views, biases, prejudices etc.) has been etched into our brains in gradual steps in response to stimuli from life experiences following this process.

Since all the above involve physical changes within the brain, the shape and size of the neural mass, and therefore of the brain, changes.

A tremendous (synaptic) growth spurt occurs in the brain of the newborn during the first few years following birth. One of the important results of this growth spurt is that *the core neural wiring needed for numerous important mental mechanisms such as the response to sensory stimuli, language and social skills is completed or nearly completed by about age six.*

From the above, it is easy to see that *in the postnatal and formative years of the newborn, the environment (nurture) plays a crucial role in its development.* In fact, during this phase, nurture is the dominant factor and nature takes a secondary role, in exact reverse to the emphasis in prenatal development. Hence, **it is critically important that a newborn be provided with wholesome stimulation (love, security, laughter, warmth etc.).** Such stimulation builds neural patterns in the newborn that support traits of strength like confidence, motivation, courage and resilience. For this to happen, *the primary caregivers must (a) be aware of the need to provide wholesome stimulation and (b) know what wholesome stimulation is.* Those who are thus equipped are nurturing newborns with wisdom.

On the other hand, unwholesome stimulation (insensitivity, neglect, abuse, anger, etc.) builds neural pathways that support negative traits in the newborn such as anxiety, pessimism, lack of confidence and antisocial behavior. Primary caregivers in this category are obviously driven by ignorance.

Earlier we said that the neurons of the newborn await experiential stimulation to spread out networks as a dry sponge awaits water to expand. We can add that, if the water is clean, we have a clean wet sponge and if the water is dirty, a dirty wet sponge. Likewise, if the stimulation is wholesome, the newborn's neural wiring will be to his/her wellbeing, but if the stimulation is unwholesome, the newborn's neural wiring will be to his/her disadvantage. Stated differently, *the nurturing environment can do immense good or immense harm to the new life depending on the quality of the environment.* A hostile environment can overburden the stress-response mechanism, resulting in proneness to anxiety, depression, and other emotional handicaps, often throughout life, *unless strong remedial action is taken.* However, let's hasten to remind ourselves that it's not only nurture that determines the life course of the newborn but also nature (genetics) and one's karma.

Also, let's not rush to the easy conclusion that the primary caregivers or influential others are to be *blamed* if the nurturing environment that prevailed and the end results were unfavorable. If we do blame, which unfortunately is a common and universal practice, it is due to *our* ignorance of reality and myopic thinking. Hence this subject – blame – being critically important to position things in the right perspective, and alleviate much distress in individuals and society, is discussed in detail in Section C.

During this period of development, the brain produces trillions more synapses than the new life actually needs. Then the 'work-or-leave' (or 'use-or-lose') principle is applied ruthlessly. Those synapses that have been industrious responding to stimuli are retained and the others are eliminated, like employees in a company. In fact, this *pruning* process (also referred to as *sculpting*) escalates to a ruthless tempo at about age 10. By about age 13, the sculpting process is more or less completed leaving marks (about 100 trillion synaptic connections) on a brain/mind that will maintain its uniqueness amongst billions. Why 'more or less completed'? Because, **the ability to modify or create new neural pathways and synapses in response to experience remains throughout life, although the work becomes harder as the person advances in age.** In the final analysis, any method (be it meditation or any form of psychotherapy or other 'technique') that claims to provide a lasting solution to existential stress (mental distress) should utilize this ability. Importantly, the method must create neural changes as a result of *new thinking and experience that is in touch with reality.*

(An interesting point of comparison to note at this juncture is that the growth spurt during the prenatal period involved *neurons* whereas during the postnatal period it is the *pathways*, but both neurons and pathways are subject to the pruning process subsequent to the growth spurt.)

During one's life span, behind all mental processes (e.g., perception, thinking, feeling and memory formation and recall) there is bustling neural activity including traversing established pathways, creating new pathways and modifying existing pathways. Underlying every new memory is some new neural formation that records it. In short, the brain/mind phenomenon is a hive of incessant bustling activity, confirming the Buddha's pronouncement 2500 years ago about the changing nature of the mind.

With the recent (specifically post-1990) explosion of scientific data on early childhood development, a 'gold mine' is now available to educators, parents and others involved with postnatal growth to make the developmental years of children the most rewarding. In the long history of human existence on this planet, we are certainly lucky to be living as parents or children in this era because there is so much valuable information to guide us regarding right mental development.

In this chapter, we have provided a glimmer into the tremendous wealth of information that is emerging to assist in raising mentally wholesome children, thanks to the exponential growth in neuroscience. However further discussion of the subject of early childhood development is outside the scope of this book, because our focus is on the person who has already gone through the developmental phase (conception to adulthood) and is presently facing existential distress. For parents-to-be, parents of infants and other caregivers interested in early childhood development and how to raise mentally healthy children, there are plenty of books available on the subject. We can conclude this aspect of the discussion with a message to these caregivers: *the shortest and ideal Way to Inner Peace is to be first raised in a wholesome (ideally no-self) environment during early childhood years.*

Now, let's revert to our discussion about adults. ***The way we adults respond to sensory stimuli throughout our lives was wired into our brains at a time when we had no say in our destiny.*** *This was when we were an embryo/fetus followed by our formative years. Depending on whether the stimulation we received during the growth period was wholesome or unwholesome, the wiring was one of two formats: (a) that which responds to current sensory stimuli resulting in happiness and peace or (b) that which responds to current sensory stimuli resulting in stress (distress).*

For adults the above leads to a seemingly fundamental paradox (Catch-22). **When our wiring is that which responds to sensory stimuli resulting in stress (which happens for the vast majority of us), it seems that we are doomed to suffer until the end of our lives, even though we had no input into the way in which we have been wired.** "That's not fair!" one might yell in desperation. Or, is there a way out of this seeming hopelessness, a Way to Inner Peace?

There is a Way to Inner Peace. When the early environment has been unfavorable, satisfactory reparative measures can be taken in adult life, which is what this book is all about. *The Way to Inner Peace* is to repair the problem wiring, which will be covered in detail in Section C. When viewed through the eyeglass of modern science, it can easily be seen that this re-wiring is exactly what Buddhist Insight Meditation achieves.

Chapter Insights and Highlights

1. As a harmonious team, genes (nature) and environment (nurture) govern our development. During gestation, nature is the predominant factor. After birth, nurture plays the more influential role.

2. Brain development starts the beginning of the 3rd week. Neuron production occurs, and is completed, during the gestation period, with an end total of about 100 billion neurons.

3. Some neural wiring takes place during gestation, giving enough circuitry for the newborn to start life at birth.

4. At birth (a) only the brain stem is completely wired to support essential life processes and (b) the newborn can respond to sensory stimuli only dimly.

5. During the first few years after birth a tremendous synaptic growth spurt (wiring) occurs.

6. Excess production, of neurons (during prenatal development) and synaptic pathways (during postnatal development), occurs and the unwanted (unused/underused) pruned later.

7. In response to environmental stimuli, the core neural wiring needed for important mental mechanisms (such as language and the manner of future response to sensory stimuli) are completed or nearly completed by about age six. Thus, in the postnatal and formative years, nurturing plays a crucial role in the development of the newborn.

8. It is critically important that a newborn be provided with wholesome stimulation (e.g., love and caring) during the formative years so that the resulting brain wiring is that which supports wholesome traits. Unwholesome stimulation (e.g., insensitivity and neglect) produces the opposite result.

9. Although primary neural pathway formation is over by about age 13 (leaving marks of a unique personality), **the ability to create new neural pathways and synapses (or modify existing ones) in response to experience remains throughout life,** thereby making it possible to modify personality/behavior throughout life. *Any*

credible technique for overcoming existential stress (mental distress) and maintaining lasting peace __must__ use this ability.

10. The way we respond to sensory stimuli was wired into our brains at a time when we had no say in our destiny. Depending on the stimulation received in the formative years, the wiring in an adult will be in one of two formats: (a) that which responds to sensory stimuli resulting in peace or (b) that which responds to sensory stimuli resulting in stress.

11. In the case of an adult, when the wiring happens to be (b) above, (which it is for the vast majority of us), lasting relief can be obtained by using Insight Meditation to re-wire the problem pathways, and therefore changing to (a) above,. However, this requires diligence and time.

12. That is *The Way to Inner Peace.*

27

The Birth and Growth of the Self

I am not a thing, a noun
I seem to be a verb,
An evolving process -
An integral function of the universe.

Buckminster Fuller,
From the epigraph to 'I seem to be a verb' (1970).

The notion of self has two important, but divergent, characteristics: (1) It projects the *appearance* of stark reality to *all* human beings and (2) For anyone who cares to investigate it deeply, transcending sensory perception, the truth is revealed that it is fallacious.

The first characteristic makes it necessary for all human beings to use the notion of self ("*my* house" or "Hello *John*") as mere convention to conduct the 'business' of living in the world. On the other hand, our inability to simultaneously be aware of the second characteristic (that 'self' is fallacious in Reality) lands us in the mire of existential stress, because what makes us stressed or peaceful are the undercurrents driven by Reality.

Earlier we have discussed the crucial subject of *self* to some degree. However, one aspect we have not considered so far, is how the notion of self is *born*, embedded and grown to maturity in each of us as a specious entity. This aspect also appears not to have been dealt with in related writings so far. An understanding of the birth and growth of the notion of self will undoubtedly facilitate the exploration of the notion and help us significantly in our efforts to eradicate our existential distress as the notion of self is the root cause of all our distress.

Let's start by noting that virtually everything that's important in our lives has two complementary components or layers. They are (1) the genetic (evolutionary) component and (2) the environmental component. The first is usually referred to as nature and the second as nurture. In fact, in the last chapter we saw how the whole human being develops under the control of these two factors – one a blueprint carried through genes and the other, the "sculptor" (environment) that finishes the job.

What applies to the whole being applies equally well to its parts, whether it is an organ (e.g., the heart), a mental condition (e.g., fear) or some other feature of our existence (e.g., the notion of self). The blueprint for the human heart, for example, is passed on as genetic instructions (nature) but the creation of a real heart from that is the work of nurture or environment, nourishment being part of that environment. Again, the blueprint for fear is a genetic transference but how that fear manifests in each grown human being is the work of the environment. The same rules apply to the notion of self, which after all, is some form of a meaningfully set collection of neural wiring. We will now discuss how nature and nurture collaborate (or become "accomplices") to create the notion of *the self* – the cause of all our distress.

(A) <u>NATURE</u>

To understand the role played by nature in the creation of the erroneous self we need to go back to the earliest times in the Darwinian evolutionary history of life itself. Let's once again remind ourselves that there is just one goal in Mother Nature's grand scheme for life forms in the universe and that is propagation of species and not the intimation of reality. Propagation of species entails survival. To survive, life forms need a sense of intense *craving*, a driving force. *That intense craving is the sense of self.* In the case of the lowest and smallest forms of life – our very first ancestors - this sense of self had to be the most rudimentary phenomenon that surpasses our imagination. In other words, the earliest microscopic life forms had a sense of self, commensurate with their microscopic existence. A fundamental attribute for any life form is that when it senses that the self is threatened, it does all it can to survive.

As life evolved, the footprint of the sense of the specious self was passed genetically from generation to generation, with proportionate refinement. A unicellular life finds the current environment becoming hostile, so it moves away from it. A fox finds a crow approaching the carcass it wants to have for dinner and chases away the crow. (Effectively, and instinctively, the fox is telling the crow "You get out of here, this is <u>my</u> dinner). So, all this to protect the self – for survival – and this happens with all life forms. Human beings also have this genetically transferred sense of self, but in our case there is more – and that's the superimposing of a second layer that develops after the birth of the human baby which places the *self notion* in the human being in a class by itself. This gigantic leap to form a human being's 'I-am-the-center-of-the-universe' sense of self is the result of unique human nurturing that uses the phenomenon called thinking (fuelled by views). So we move on to consider this second (complementary) layer that forms our sense of self. This is the layer of *Nurture*.

(B) NURTURE

The first layer of the self notion, created by nature as detailed in the section above, is genetically transferred and appears in the new life initially as genetic code in the just formed embryo and is upgraded to neural wiring thereafter.

The rudimentary sense of self created by nature is now ready to be gradually transformed into a more powerful and mature self by the "sculpting" work of the environment (nurturing). Now let's explore this "sculpting" process in some detail.

For some months after a baby is born, the sense of self is no more than that provided by nature and remains dormant. Then it begins to emerge, but is not much different than the natural sense of self in animals. Thus a puppy barks in fear upon seeing a stranger. A baby cries when a stranger tries to carry her.

The fact that our senses are truth-distorting was established in Chapter 16: Perception and Reality. Whether we are an infant, child, youth or adult, we always perceive the world as made of entities (chairs, walls, trees, clouds, people, selves etc.), while in Reality it is comprised of ever-changing processes. Thus, while our truth-distorting senses satisfactorily serve nature's design intent of survival and procreation, they contribute to our erroneous perception of processes as entities. And we communicate with fellow human beings using distorted truths, because all 6 billion of us have the same truth-distorting senses.

▶ *Digression*

ENTITIES AND PROCESSES

We use the terms *entity* and *process* in this chapter and elsewhere in the book. Before we proceed any further, let's try to understand what we mean by these two important terms, within the context of this book.

A *process* is a collection of changes that bring about a result whereas an *entity* is something that is perceived to exist as a discrete and tangible unit. If we analyze any entity into its constituent parts and those constituent parts into their parts and so on, on a downward hierarchy, at some point we should be able to observe (invariably with the help of instruments) processes that make possible the entity with which we started.

Let's illustrate using an example, aptly relevant to the subject matter of this book. A human being ("self', "me", "John" etc.) is, to our minds, a discrete (living) entity. He/she is made up of entities called organs (heart, liver, lungs, skin etc.). The organs are again made of entities called tissues. The tissues in turn are made of entities called cells. At the level of cells we can observe (under a powerful microscope) incessant changes (movement), which reflect the underlying cellular processes (the undercurrents). Included in these processes are digestion, excretion, circulation etc. If we were to further break down cellular processes, we would enter the domains of molecular, atomic and sub-atomic processes. Thus there are no entities in this universe (except as seen through our truth-distorting senses); in truth there is only incessant change.

From the foregoing we can conclude that the human being is ultimately made up of phenomena that are governed by incessant change, i.e., processes. However, to our truth-distorting bare senses, the human being appears as an entity, i.e., as a self. In summary, a human being is not a 'self' but an aggregate of processes.

A meaningful way to think of a process is as a *happening* with no definable doer. A good example of a process is breathing. Although we are accustomed to say "I am breathing" or "my breath" it is simply a happening.

Also in reality there is no "I" that owns the breath, but merely other processes working in harmony that give rise to, and support, the process of breathing.

In the end, (at the microscopic building-block level) what is important is not the differentiation between entities or processes, but that there is change behind what we perceive as unchanging entities.

As the six (truth-distorting) sensory mechanisms gradually acquire functionality, the newborn begins to recognize form, color, movement, sound etc., by virtue of mere biological capability (nature). It does not perceive (and *need not* perceive in Mother Nature's intent) the incessantly changing processes (the truth) behind these perceptions.

The perception of the specious self, appearing true to the newborn (in the rudimentary form already set in place by nature) is now ready for 'fine-tuning' by nurture. This work is unwittingly abetted by the adult humans who comprise the growth environment of the newborn. Bear in mind that the notion of self is unchallenged and believed as gospel by these adult humans who have already traversed the growth process of newborns. Thus, the notion of self is further solidified in the mind of our newborn, now on a uniquely human plane using the higher mental faculties. At this stage (when the baby is about nine months old), linguistics begins to appear on the scene.

"Momaaaa[85]"   "Daaaaad"

Neurologically speaking, each communication helps to etch deeper, in the newborn's brain, the fallacious notion of self or identity.

A name is given to the newborn: "Colin". When Colin is about a year and half old, Mom says "This is Colin" and Colin repeats "Colin". Then follows combinations of words like "Baaaaby Colin" or a little later "This is Baaaaby Colin." This is recorded in new neural wiring and the self-notion is further reinforced.

The next stage of evolution of the specious self (at about the age of 18 months) is extension of "me" to "my" and "mine". "My Momaaa." "The ball is mine." In addition to neurally recording the idea of a "me" different from the rest of the world, the concept of ownership sets in and gets reflected in neural wiring.

Somewhere along the line, comments like "Colin, surely you can do better than Johnny – for that matter, you can easily be at the top of the class. I am very disappointed with you." Now, not only is the self-notion reinforced, fertile ground is laid for many unwholesome attributes such as competitiveness, jealousy and anxiety-proneness to mature progressively with time.

---

[85] This kind of speech 'language' spoken by parents to their newborns is sometimes referred to as 'Parentese'

This process of strengthening the neurological etching continues endlessly as the growing being interacts with the outside world and the erroneous notion of self becomes a 'given'. Its constant use in daily living is now involuntary, that is, unquestioned habit. The notion of self becomes the commanding factor behind one's behavior hereafter.

As the years pass by, countless associations of the nature of 'me' and 'mine' make of this being a *seemingly* unshakable entity, a 'fixture'. "Angelica, Colin's girlfriend." "Columbia – Colin's University", "Colin, the dentist" etc.

Imagine a microscopic counter inside Colin's brain that advances its count each time a *self*-affirming association is made and one more etching is made on the 'self groove' in the brain. When infant Colin makes his very first association the counter reads 1. By the time Colin is able to say "Me, Colin" somewhere close to age two, the counter reads a large number, let's say 85,321. On the day Colin becomes a dentist, it reads a much larger number, say 1,253,652. (Obviously these numbers are arbitrary, but help to get across the message that the reinforcement of the erroneous self notion is a relentless process, with hundreds, perhaps thousands, of reinforcements occurring daily, each time etching *self* deeper into its secure place in Colin's neural maze). Then, is it any wonder that the (specious) self is taken as the truth and becomes the predominant influence in Colin's life (and the lives of all other humans)?

Now, from the discussion so far, how can we summarize the answer to the question "How is the sense of the specious self born?" The answer may be stated as follows:

"The specious self is born to serve as the object of the driving force (the intense craving) within all life form for survival. It is Mother Nature's way of ensuring propagation of the species - no more and no less."

The sense of self in any particular life is the result of a genetically transferred blueprint and its refinement by the environment.

It would be appropriate now to revisit some points previously discussed and compare the effects of the two diametrically opposite environments that are based on *no-self* and *self,* on the development of the newborn. Recall that both no-self and self are pivotal beliefs on which depend all other beliefs relating to peace and distress respectively in human existence.

Because the principle of no-self is in touch with reality, caregivers who live according to that principle will generate a wholesome environment. For example, unconditional love towards all beings is a characteristic of no-self living. Hence, a child growing up in such an environment will possess the foundation for the extension of unconditional love to all beings as he/she grows up. On the other hand, love on the condition that the loved one must be 'mine' is a characteristic of a life lived on the belief of self, which is not in touch with reality. Self-based living is fertile ground for the promotion of unwholesome characteristics such as jealousy and hatred towards others who are not 'mine'.

Along similar lines, it can be easily established that a child growing in an environment created by primary caregivers whose lives are based on the principle of no-self will be mentally wholesome, not just in love, but in *all* aspects because no-self is a core belief. Such a being, as an adult, will have a tremendous advantage not only in living a life of happiness on worldly terms, but also in traversing the higher path to Sublime Peace.

From the vantage point of reality, the notion of self should be viewed as a gross 'error' in our mental development, the joint 'perpetrators' being nature and nurture, taking place at a time when our will was not available to guide that development. In the final analysis, we all pay dearly for that gross 'error' whether by committing an evil act or by feeling distressed.

In the next chapter, Anatomy of the Self, we take an in-depth look at the crucial manner in which the erroneous notion of self affects our lives.

Chapter Insights and Highlights

1. A *process* is a collection of <u>changes</u> that bring about a result whereas an *entity* is something that is perceived to exist as a discrete unit, usually something tangible.

2. Entities and processes are related but an entity is specious. Closer to the truth are the constituent processes, though our truth-distorting sensory mechanisms can notice only the entity (primary example: *self*) and not the underlying processes.

3. A newborn is equipped with the perceptive capability to recognize entities in hazy and bare format: form, color, movement, sound etc. – thus a faint and immature notion of self. Formation of this rudimentary notion of self is the first of two phases in the creation of the specious self, the dominant factor being *nature*.

4. Thereafter, interaction with the environment (with linguistics playing a prominent role) solidifies the notion of the specious self. This is the second phase in the creation of the specious self. The dominant factor is *nurture*.

5. Neural wiring takes place both before and after birth and is the underlying 'hardware' behind the birth and growth of the notion of the specious self.

6. A nurturing environment based on the *no-self* principle would create the ideal wholesome stimulation for the newborn to develop wholesome traits.

28

Anatomy of the Self

> You cannot step twice into the same river,
> For other waters are continually flowing in.
> *Heraclitus (circa 500 B.C.)*

Now that we know how the self was born and grew, it's time to get a closer look at it by studying its 'anatomy'.

The truth-distorting characteristic of the senses does not become an issue as long as we contain our 'business of living' to procreation and survival. Distress is inherent in that system, and Mother Nature does not care whether beings suffer or not. However, the speciousness of self only becomes an issue because human beings (not Mother Nature) do not want distress and desire its eradication. To realize that goal, then, it becomes necessary for us to transcend the truth-distorting senses and know the truth. To overcome distress one must realize and integrate into one's daily living, the truth of the notion that there is no self.

In the scriptures there are many terms – such as aversion, desire, craving, attachment, clinging and ignorance – described as unwholesome traits leading to distress. But these traits belong, it appears, to the one who suffers – me, the self. Therefore, it is clear that if we can get rid of the self-identity, then we automatically get rid of *all* these unwholesome traits. It's like the many branches of a tree that provide unwanted shade to a house. Instead of felling two dozen branches, we can chop just the one trunk, which will bring down all the branches.

Referencing everything we experience to a self, we perceive a distorted version of the world. To transcend that distortion, we need to shed that notion of self. That means, we need to disable the neural wiring that corresponds to the notion of self. (How to do that will be discussed elsewhere in this book.) It is similar to a person who has been wearing gray sunglasses all his/her life and has always seen a color-distorted (gray) world. To see the world without that color distortion, the person has to remove the sunglasses. The notion of self is 'our sunglasses'.

When we get rid of the notion of self, we see the world without distortion, that is, the way it really is.

All human beings pay dearly for not realizing that self is only a distortion of reality and that in absolute reality there is no self. Here's an analogy to illustrate how ignorance of the truth of no-self leads to distress.

A man approaches a frozen lake. His sensory perception tells him that the ice is solid, because all that his eyes can see is solidity. The appearance of solidity leads to an involuntary conclusion of safety. Now he ventures out on the ice. When he has walked some distance, the ice gives way and he perishes by sinking into the frigid water below. He perished because he did not have the mental capability to transcend immediate sensory reality (for example, by checking with the official Weather/Marine Advisory before embarking on his walk).

The same for self and no-self. A person will suffer so long as he/she believes in self, the illusion created by truth-distorting senses. If the person has the wisdom to transcend "self" and realize "no-self", he/she will not suffer any more. The unique contribution of Dhamma to the human healing process is the profound doctrine of no-self. This uniqueness and profundity, compounded by a lifetime of conditioning to the opposite notion of self, makes no-self one of the most difficult Dhamma concepts to comprehend and integrate into one's life. Hence we have dealt with the notion of self from different angles, from different perspectives and in depth.

The assertion 'there is no self' without qualifiers is incomplete and misleading, though unfortunately this is the way the message exists in the usual Dhamma deliberations. An accurate way to state the principle of self/no-self is in a two-pronged format as follows:

> (a) *There is a self*, **only as perceived by our truth-distorting sensory mechanisms, and**

> (b) *There is no self* **in Absolute Reality (truth), that is, upon transcending the senses.**

Now we have no confusion, no mysticism and no half-truth. We have stated the filtered essence of the principle of self/no-self exactly as it is. There is no longer any flavor about the no-self idea that is mystical, occult, metaphysical etc. It is plain and simple, and at the same time, rational and scientific. Therefore we have a clear basis on which to examine some important corollaries of the principle.

The first corollary follows directly from (a). Because we have no choice but to use the truth-distorting senses to interact with the world in daily living, we have to live as though there is a self. Whether we are unenlightened or enlightened, we all have to do so.

The second corollary follows from (b). While interacting with the world as though there is a self, a person who is enlightened will always be additionally aware that in truth there is no self. Such a person will also *experience* no-self in his/her inner life, aware that all the undercurrents that control existence are driven by the principle of no-self.

The third corollary reveals the fundamental difference between Buddhist psychotherapy and all other forms of popular psychotherapy (including religious formats).

All non-Buddhist psychotherapy takes the existence of the entity - *self* - as a given. Thus they are based only on (a) above, and that too only partially, in that the truth-distorting qualifier does not come into consideration. Simply stated all non-Buddhist psychotherapy is built on the premise 'There is a self'. For example, Western psychotherapy is built on notions such as self-esteem, self-image, self-control, self-respect, self-assurance, self-sufficiency, self-discipline, self-love, which are part of a much longer list. The immediate conclusion that we can draw is that in such psychotherapy or healing systems the treatment is incomplete because they are based on just a *perceived* truth, i.e., part of (a) above. Therefore, any resulting therapeutic benefits are also incomplete. By not considering also (b) above, the undercurrents of existence are not taken into account, and that will result in failure of the treatment in the long run, even if there are short-term benefits.

Buddhist psychotherapy also advocates some *preparatory* practices based on the notion of self, such as development of self-reliance, fully aware, and acknowledging, that self is only a conventional or worldly reality, i.e., (a) above. Therefore, most importantly, and as the last and crucial step – and this is the fundamental difference – Buddhist psychotherapy proceeds on to practices that enable one to shed the notion of self in accordance with (b) above, the truth of no-self. The result is completion of the healing 'journey' of the mind, that is realization of the goal of Sublime Peace, eventually. Stated simply, Buddhist meditation takes the healing process to a *completion*.

Before we close this chapter, there are a few sundry observations to cover regarding the self/no-self topic.

(1)   When someone suffers, there is a tendency to label and look at the distress as 'my distress'.   Such labeling and association enormously exaggerates the distress into an 'Everest'.   With the understanding of no-self and its integration into one's life, one abstains from owning the distress (as 'mine').   And the attitude towards the distress changes to echo the famous scriptural line, "distress is there, but no I that is distressed" – an acceptance, but no more ownership.   With such practice, psychological distress abates and eventually only physical pain will remain.   Physical pain is universal – it is a fact of life for all of us.   We all have to bear physical pain at certain times in our lives.   Even Enlightened Beings have to bear physical pain.   For example, it is on record that The Buddha suffered grievous bodily pain when a splinter injured his foot[86]

(2)   To use a simple and practical term, we can say that living based on the notion of self means *personalization* of life events.   All personalization leads to distress.   Thus, in a practical sense, if we live our lives with less personalization, we will be living with greater inner peace.

(3)   An analogy.   Seated by the ocean, we watch the waves.   Millions of these waves make up the surface of the ocean.   For a moment, imagine the waves had human-type minds.   Then individual waves will think such thoughts as "I am a tall wave", "I am a short wave", "I am pretty", "That wave is ugly" and "I have a wealth of foam".   Each wave will be unique and will be recognized as such by other waves.

Now imagine the minds disappear reflecting the real nature of waves. The intelligence that labeled, individualized, made comparisons and judgments is gone.   Then, what is left is nothing but process.   Waves (processes) arising from the great ocean, existing for a moment and ceasing as they merge back again into the great ocean.

The arising, existence and ceasing of human beings (6 billion presently) from the 'ocean' (the Universe) is similar.   It's only our (human) mind that gives labels, individualizes, makes comparisons and judgements, pivotal on the *self notion*.   And we behave

---

[86] Samyutta Nikaya , Vol. 1, page 110, #3

accordingly. Remove the human intelligence factor and what is left are processes arising from the great Universe and ceasing as they merge back with the great Universe. Besides that, there is nothing (no identity, *no-self*). And, no-self implies *oneness* of the Universe.

(4) A question often asked is: "When I believe in a self, I am motivated to do things. Then I work for the welfare of myself, my children and so forth. I want to build a nice home for my family, educate my children, advance in my career etc. When I realize no-self, where do I get the motivation from?"

The answer to this valid question can be as follows:

- As we have seen above, no-self implies oneness. Our motivation does not disappear, but becomes *different*. Whereas earlier the motivation was driven by the self-notion (me, mine), now it is driven by the notion of oneness. And there is an abundance of things that can be done under the notion of oneness.

- The primary guideline for the new action is to do things that cause no harm to oneself or others.

- Since one individual obviously cannot do things for the welfare of the whole world, the meaningful and practical way is to adopt the action words of the environmentalists: Think globally, act locally[87]. In our case, then 'Think oneness (universe), act locally'. Thus, we can still continue to do the important things that we did before for oneself, one's children etc., but one's *mental* attitude will now be oneness (no-self) rather than self. The beggar sleeping on the street downtown will be thought of with the same compassion and love (called unconditional love or *metta* in Dhamma) that one has for one's own child. Wherever, and whenever possible, more and more will be done for the actual welfare of 'others'. Earlier one may have looked the other way upon seeing a beggar as when filth was seen. Now the beggar gets a dollar with love, since he cannot be given a room in our house in which to sleep. And another beggar. All human beings. And the child's university

---

[87] Attributed to French-born American bacteriologist and 'father of modern medical ecology' Dr. René Jules Dubos (1901 – 1982).

education is still paid for, but the idea of the new wing to the already comfortable house is abandoned.

- Other examples of things that can be done under the notion of oneness are:

    - Do things that enable one to keep the mind and body healthy.

    - Earn a right livelihood.

    - Do things that bring about harmony.

    - Take action that helps to save the environment.

    - Do things that are needed to move forward towards Sublime Peace.

And that's a workload enough to keep anybody busy through more than one lifetime.

(5) Happiness can be promoted in individuals by a happy 'growth environment' that still operates on the basis there is a self. However, even those we normally refer to as happy individuals, and who invariably conduct their lives based on good morals and ethics, can realize the higher states of inner peace and Sublime Peace only with eradication of the notion of self.

(6) Because of our belief in a self, and the consequent build up of life's practices on that belief, Dhamma posits that all worldly beings have impure or diseased minds. Making this point clear,

The Buddha said[88] that it may be possible for a person to claim to have been free from physical disease even for a hundred years, but from mental disease not even for one day, except for an Arahant or a Buddha. The Arahant and The Buddha have fully rid their minds of the notion of self, hence their minds are completely pure, i.e., disease free.

Concluding this chapter, we can say the following. In the end, the most important study of all for a human being becomes the study of self, until

---

[88] See *Anguttara Nikaya*

one realizes the truth that there is in fact no self. Then one has moved away from existential stress into the territory of true Enlightenment.

Chapter Insights and Highlights

1. The notion of *self* is the root cause of our distress. Stated differently: *ignorance* of the fact there is no self is the root cause of our distress.

2. When we rid ourselves of the notion of self, all our unwholesome traits such as aversion, desire, craving, attachment and clinging disappear, as when a trunk of a tree falls, all the leaves fall.

3. The accurate way to state the principle of self/no-self is:

    (a) *There is a self*, **only as perceived by our truth-distorting sensory mechanisms, and**

    (b) *There is no self* **in Absolute Reality (truth), that is, upon transcending the senses.**

4. To live in this world, we have no choice but to use the truth-distorting senses. Hence we have to live as though there is a self.

5. However, to overcome distress, we need to be constantly aware that the truth, operating as an undercurrent, is the fact of no-self. To be thus aware, and to integrate that awareness into one's existence, is to be enlightened.

6. The fundamental difference between Buddhist psychotherapy and other forms of psychotherapy is that only the former takes the healing process to a point of completion based on the principle of *no-self*.

7. Human life can be compared to the waves in the ocean. Arising from the ocean, existing for a brief time and ceasing upon merging back into the ocean. There are just processes, no selves (no waves) except as a label or convention in the human mind. And no self implies *oneness* of the Universe.

8. When we realize no-self, our motivation for existence does not disappear, it simply becomes different. The motivation which was earlier driven by a notion of self is now driven by a sense of oneness with the Universe, in which each one of us is an essential, integral part.

29

X-Conditions

No god, no Brahma[89], can be called
The maker of this wheel of life;
Empty[90] phenomena roll on,
Dependent on conditions all.

Quoted in *The Path of Purification*
(Visuddhi-Magga) XIX

Learn to wish that everything should come to pass exactly as it does.

Epictetus

We may render the above verse from Buddhist scriptures in simple prose as follows. *Behind this life of ours there is no supernatural maker, but just no-self processes that roll on dependent purely on conditions.* What we shall attempt to do in this chapter is to investigate more deeply this profound statement, as it has a number of important ramifications for our daily living.

The basic premise on which the present analysis of conditionality starts is the following statement:

If with A as condition, B exists, then when A ceases, B ceases.

While the truth of the above statement is obvious, in practice we will find that the existence (and therefore the cessation) of any event depends not on one condition but on many. Two important corollaries that follow from the above statement are:

(1) A, the condition (or cause), is the result of conditions preceding it.
(2) B, the present result (or effect or event), becomes a condition for one or more future results.

Let's commence our investigation by revisiting and examining more closely, the example of the bonfire quoted in Chapter 8, where it was stated that on a heedless response one would say that the bonfire exists

---

[89] Creator god.
[90] Here empty implies empty (devoid) of a self.

because of the firewood. However, if one were to deeply investigate the conditions for the existence of the bonfire, one would find that there are many other conditions needed besides the firewood such as the air (oxygen) and dryness. If any one of these conditions is absent (e.g., absence of dryness due to rain), then there will be no bonfire. A diagrammatic representation of this dependency on multiple conditions follows.

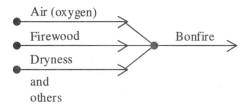

(Note from 1 and 2 above that although we use various terms – condition/cause and result/effect/event – to describe two consecutive stages of happenings, in the final analysis they all refer to different manifestations of *conditions*. Given this fact, we use one symbol •——> to represent both stages in the diagram.)

If we ponder to see how each one of the multiple conditions came to be, we will identify a second group of multiple conditions preceding that condition in turn. For example, at the bonfire site firewood will exist when all the conditions, i.e., the tree, the means for chopping the tree, the means to transport the wood to the bonfire site and other pre-requisites are available. This idea is depicted in the next diagram.

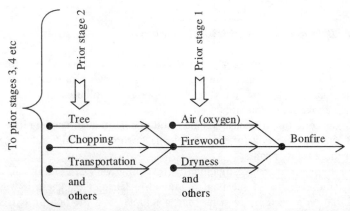

Picking any one condition from this *prior stage 2* (e.g., tree), we will see a number of needed conditions at *prior stage 3* (e.g., soil, moisture, sunlight, temperature etc.) and so on ad infinitum, backwards in time. If we were to represent this phenomenon in a general template we will have a presentation akin to what appears in the next diagram.

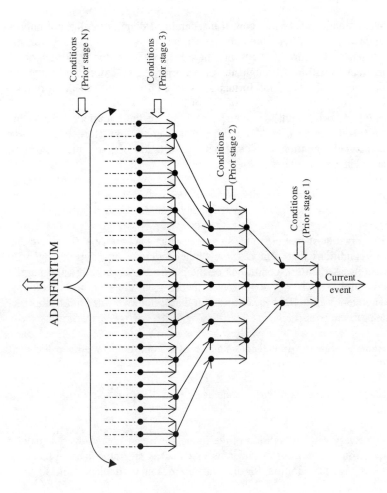

What we refer to, as the current event can be any phenomenon or entity – *anything* without exception. Thus the bonfire (in the last example) is a current event as would be a person or an emotion (such as anger) experienced by someone, in other situations.

(Note: Because of space constraints, we have used a constant arbitrary number of three conditions throughout the diagram as comprising each preceding set. In actuality, the number varies from event to event, is usually more than three and often is very large.)

What we can easily see from the generalized diagram is that not only is there a set of direct prerequisite ('prior stage 1') conditions for the existence of a current event, but there is an ever-expanding formation of indirect conditions (through successive prior stages) extending backwards in time to infinity. This formation is an enormous funnel-like (or cone-like) collection composing of zillions of conditions. For the sake of brevity and for want of a name, in the rest of the book let's refer to this funnel-like collection of conditions as *x-conditions* (for eXtended, or eXpanded conditions). Then, the manifestation of x-conditions, can be stated as a principle as follows:

> *An ever-expanding funnel-like collection of conditions that extends endlessly back in time precedes any event in this universe.*

[As a matter of interest in passing, the reader may notice at this stage that the conditions that comprise the funnel fall into three types – genetic conditions (nature), conditions of the environment (nurture) and karmic conditions. That is, x-conditions = nature + nurture + karmic conditions. Though not important for our present discussion, we will refer to this fact later in the book]

Accentuating the funnel-like feature of x-conditions, we have the next diagram (following page).

Some important corollaries emanating from the principle of x-conditions are:

(a) Every single condition in the funnel, however far removed it may be from the current event, is as essential as an immediately preceding (stage 1) condition, for the existence of that particular event.

(b) With the truth-distorting senses of human beings, we usually recognize only the immediately preceding conditions (and sometimes only one or two of these) and are 'blind' to the conditions at stage 2 and beyond.

(c) Even with the greatest insight, one cannot (and does not need to) identify all the conditions relating to an event, as the funnel-like collection of conditions is endless.

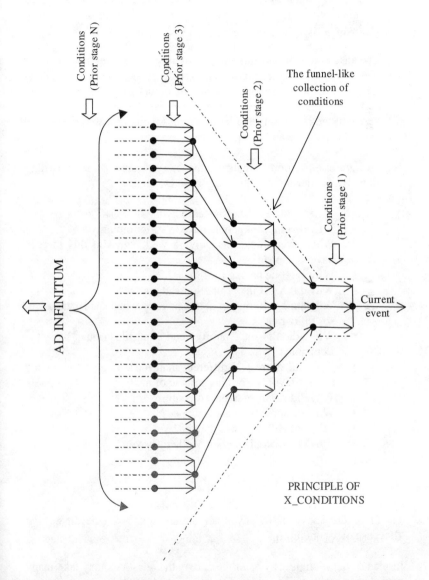

(d) Every object ('thing') in this universe is unique. So is every happening (or event). Understanding this fact is critically important to leading a life that is harmonious and in touch with reality. (Even so-called identical twins are not really identical. One significant contributory factor is that the sum total of the life experiences of one is different from the other. Thus, they are identical only as perceived by others via their truth-distorting senses and only in their physical characteristics.)

(e) The discussion of x-conditions irrefutably establishes the fact that beliefs in fate, chance, luck and similar phenomena are based on fallacy. *Every happening was meant to happen exactly the way it did and is the result of a unique collection of conditions.* We just do not know all the conditions that led to the happening. So we erroneously call it fate, chance and so on.

Now we are in a position to realize satisfactory closure to many baffling questions we ask during the course of our lives, such as:

- …., why me? (e.g., Cancer, why me?)
- Why do innocent people have to suffer brutality?
- When everything was moving well, why did this tragedy have to happen?
- Why can't he be like me?
- Why did X get the promotion and not me?
- Why am I suffering in abject poverty when she is (they are) so 'filthy rich'.
- Why didn't our family end up illustrious like the Benjamins?
- Why did X treat Y different than me? (e.g., why did my parents favor my brother instead of me?)
- Why did …. have to die so young?
- Why are some born handicapped?
- Why did Hitler do what he did?
- Why can't people be like Mother Theresa?
- Why do people destroy our planet?
- Why ……. ?
- Why ……. ?

To all of the above or to any other similar questions the answer is: "Because of x-conditions."

Instead of questioning why as in the above, the questions may take many other forms such as "What have I done to deserve this?" The answer, to this specific question, is "Hardly anything. It happened due to operation of x-conditions."

The common advice is, "This is the way it is (or, this is Nature), so let's accept it and move on." But the mind does not want to accept it because it is in the nature of the mind to want *reasons*. The mind wants to know *why* something is the way it is. x-conditions gives us that reason. With x-conditions the advice takes the more complete form "Due to x-conditions, this is the way it is. So let's accept it and move on." Now the mind is less inclined to hesitate or doubt, because it has a reason and one that is in touch with reality.

Having attributed happenings to x-conditions, do we sit back and do nothing about all dislikable things that happen to us during our lifetimes? Absolutely not! The action to be taken is along the lines quoted in the serenity prayer referred to earlier with one addition – we provide the reason why we need to accept certain things, which is x-conditions. For therapy, it is important to know the reason. Stated in a practical manner, the formula for action would be as follows:

I.   *Accept* all that has happened up to now as the way it is, the reason being x-conditions.
II.   *Act* to improve things from now on, where feasible, with data ("lessons") from past happenings contributing to formulation of this action.
III. *Accept* what cannot be done to improve things from now on, also, as the way it is, the reason again being x-conditions.

In the rest of the book, for brevity we will refer to the above as the Triple-A formula (or method) – for Accept, Act, Accept. The formula is of universal applicability, and its application to problems of human existence (distress) will be our primary interest.

Note that there is a lot of *acceptance* here (steps I and III). For a tiny speck of a human being to live in this immense universe, with a myriad of external forces/factors (physical and mental), it should come as no surprise that we do need to accept a lot of things – there is no other way. Acceptance, as we will discover, is tremendous therapy. This acceptance means saying to oneself "This is the way it is". It can be the worst or the best or anything in between and for all our response is, *"This is the way it is"*. Reason: x-conditions.

Once again recall the story in Chapter 4: Living Through Change about the king whose distressful emotional life was changed to one of tranquility upon deep realization of the truth in the statement "This too will pass". Now, we can combine that truth with the above revelation resulting from x-conditions, along with the fact of no-self and say:

"This too will pass. This is the way it is. There is no I that owns this." Whenever we are in distress let's remember to deeply contemplate this statement of eternal truth. And there is no doubt that it will help us overcome the distress and realize tranquility, given proper contemplation.

Step II is the 'action step', the action being *will*ed (or *volitional*). Some important notes about this step follow:

(a) Recall from earlier chapters that volitional action is referred to in Dhamma as *karma* in Sanskrit (or *kamma* in Pali). It could be wholesome or unwholesome whether driven by wisdom (pivotal on the no-self concept) or ignorance (pivotal on the self concept) respectively. Action always produces consequences (Pali: *vipaka)*, which will be correspondingly wholesome or unwholesome. A very important corollary of 'no-self' action is not to willfully cause harm to oneself or others, because all ethical action (the 'good ' and 'bad') is based on it.

(b) Any volitional action taken becomes a new x-condition injected into the funnel of x-conditions. This is the only place where the immense natural flow and formation of x-conditions is alterable by volitional human action. Due to the chain-reaction effect of conditions, the effect of this action will be felt for all time to come.

(c) In view of (b) above, our only opportunity to change our destiny for the better, within limits, lies in thoughtfully (wisely) choosing wholesome action. Where applicable, we must use the 'lessons' from what has happened up to now as important determinants of the willed action we propose to take.

(d) Again, in view of (b) above, any unwholesome volitional action taken (which is always driven by ignorance) will be followed by its proportionate consequences – some form of distress, the intensity depending on the gravity of the action. This distress must run its due course.

Punishments meted out to any human being by another human being or any form of human society are not a substitute, equivalent or alternative for distress meted out by nature under karmic law. The judgement of an ignorant human being or a group of them (society) can never be superior to the judgement of Nature under the karmic law of ethical action-consequences. However, from a worldly point of view, social groups may deem punishment necessary to maintain law and order as defined by each such social group.

(e) A forest fire starts with one spark. A tree burns down, then another tree, then another and eventually the whole forest. A similar fate can, and often does, befall human beings. One action (well-intentioned or not) driven by ignorance can start a chain-reaction resulting in vast damage to oneself, one's family, society or the world at large. The case of well-intended action driven by ignorance brings to mind the children's story of the friendly bear. Intending to kill a fly hovering over the face of it's sleeping friend (a man), the bear hurled a huge rock at the fly. The fly flew away. The bear's friend died. So the corrective action for us is to replace ignorance with wisdom.

(f) Fortunate beings will do the utmost to rid themselves of the ignorance (i.e., develop wisdom based on the fact of no-self) so that the force (ignorance) that propelled the unwholesome volitional action is eliminated from now on. The technique is Insight Meditation.

(g) The karmic law of ethical action-consequences precludes the doer from justifying unwholesome willful action.

(h) Now, for an important point worth repeating. Any action taken to change unwholesome habitual reactions (such as in blame, anger, jealousy, guilt and depression) into a long-term solution needs repetition of the new willed action over time, until the new pattern has completely overwritten the old. Then the new pattern of reaction is no longer willed (voluntary), but involuntary. Thus, Step II action must initially be taken on events that have *already happened*, obviously not as a solution to these but to generate a long-term cure for those that will happen in the future. Until the long-term cure is in place, short-term help may be used for the immediate events. For example, while a person is practicing techniques based on Insight Meditation for long-term anger-control, he/she can use provisional methods such as breathing meditation and 'counting-to-ten' to manage current triggers of anger.

Before we conclude this chapter, we present (in the form of a Digression) the inspiring story of how one courageous human being provided the answer to the common question "Why me?"

▶ *Digression*

WHY ME?

The interesting cover story in Canada's weekly newsmagazine *Macleans* of May 21, 2001 was titled "Cancer, why me?" The June 4th issue of the magazine carried the following 'letter to the editor' from Gizzie Burkett[91] of Toronto. In it is a lesson that is clear, moving and impactful for those of us who may ask the question "Why me?" (not necessarily regarding cancer but anything else in life).

"After six cancers in the past 18 years – and I'm only 39 – I've never asked the question "Why me?" When I get to the place where the question could be answered, it really won't matter anymore. My father told me upon my first diagnosis, ovarian cancer while I was pregnant with my son, that if I was able to help just one other person going through the same thing, that was my answer to "why?" In October, I opened a breast cancer awareness store in Toronto, and in February, I launched an adult wish foundation for people living with breast cancer. Instead of asking why, I made lemonade from lemons."

Thanks Gizzie – you have helped more than 'just one other person' through your Acceptance, Action and Acceptance

---

As we shall see in future chapters, the principle of x-conditions exposes, or helps to expose, the fallacies behind a number of common beliefs and habitual practices (such as blaming, anger, hatred and jealousy) existing in humans due to our truth-distorting senses. Thereby, the door is opened to corresponding revelations in touch with reality from which we can benefit enormously in daily living. We will explore this further in Part C.

Chapter Insights and Highlights

1.   Every event in this universe is the result of *multiple* conditions.

---

[91] Gizzie's letter is quoted here with her permission.

2. An ever-expanding formation (funnel-like collection) of conditions extends endlessly back in time and precedes any event. For brevity, we will refer to this phenomenon as the principle of *x-conditions*.

3. Every indirect condition, however far removed from the present event, is as essential for that event to arise/exist as an immediately preceding condition.

4. With our truth-distorting senses we usually recognize only the immediately preceding apparent condition (or conditions), and mistakenly attribute the existence of the present event only to it (them). This leads to many human fallacies, some of which, such as blame, precipitate dire consequences.

5. X-conditions give us a definitive basis for resolution of problems, particularly those associated with stress via the following Triple-A (Accept, Act, Accept) formula:

    I.   *Accept* all that has happened up to now as the way it is, the reason being x-conditions.
    II. *Act* to improve things from now on, where feasible, with data ('lessons') from past happenings contributing to formulation of this action.
    III. *Accept* what cannot be done to improve things from now on, also, as the way it is, the reason being x-conditions, again.

    To illustrate the Triple-A method let's consider a person who is concerned about heart disease. I. He *accepts* genetic factors such as history of heart disease in a parent. II. He *acts* to change his lifestyle in applicable areas such as eating a healthy diet, getting regular physical activity, maintaining ideal body weight, abstaining from alcohol and quitting smoking. He may also take medication (e.g., to lower cholesterol or high blood pressure) if deemed necessary by his physician. III. He *accepts* the inevitable future increase in risk of heart disease that accompanies aging.

6. Our only opportunity to change our destiny is by willful action (in step II above), which becomes a new x-condition fed into the immense funnel of x-conditions, with impact for all time to come. Depending on whether the action is wholesome or unwholesome, the ethical law of action metes out appropriate consequences that have to be lived through to completion.

7. The judgement of an ignorant human being or a group of them (society) can never be a substitute for the judgement of Nature under the karmic law of ethical action-consequences.

8. The karmic law of ethical action-consequences precludes the doer from justifying unwholesome willful action.

9. Whenever we are distressed let's help the process of bringing peace to ourselves by deeply contemplating the filtered essence of three important truths that we have discussed (stated below in capsule):

    This too will pass *(Reason: impermanence).*
    This is the way it is *(Reason: x-conditions).*
    There is no I that owns this *(Reason: truth-distorting senses, hence no-self).*

    Let's carry this capsule in our minds wherever we are, as the king carried the first statement as an inscription on his ring.

~

Distress Relief

~

Sub-Preface to Part C

Here are some snapshots of human existence in today's world that are representative of a typical day. Some are similar to media reports and the others are just 'common' events:

- The only breadwinner of a family, a cancer patient, is hospitalized after a heart attack ...now awaits triple by-pass surgery, while a distraught family .....
- Nine people and a suicide bomber perish in .....
- The millionaire Chief Financial Officer of giant corporation ... is arrested on charges of defrauding .... if convicted, a maximum prison sentence of 10 years ....
- .... drops out of university as he is unable to cope with the stresses of personal life and higher education.
- Construction worker ... undergoes severe spinal injury from a fall, is paralyzed from waist down ...
- ... , terminal AIDS patient, spends his last days in a hospice and is pre-occupied with fears of his impending death.
- Distraught about the impending divorce and separation from his family, a man kills his wife, two daughters and himself.

Sounds distressful? Very much. But this is part of our existence. At sometime or other each of us will be affected directly or indirectly by one or more events similar to those listed above.

Our present goal is not to get into details of any of the above events but to note that amongst them we can find some familiar elements either as an apparent cause or a precipitating result. The elements include blame, anger, hatred, guilt, depression, anxiety, sickness, injury, dying and death and serve as chapter topics in Part C. As we go through the chapters, it will become abundantly clear that what is needed to overcome the maladies is a handful of profound insights that were encountered in Parts A and B. Foremost amongst these insights are impermanence, no-self and x-conditions. The proper integration of these insights into our lives, which is crucially important, is dealt with in the closing chapters.

PART C

DISTRESS RELIEF

30

Blame

Listen Atula. This is not new.
It is an old saying –
"They blame you for being silent.
They blame you when you talk too much
And when you talk too little."

Whatever you do, they blame you.

The world always finds
A way to praise and a way to blame.
It always has and it always will.

The Buddha[92]

Walk in your brother's moccasins for a mile before criticizing him.
Ancient American Indian Proverb

In the few seconds it takes to read this sentence, many relationships will be embittered and many acts of violence committed on this planet because someone blamed another. Before the sun rises tomorrow, many human beings will be injured or killed by fellow human beings on this planet, because some person or a group of people felt it necessary to blame another person or group of people. With that being the immense cost of blame, let's then ask the basic question: "Is blaming in touch with reality or is it a meaningless and groundless practice?" The objective of this chapter is to search for an answer to that question.

It will be best to start the discussion of the subject of blame with an example. For that purpose, we will borrow the story of Adeline and Barnaby from Chapter 1.

To briefly recap the story, we have an initially happy marriage that turns into a sour relationship for Barnaby and Adeline and the fallout is distress not only for the two adults but also for their two lovely children. Each blames the other for the distress. Divorce proceedings are looming.

---

[92] The Dhammapada verses 227 and 228.

For our present purposes, we will pursue the story as perceived and presented by Barnaby, wherein he blames Adeline for his distress. Is Barnaby in touch with reality in taking this position? If he is not, then first and foremost it is in the interest of *his* emotional health to take corrective action. That would be to discard his present view and substitute that view with what is in touch with reality. This is the stuff of Insight Meditation practice, and in Barnaby's present predicament, the essential therapy for him. Let's continue.

First let's consider Barnaby's present perception realized via his truth-distorting senses, which, as we have seen earlier, scan no further than the immediately preceding set of conditions, and often considers only one condition. In the Barnaby case, that one condition is Adeline. To Barnaby, who has not pursued the transcendental approach yet, the 'convincing' truth is that Adeline is blamable for his distress. This, then, is the worldly perception, a perception appearing through truth-distorting senses.

Next let's pursue the transcendental view, first in respect of conditionality, then in respect of the self-view. We will use the principle of x-conditions to facilitate our analysis and also to emphasize the unfathomable vastness of conditions that collectively determine Adeline's situation. Three examples will be sufficient to establish the reality. The first addresses conditions immediately preceding Adeline, the second illustrates a condition some steps back and the third, a condition closer to infinity back in time. The second and third are conditions *arbitrarily* picked from the funnel of conditions, simply to help us with our analysis.

1. The conditions immediately prior to Adeline are many and include the influences of her mother and father. So, her mother and father are (direct) conditions for her existence.

2. Let's arbitrarily consider Adeline's maternal Great-Grandma #11. On an ancestral line we have to go back over a dozen stages to 'meet' her. If Great-grandma #11 did not exist, Adeline would not be existing. So Great-Grandma #11 is an *indirect* condition for the existence of Adeline, as significant as her mother is.

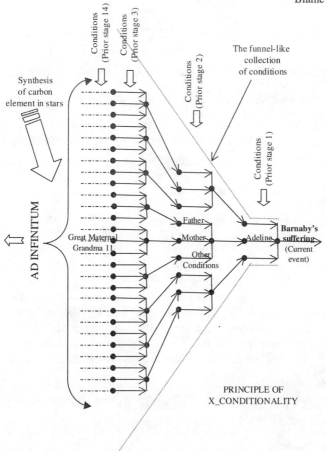

If Great-Grandma #11, as a lass of sweet seventeen did not by 'chance' meet a comely young visiting foreigner at the harvest dance, the latter would not have become Great-Grandpa #11 and there would be no Adeline. So that harvest dance is also an indirect condition for the existence of Adeline.

3. All living things – plants and animals (including human beings) – are carbon-based, meaning the key element of which these organisms are made is carbon. Planet earth received its carbon from material that was synthesized from lighter elements in the first generation of stars, millions of years before our solar system spun out into existence. Not only were lighter elements essential for the synthesis of carbon, but also needed was a *rare* coincidence (now well known to scientists) involving the energy levels of the atomic nuclei of these

lighter elements. Now just imagine what it would be like on our planet if the rare cosmic coincidence had not occurred and therefore the carbon supply was unavailable – it will be a barren planet with no life forms (including of course Adeline!). Thus, the cosmic coincidence, the lighter elements and carbon synthesis are (indirect) conditions for the existence of Adeline.

Likewise, we can easily show that Adeline's *emotional* make-up (be it anger, hatred, jealousy, depression or any other) at any given moment is also determined by the corresponding x-conditions applicable at that moment. The same for Barnaby. The same for the rest of us.

Armed with the above information, let's now move towards a closure on the Adeline-Barnaby case.

Firstly, we can conclude that, due to his truth-distorting senses Barnaby perceived Adeline's behavior as *the* cause of his distress. The truth is that a myriad of conditions (direct plus indirect) collectively caused it. The immediately preceding condition (Adeline) was the 'delivery person' for a multitude of preceding conditions. Blaming Adeline for his distress is like blaming the delivery person for a parcel of spoilt chocolates. Or, like blaming the last runner in a cross-country relay race, for losing the competition.

In view of what we have discussed, the reader will now be able to see the reasons for the following comment that appeared in Chapter 1.

> ".... Dhamma would point out to Barnaby that Adeline is not the *root* cause of his marital chaos. Whatever Adeline may have done, whatever she may be as a person, all that Barnaby went through emotionally was created by how he *perceived* Adeline and her actions. Adeline's actions, at most, are to be *associated* with what Barnaby has gone through, but *letting* her actions ruin him happened totally within his own mind. To Adeline, Dhamma will bring the same revelation, in principle. So the work both have to do, if they want to eradicate their mental distress, is to learn how to change the way they perceive the world, so that they can be in touch with reality; in Dhamma terms, purify their minds. And showing the way to do it is essentially what Dhamma is all about."

Now for a different analysis using the no-self principle. The entities Adeline and Barnaby ("selves") do exist as seen from the truth-distorting senses (as discussed in detail in the chapter titled 'Anatomy of the Self'). However, seen from Truth, they do not exist. Both are ever changing aggregates of processes. Hence, in Truth, assigning blame to entities Adeline (or Barnaby or any other) is impossible.

Furthermore, we saw in Chapter 27: Birth and Growth of the Self, the notion of self was wired into us by nature and nurture both at times when we had no control over our destinies. And the errors committed by us or others in life resulted, in the final analysis, from that notion of self – a case of deep-rooted ignorance. Therefore, in reality, we cannot blame anyone[93] (including ourselves) for errors committed. However, what is incumbent upon us is to *take action* to eradicate the belief in a self (i.e., practice Dhamma) so that we will not continue to make the same errors during the rest of our lives.

The same principles discussed above in regard to assigning blame to people apply to blaming anything else, be it such targets as the lousy weather, the misuse of taxpayer's money by the government or the dog next door that barks at 2 am.

We can now answer the original question we posed in paragraph 1: "Is blaming in touch with reality or is it a meaningless and groundless practice?" The clear answer: *blaming is __not__ in touch with reality and is a meaningless and groundless practice.* Yet, virtually all of us do it to some degree. Why? Because our 'shortsighted' and truth-distorting senses create illusions of blameworthiness (as in the Adeline-Barnaby case) and life-long conditioning has made it yet another human habit, though erroneous. One who realizes the shortcomings of the sensory mechanisms and transcends the senses by insightful thinking as outlined in this chapter becomes a person with wisdom (on the issue of blame). Such a person blames neither others nor oneself for any happening. All things happen because of x-conditions – the continuous flow of nature from beginningless time to the present event.

Now let's see how a rational and meaningful approach can be developed to resolve the Adeline-Barnaby case using the Triple-A method (from the chapter on x-conditions), with the spotlight on Barnaby.

I.   *Accept all that has happened up to now as the way it is, the reason being x-conditions.*

        Barnaby (having contemplated the manifestation of x-conditions) accepts all that has happened up to now as the way it is. He does not blame Adeline any more.

---

[93] Coming from a different angle, but emphasizing the same principle of non-blame on account of ignorance, recall Christ's statement in respect of the men who were about to crucify him: "Father, forgive them, for they know not what they are doing."

It is important to recall from Chapter 29: X-Conditions, the difference between blame and accountability. Blame is a meaningless and groundless practice because of x-conditions which run backwards to beginningless time, and which give rise to involuntary actions in an individual. On the other hand, the individual is accountable for willed unwholesome acts committed by him/her and the pay-back happens under the karmic law of volitional action-consequences *(karma-vipaka)*. It is an accountability that takes place between a human being and Nature, not between one human being (e.g., Adeline) and another (e.g., Barnaby). Factors such as partiality, hatred, revenge and vindictiveness that influence the act of blaming do not occur in accountability.

II.   *Act to improve things from now on, where feasible, with past happenings contributing towards formulation of this action.*

Barnaby, anger gone and calmer with his new attitude (item I above), is able to convince Adeline to attend a joint session of counseling, which includes the principles discussed in this chapter on blame. Adeline too is now convinced that blaming is a meaningless practice. They agree to give their marriage another try.

To completely overcome the ignorance that gave rise to blaming in the first place, both Barnaby and Adeline decide to diligently pursue Insight Meditation

III.   *Accept what cannot be done to improve things from now on, also, as the way it is, the reason again being x-conditions.*

Both accept the uniqueness of human beings, by virtue of x-conditions, and therefore the right of each to continue to be different, particularly in matters of the mind.

The above process applies to any other situation where blame is involved. As one other common example let's briefly look at the case of a person (say, Angelica) blaming the 'poor nurturing' provided by a parent for all her present misfortunes. Applying the Triple-A formula, Angelica learns to accept all that has happened as the way it is, also acknowledging that the parent was merely the 'delivery person' for the relevant x-conditions. That the nurturing environment left much to be desired is not questioned, but there is no more finger-pointing at a single, immediately perceivable condition, the parent. With the blame and anger gone, and a mind that is calmer, she takes responsibility for her own life. Angelica draws out a plan of action depending on her unique circumstances and identifies what she cannot do, also as the way it is. The result: much peace for Angelica.

Finally, before we close this chapter, we need to touch on the subject of *praise*, being the opposite of blame. If blame is a meaningless and groundless practice (as we have clearly established) in reality, then so is praise. Most of us would not like that. We like to be praised but not blamed. But nature, truth, does not exist for the sake of being liked by humans. We cannot have one side of a coin without the other. Any 'praiseworthy' happening is primarily due to manifestation of x-conditions and not due to any single immediately preceding condition. For example, Einstein did not attain the praiseworthy scientific heights he did all because of his mother or father (who were merely 'delivery postmen' like any parents) but primarily because of x-conditions relevant to his achievements. Any contribution made by the parents was limited to willed action conducted by them, through wisdom and not ignorance. That contribution is only one of a myriad conditions that comprise the funnel of x-conditions pertaining to Einstein's achievements.

The Buddha's recognition that both blame and praise are meaningless and groundless comes clear in the Dhammapada 81: "Even as a great rock is not shaken by the wind, the wise man is not shaken by praise or by blame."

We close this chapter with an interesting digression on the next page.

▶ *Digression*

OUR NEAR-IMPROBABLE EXISTENCE

Investigation of the principle of x-conditions leads us to numerous supplementary revelations, one particularly interesting case which we will examine here. We started the analysis by saying that a direct condition for Adeline's existence was her parents. Now, in accordance with the principle of x-conditions, the condition 'parents' branch off into other conditions in a limitless fashion. The near improbability of Adelaine's existence and, for that matter, the existence of all of us on a mere single condition is brought to light in the following analysis.

When a man and a woman get together to create a new life, about 300 *million* sperms partake in a competitive swim and just one sperm penetrates the single ovum, starting the new life. Had it been another sperm that won the competition, the result would be another person, with unique physical and emotional characteristics. In our example it would be not Adeline but another. Our existence, based on this one condition alone (of a specific sperm from 300 million penetrating the single ovum), is so near improbable that we may *perceive* it as 'miraculous' and therefore 'precious', though in reality there are no miracles and the cause of our being here is x-conditions.

In view of the foregoing revelation, we can make an important practical conclusion: each human life almost did not come to be. Therefore, the life of each one of us is too 'precious' to be wasted on unwholesome practices such as blame, anger and hatred. Those with wisdom will instead use every possible moment in it to practice Dhamma and realize inner peace.

Chapter Insights and Highlights

1) Human beings are prone to assigning blame, often with disastrous consequences.

2) Seen from truth, blaming is not in touch with reality and is a meaningless and groundless practice.

3) A meaningful alternative to blaming can be realized by application of the Triple-A formula.

31

Anger, Hatred and Jealousy

Watch for anger of the mind; let your mind be self-controlled.
Hurt not with the mind, but use your mind well.

The Dhammapada 233

Do not wish to be anything but what you are,
And try to be that perfectly.

St. Francis De Sales

I complained because I had no shoes,
'till I met a man who had no legs.

Author Unknown

Like blame, the price we have to pay as individuals and society for emotions of aversion, particularly anger, hatred and jealousy, is enormous. We will investigate these emotions in this chapter.

The important common thread that runs through all these emotions is the strong belief (or wish) that an object or event perceived should not be the way it is. The stronger the wish, the stronger the emotion. Let's illustrate with examples.

Anger. When Adeline arrives home with the groceries her husband Barnaby discovers she has forgotten to bring the club soda, an item important to Barnaby, because he has to have soda with his scotch. Barnaby gets angry and yells at Adeline. A heated argument ensues with excursions to unpleasant subjects that have no connection to club soda or the human condition of forgetfulness. Emotions escalate with no end in sight. The two do not talk to one another for the rest of the day. At bedtime they try to fall asleep staring at opposite walls and both did not sleep well that night. The psychological underpinning that triggered this episode is Barnaby's thought: "Adeline *should have* remembered to bring the soda."

Hatred. Since the day an unpleasant argument arose between the two, long time ago, Sammy has formed a perception of neighbor Neil as an obnoxious person and has developed resentment and hatred towards Neil over the years. Sammy's underlying thought: "Neil is obnoxious. He should not be." Whenever Sammy has to meet Neil or thinks of him, he feels quite anxious. At times, his hatred of Neil was so intense that Sammy 'felt like punching Neil in the head'.

Jealousy. Angelica (just turned 20) and Nadine were best of friends at one time. Later events made their relationship sour. Worse, as time passed, Nadine fell in love with Angelica's boyfriend and their engagement is scheduled for November. Angelica is overwhelmed with jealousy towards Nadine to the point of her health being seriously affected. Angelica's final law school exams are a mere three months away. Anxiety about the possibility of failing her exams due to this emotional turmoil has thrown her into a destructive vicious cycle including severe insomnia. Angelica's underlying thought: "Nadine shouldn't have done what she did." In addition perhaps: "I wish I had her blue eyes and blonde hair. And I wish she was dead."

In all the above cases, we can see the following facts.

1. There is a wish for things that have already happened to not have happened. This is impossible because we cannot reverse the clock of nature. Thus Adeline did forget the club soda, Neil has been and is obnoxious and Nadine did what she did. All these cannot be undone even if wished a zillion times.

2. Even more importantly, by virtue of x-conditions, all these happenings had to come to pass <u>exactly</u> the way they did. Conditions were so arranged, lined up and primed by Nature, from beginningless time for Adeline to forget the club soda, for Neil to be obnoxious and Nadine to do what she did.

    1 and 2 above clearly tell us that, if they are to be in touch with reality and not continue to suffer, the parties concerned need to *accept* the way things are, up to this point.

3. There is a pervasive *failure* in humankind to see the uniqueness of all things in this universe, particularly in others, and to accept differences amongst people as the way things are (by virtue of x-conditions).

4. The common fallout from these emotions – anger, hatred and jealousy – is (unnecessary) distress, certainly for the one who harbors the emotion and possibly for the object.

Furthermore, the fact that in reality there is no-self in both perceiver and perceived again makes all these emotions meaningless and groundless, as in the case of blame. The vast majority of us display these emotions because of the messages we have received via our truth-distorting senses.

As with blame, if we are to be wise and be in touch with reality and thereby live in peace, what we have to do is to *accept* all the things that we cannot change or control, which includes other people. Furthermore, we need to *act* appropriately when possible. This process was explained earlier as the Triple-A formula.

To illustrate the technique of problem resolution using the Triple-A method, we will briefly go through the three examples listed earlier.

(A) <u>ANGER</u> (Adeline/Barnaby case)

Goal: Barnaby to overcome his anger.

I.   *Accept all that has happened up to now as the way it is, the reason being x-conditions.*

What has happened in this case is that Adeline did not bring the club soda, period. No blame. No anger. Just acceptance.

II.   *Act to improve things from now on, where feasible, with data ("lessons") from past happenings contributing to formulation of this action.*

Adeline and Barnaby agree to maintain a "to buy" list in the kitchen. This list will be taken on shopping trips hereafter, so there is no further dependency on a mental list.

III.   *Accept what cannot be done to improve things from now on, also, as the way it is, the reason being x-conditions, again.*

For example, Adeline 'making a resolution' to remember all items hereafter is not viable because more complex conditions than a mere resolution are at play in the mental act of remembering.

(B) <u>HATRED</u> (Sammy/Neil case)

Goal: Sammy to overcome his hatred of Neil.

I.   *Accept all that has happened up to now as the way it is, the reason being x-conditions.*

Neil is exactly what he is supposed to be, not an iota more, not an iota less. And that includes everything about his personality. (In fact, the same applies to Sammy too). No blame. No anger. Just acceptance.

II. *Act to improve things from now on, where feasible, with data ("lessons") from past happenings contributing to formulation of this action.*

With his acceptance of the way things are, and therefore a mental barrier removed, Sammy decides to open communication with his neighbor not artificially but in a natural manner.

III. *Accept what cannot be done to improve things from now on, also, as the way it is, the reason being x-conditions, again.*

Sammy accepts that the purpose of his existence in this universe is not to change others' personalities.

With his new way of thinking, Sammy is able to overcome his hatred of Neil. In fact, with persistent practice of the above method in similar situations involving others, Sammy is eventually able to replace his hatred with love for all beings and live in harmony. Here are the Buddha's words[94] on hatred:

> "*Hate is not conquered by hate but by love;* this is a law eternal. Many do not know that we are here in this world to live in harmony. Those who know this do not fight against each other.
>
> *Victory brings hate, because the defeated man is unhappy.* He who surrenders victory and defeat, this man finds joy."

---

[94] The Dhammapada verses 5 and 6

War (to which the vast majority of us comprise a reluctant audience in today's world of radio, TV and the Internet) is very much an outcome of hatred (and anger). Of war, the well-known Buddhist author and British judge Christmas Humphreys had this to say: "Why is a world that should be learning by experience ever at war? Because each man is at *war within*". Can we, and future generations, ever hope to eliminate war on this planet and live harmoniously? The answer, unfortunately, has to be a question: Can (and will) all the warmongers win the *war within* themselves, that is, their ignorance of the truth?

(C) <u>JEALOUSY</u> (Angelica/Nadine case)

Goal: Angelica to overcome her jealousy.

I. *Accept all that has happened up to now as the way it is, the reason being x-conditions.*

Nadine is exactly what she is supposed to be. And that includes everything Angelica perceives about Nadine but wishes were not there – the latter's blue eyes, blond hair, flirting ways and so on. No hatred. No jealousy. Just acceptance of another person as a unique 'component' that contributes to the make-up of this immense universe.

Angelica also realizes, with wisdom, that all the factors upon which her jealousy is built (such as the perceived beauty of Nadine) are devoid of real value. They are worldly perceptions made through truth-distorting senses and are therefore not in touch with reality.

II. *Act to improve things from now on, where feasible, with data ("lessons") from past happenings contributing to formulation of this action.*

With her new attitude towards Nadine, Angelica feels an enormous weight off her mind. She regains her confidence and focuses her attention and energy on the final exams. After all she is young and when she finishes law school she may look out for a new partner – in a world with millions of young men, that should not really be a concern.

III. *Accept what cannot be done to improve things from now on, also, as the way it is, the reason being x-conditions, again.*

Angelica accepts that it takes two to form any relationship and because impermanence applies to both parties, the relationship itself is subject to impermanence. Now she has the wisdom to gracefully accept inevitable changes that are sure to affect even her future relationships. Next time around, she will have the strength of being in touch with reality to guide her.

Now to an important point regarding the practices we outlined above. The goal of the Triple-A method is to change wrong views that drive the behavior of aversion and it will take much practice and time before the new views in touch with reality take effect. Until then, and while practicing the Triple-A method, one can obtain some temporary relief by resorting to breathing meditation practice (Chapter 12).

Chapter Insights and Highlights

1) The important common thread that runs through the emotions of anger, hatred and jealousy is the strong belief (or wish) that an object or event perceived should not be the way it is. The stronger the wish, the stronger the emotion.

2) However, the reality is that objects and events are the way they are because of x-conditions.

3) Anger, hatred and jealousy can be overcome by applying the Triple-A method.

32

Depression and Anxiety[95]

"I am now the most miserable man living. If what I feel were equally distributed to the whole human family, there would not be one cheerful face on earth. Whether I shall ever be better, I cannot tell; I awfully forbade I shall not. To remain as I am is impossible. I must die or be better, it appears to me."

Abraham Lincoln
The 16th President of the United States of America

NOTES OF CAUTION

1. Depression (and anxiety, to a lesser degree) can be life threatening. A number of factors, including a person's medical/psychological history, present health condition and any treatment regimen currently in place will determine the unique health profile of the person and therefore the course of treatment. Hence any actions for the management of depression and anxiety, including changes to the present treatment regimen, must be taken only under the guidance and supervision of a qualified physician or other recognized healthcare professional.

2. Dhamma (in particular Insight Meditation) can provide extraordinary capability for alleviation (and eventually a lasting relief) for depression caused by erroneous thinking. If you are suffering from depression or anxiety and wish to try out suggestions in this book to obtain relief from these disorders, consult your current healthcare professional (typically your physician) and proceed only with his/her approval. In particular, do not abruptly stop your current treatment regimen in deference to the techniques described in this book.

---

[95] We have grouped depression with anxiety in the chapter title as they are related; this will become clear later in the chapter. To start with, at this point let's note that depression and anxiety have an underlying biology that's similar.

B ecause it is a very common emotional problem in the general population, depression has been called the "common cold of psychiatry". It is estimated that currently over 100 million[96] people worldwide are affected by the disorder and the number is rapidly increasing. It strikes people in all walks of life – the rich and the poor, the scholar and the illiterate, the famous and the obscure, the powerful and the powerless.

Among the well-known, those who reportedly[97] suffered from it include:

- Abraham Lincoln, the 16th President of the United States of America.
- Winston Churchill, the wartime Prime Minister of Great Britain.
- Isaac Newton, pre-eminent scientist.
- Ernst Hemingway, Virginia Woolf and Charles Dickens - famous novelists.
- Rod Steiger, Oscar-winning best actor.
- Beethoven and Hector Berlioz - classical music composers.
- Julian Huxley, famous biologist.
- "Buzz" Aldrin, astronaut and the second person to walk on the moon (minutes after teammate Neil Armstrong, on 20 July 1969).

When we look at the symptoms of depression it is easy to understand why untreated depression can have a devastating effect on the life of the sufferer. Some symptoms of depression are: inability to concentrate, cognitive impairment, unrelenting anxiety or sadness, loss of appetite, insomnia, loss of interest in activities which were earlier interesting and pleasurable, feeling guilty, excessive crying, apathy, feelings of hopelessness or worthlessness, and thoughts of suicide. In modern-day terms, a person is considered to be depressed if he/she has, within a period of two weeks or more, experienced:

(1) a sad or empty feeling or loss of interest or pleasure most of the time, and

(2) at least five of the symptoms listed above [in addition to (1)].

---

[96] At the time of this writing, it is reported that the incidence of depression in Canada is 36%, that is, more than one person in three.

[97] The term depression, as used to signify the mental disorder, is of recent origin and the diagnostic criteria have been evolving over the years, primarily due to the complex nature of the disorder. Thus, in the case of most of the persons listed, the current belief that a person suffered from depression is an *extrapolation* realized from recorded information pertaining to the suffering of the individual, rather than a professional diagnosis of depression made during his/her lifetime or time of suffering.

Before we can assess the nature of relief Dhamma[98] can provide for depression, we need to discuss two broad categories to which depression may be assigned. For our purposes, we can define these two categories simply as:

(A) Depression that is caused by erroneous thinking.

(B) Depression that is caused by factors other than erroneous thinking.

Dhamma can provide relief for depression is when it is type A. Erroneous (or distorted) thinking is thinking that is fuelled by wrong views (primarily the view of *self*), i.e., thinking that is not in touch with reality. So the theory behind the Dhamma approach is very clear: *replace the wrong views (that cause depression) with the corresponding right views and the depression will be rooted out.* Thus, the antidote for type A depression is Insight Meditation. Most cases of depression can be traced to some form of distorted thinking (type A).

Depression can be caused by factors other than distorted thinking (Type B). These factors include:
- *some organic illnesses* (e.g., brain tumors, some types of cancer, pneumonia, epilepsy, some infections, migraines, multiple sclerosis, Parkinson's Disease, postmenstrual syndrome, rheumatoid arthritis, stroke, thyroid disorders, tuberculosis, certain vitamin deficiencies, dementias and AIDS).
- *prescription drugs* (e.g., oral contraceptives, sedative/hypnotic drugs, some anti-migraine medications and drugs for high blood pressure treatment).
- *'street' drugs* such as cocaine.

In view of the foregoing, it is very important to consult a qualified healthcare professional to rule out type B depression. If the depression a person is suffering from is diagnosed as type B, the only individuals who can provide proper care are qualified healthcare professionals. They must also be made aware, and consulted, in the ongoing management of depression even if the depression is not type B.

When we read Abraham Lincoln's words quoted above, we get some inkling of the intense emotional pain suffered by a depressed person. In

---

[98] As noted earlier, *depression* is a term of recent origin. The condition closest to depression described in Buddhist literature is referred to by the Pali word *domanassa,* meaning 'mentally painful feeling'.

the end, it's evident that Abraham Lincoln turned things around with his willpower and did well.

As an endowed feature of the species, the typical human being has the *potential* to lead meaningful lives and to achieve greatness. However, for many people, depression can annihilate that potential replacing it with immense distress (for some lasting a lifetime), if remedial action is not taken to tame this energy-sapping 'monster'. As we shall see in this chapter, help is available.

According to The World Health Organization (WHO), depression is among the leading causes of disability worldwide. WHO also reports that fewer than 25% of those affected (in some countries fewer than 10%) have access to effective treatment.

Having explored the general background of depression, we will now proceed to see how Dhamma principles can be applied to obtain relief from depression (and anxiety).

We have seen (in Chapter 25) that the mind uses existing memory (primarily views) to interpret sensory input from the world resulting in a specific neuro-chemical make-up. This eventually translates into emotions (in the mind) and physiological changes (in the organs of the body). Now let's focus on the emotions, specifically addressing depression. If the views in memory are in touch with reality, then the resulting emotion will be peace. If the views are not in touch with reality, and certain other conditions prevail (e.g., persistence in activation of the damaging views and the views being intense in nature), then the resulting emotion can be depression.

Usually depression is not a stand-alone emotional condition, but is associated with other persistent disabling emotional conditions such as stress, anxiety and guilt, which in turn are products of views that are not in touch with reality. Let's review two of these erroneous views, which are significant for the present chapter. One is a view that directly leads to guilt (self-blame) and the other is self-view, which is the root of all thinking-caused emotional distress, including depression.

(a) *The View That Leads to Guilt.* The self-blaming view "I did that but I shouldn't have", is an expression of guilt. Prolonged and intense guilt may eventually escalate to depression. In fact, one of the primary routes to depression is via guilt. Chapter 29: X-Conditions clearly show us that feeling guilty (self-blaming) is meaningless and groundless as is the practice of blaming the outer world. If one ponders the view "*I* did that but *I* shouldn't have", it should become clear that the view that leads to guilt, in the final analysis, also is dependent on one's self-view. However, we will examine these two views separately, for practical benefits.

An objective and health-promoting alternative to the meaningless practice of guilt is provided by the Triple-A formula and is illustrated with an example, which also shows the connection to depression and its alleviation.

Cynthia was returning at night with her 7-year old son Michael to her home in Oakville from Ottawa. Roads were clear and dry in Ottawa but there was freezing rain in Oakville and surrounding areas. Cynthia decided to take Highway 427 instead of the usual 403 as it appeared to her that 427 would have less traffic and be much quicker. Within minutes of turning on to 427, Cynthia's car collided with an overturned tractor-trailer, lying on the highway as a result of an accident seconds earlier. Cynthia escaped with a whiplash but her 7-year old son Michael sustained multiple injuries.

The doctors informed Cynthia and her husband that the prognosis for Michael was a full recovery from all injuries, but that it would take 9 months to a year.

Cynthia blamed herself entirely for what happened, particularly for young Michael's plight. She was convinced that it was "her stupidity in deciding not to take the customary 403" that resulted in the accident. Her sense of guilt was so intense that her health and ability to carry on her daily activities were affected. In addition, she became anxious, as she often worried about what effect her condition would have on the future of herself and her family. About 2 months after the accident, she began to slide into depression.

What help can Cynthia summon, based on Dhamma and medical science? Let's use the Triple-A method to guide Cynthia. We will assume that Cynthia is alert and able to follow rational thinking required to practice, and benefit from, the Triple-A method. To that extent, she has also received the go-ahead from her physician.

I.   *Accept all that has happened up to now as the way it is, the reason being x-conditions.*

Without judging I accept that the accident did happen, Michael was injured and the car is a write-off.

However, the accident *did not* happen due to "my stupidity in deciding not to take the customary 403", but only due to x-conditions.

I did not *willfully* do anything with the intention of causing harm to myself or to others (including Michael).

Therefore there is absolutely no reason for me to feel guilty about the event, in particular, about Michael's plight.

This is the way things are.

II. *Act to improve things from now on, where feasible, with data from past happenings contributing to formulation of this action.*

In the future I will endeavor to not drive at night unless absolutely necessary. When travelling to distant locations, I will listen to weather forecasts and leave early in the morning.

I will make arrangements for home tutoring for Michael to catch up on missed schoolwork.

III. *Accept what cannot be done to improve things from now on, also, as the way it is, the reason being x-conditions, again.*

In spite of action I take to minimize accidents in the future, they could still happen. That's part of living.

Michael will have to wait till the end of the year for full recovery. The best available medical system is looking after him. There is nothing I can do to enhance that.

Immediately after this exercise, Cynthia felt a soothing effect in her mind. However, for long-lasting relief from her guilt, anxiety and depression, she will need to apply the method consistently whenever these mental conditions resurface. That is, she will have to diligently practice until rational thinking becomes automatic (involuntary) thinking and forms a shield against attempts of depression to recur. We will discuss a more comprehensive and structured approach to the application of Insight Meditation to cases such as Cynthia's in the closing chapter (Chapter 40).

While depression is primarily caused by wrong views, the *intensity* of a particular episode depends on a number of factors. These include the duration of each episode, the number of times the disorder has occurred in the past, the nature and combination of triggers and the multiplicity of symptoms.

(b) *Self view.* As we have already seen, the most damaging of views is the core view that there is a self. When happenings are associated with *me* and *mine*, that is, when they are personalized, the result is some manifestation of distress. If the distress is intense and prolonged, the outcome can be depression.

A good example that illustrates how personalization leads to mental distress is the outbreak of the deadly new infectious disease called SARS (Severe Acute Respiratory Syndrome), which is just a few months into its potential global spread as the author is penning this chapter in the spring of 2003. SARS remains a mystery viral illness at the time of this writing. It happens to be the primary focus of the majority of the people and news media around the world, with many anticipating it to develop into a full-blown scourge. There is a multitude of very important ramifications of SARS - including medical/health, economic and infrastructure issues - that the appropriate responsible groups of the world community are trying to address as best as they can. While these responsible groups are working on their respective issues, our interest, in this book, is another issue - the *mental* reaction of the typical person and the associated *emotional* impact on that person.

Today's electronic communication media bring the latest news on any topic of public interest, such as SARS, instantly to our living rooms. In a typical day, the 'latest news' on SARS may be conveyed in statements such as the following:

- SARS is a national emergency.
- The number of deaths from SARS rises to twenty.
- Businesses severely affected by SARS; the economic fallout will be 'tens of billions of dollars'.
- Tourism disaster!
- Worldwide battle is being waged against scourge of SARS.
- Beijing closes public schools as a precaution.   ....
- One of the best hospitals in the country closes as SARS infects staff.

- Nurses quit over SARS stress.
- The World Health Organization issues travel advisory listing destinations travelers must avoid.
- A nurse traveling by public transport is suspected of having SARS and may have infected other passengers …
- A health-care professional, a probable SARS case, who visited a funeral home, may have put hundreds of others at risk.

The typical person who digests such news becomes increasingly anxious. In some people the anxiety escalates into panic and even paranoia. If the anxiety is intense and persists for a long time, it could precipitate depression, particularly in vulnerable people. But why does listening to news such as the above, and pondering over them, bring about such distress? **It is because the happenings are personalized – they are associated with** *me* **and** *mine.* The way one personalizes these happenings can be seen clearly in typical self-talk sentences such as the following:

I too could easily get SARS and that would be terrible. I could die from it. What will happen to my …. if I die? What if my … gets SARS? If the national healthcare system crumbles because of SARS and I fall seriously ill, there will be no one to take care of me. If the nation's economy collapses due to SARS, that'll be the end of my life's savings. And so on, to endless worry and anxiety that could escalate to more debilitating forms of mental illness.

Note the *I, me, mine* (underlined) that signify personalization, in each of these sentences of worry and anxiety.

Our immediate concern should not be that these damaging thoughts surface but our failure to apply a rational technique to rebut these involuntary thoughts with thoughts in touch with reality. If such a rational technique is applied, the resulting dislodging of the erroneous thoughts should enable us to overcome the inordinate fear and replace the unhealthy overreaction with healthy, rational action. Then we are empowered to carry on living with courage based on wisdom in the face of SARS (and for that matter, all adversities we humans have to face).

That technique is:

(i)   In part, the Triple-A method described in Chapter 29.

(The Triple-A method was used in this chapter in the example of Cynthia's recovery from guilt and depression and has been used also in a number of other examples in prior chapters.)

(ii)   In completeness, the 'Worksheet' provided in Chapter 40.

We leave the application of (i) and (ii) to the SARS situation as an exercise for the reader, with (ii) to be tried out after the reader has read the complete book, Chapter 40 being the closing chapter. Even if we are not affected by SARS, working through the steps of the exercise will equip us with the coping skills needed to effectively meet similar eventualities in the future.

Before we conclude this chapter, we need to cover a few more points relevant to depression.

1)   The post-1980 era is a fortunate period in the history of humankind to encounter thinking-caused depression and anxiety as they can be fully overcome with Insight Meditation combined with complementary help from medical science, where appropriate. Why post-1980 era?   Because medical science provided the world, beginning in the 1980s, with (a) a good understanding of the biology of depression and anxiety and (b) effective drug therapy for these and other related disorders.

2)   To practice Insight Meditation one should be alert and able to follow rational thinking. If the depressed person is cognitively impaired, due to an aggravated psychiatric condition, he/she must obtain the services of, and clearance from, an appropriate healthcare provider (usually a psychiatrist) before enlisting Insight Meditation. The treatment likely will include drug therapy. This provisional help will assist in regaining sufficient cognitive capability to practice Insight Meditation

3)   While depression usually arises from thoughts (fears) about the *past*, anxiety usually revolves around thoughts (fears) about the *future*. For example, the thought "It is likely that I will lose my job" causes anxiety. Likewise, in our example, Cynthia's thought "It was my stupidity in deciding not to take the customary 403 that resulted in the accident" eventually precipitated her depression.

However, depression and anxiety feed one another cognitively and biologically. Usually depression follows from prolonged and unresolved anxiety. Thus the intense and prolonged pre-occupation with thoughts of impending job loss and its consequences could lead to depression in the vulnerable person. Likewise memories of prolonged depression can trigger fearful thoughts of unremitting depression (and resulting distress) in the future causing anxiety. Thus depression and anxiety, when untreated, can become partners of a vicious cycle. This is all avoidable and unnecessary because both depression and anxiety are effectively treatable as previously mentioned.

4) Like depression and anxiety, depression and sleep can also form a vicious cycle. Depression can disturb one's sleep resulting in too much or too little of it, or in creating poor quality sleep.

When we awake, the way we feel is significantly influenced by what has gone on in the mind during the sleep/dream cycle. In sleep, irrational negative thoughts can have a field day because the *will* function is dormant and therefore rationalization is unavailable, resulting in restless sleep causing the depressed person to feel worse upon waking. In that event, it will help to remind oneself as follows:

"This feeling is a residue from the sleep/dream world. As the day progresses *'This too will pass'* as it has in the past." And it will. The process will be accelerated if the person engages in some daily activities, rather than staying in bed or doing nothing.

5) Physical work (including exercise) is an excellent temporary relief for both depression and anxiety and can assist in preparation for an eventual lasting relief with Insight Meditation. In fact, physical work has in it the elements of *Calming Meditation* (a recommended prerequisite for Insight Meditation). This is because it is a healthy sensory diversion from the preoccupation with destructive and irrational thoughts (of the past) in depression and (of the future) in anxiety. The thoughts of the present involved in doing physical work are health-promoting and a form of Calming Meditation.

Any physical work (such as clearing the garage, taking a brisk walk or cooking) is better than no work and is very therapeutic. We need to remember that the mind and body are partners. When one partner is a bit down, the other partner must help, as in a marriage partnership. When the mind is a bit down, the body (with physical activity) can give the extra 'push' the mind needs to get on the path of recovery and vice versa.

6) Progress in depression management can sometimes be like a saw-tooth-curve rather than a continuously improving linear progression. Occasionally one can slide back into unwell days, but in the long term the cumulative effect will be upward progress. The key here, as with all forms of practice involving the mind, is diligence and patience. What we are trying to do is re-wire the depression-supporting neural circuits to wellbeing-supporting circuits and that is hard work. For many, it may take a long time before lasting relief is realized.

Lasting relief can be realized for distress in general, and depression caused by erroneous thinking in particular, with Dhamma practice that entails diligence and patience. This fact is borne out by the case of an inmate[99] of a U.S. Federal prison who practiced Dhamma as set out in the first edition of *The Way to Inner Peace*. The practice enabled him not only to feel profoundly better but also to no longer require prescription drugs. The first three paragraphs of his letter to the author, being relevant to our present discussion, are reproduced next.

April 10, 2002
Valued Teacher:

Thank you so much for sending me a letter. Dear sir, you don't owe me apologies for anything, most especially for being too busy. Every letter you send is a welcome gift and a wonderful surprise. As I look back now, I can't seem to find any words that would be useful to express the gratitude that I feel for you becoming a part of this life. It's like coming across the most beautiful flower in the whole world that will not ever be forgotten. The impact of our first acquaintance through your book will have a lasting effect for a very long time. The book "The Way to Inner Peace" has made a change in this life and was the catalyst to a new way that is unspeakable. If anything I owe you sir this life and the freedom that comes with the Dhamma. It's hard to explain but I will try.

When I came here to prison back in 1998 I was very sick and lost for sure. I do believe that I was locked in a mental prison a lot worse than the physical one I'm in now. The attachments I had were driving me crazy and the world was just one big bowl of suffering. I had a dual diagnosis that was Major Chronic Depression, and severe Drug and Alcohol addiction with Catatonic Tendencies. I thought that it was the world that was causing my problems and that if it would only be different then everything would be ok. I never dreamed that it was me and my views that was the real problem. When you pointed out that there is a wonderful teacher in everything and I could learn how to change, but only if I would open

---

[99] For obvious reasons, the prisoner's identity is not published

this mind, it sparked something very deep. Its been like one big scientific discovery after another, and that everything can be of helpful use on the pathway to learning real coping skills. I know now that the more the resistance the more the need for the lesson. Most of the best lessons come from heading into the uncomfortable. I've ran for so long from the teacher.

Since then I've worked very steady everyday studying and practicing Dhamma. The blessings are unbelievable and even though there's a lot of difficulties its still better than its ever been. When I first came here I was referred to a psychiatrist an taking 200 mg. of trazadone daily. Also was referred to see a psychologist no less than once a week. During that time I made some real breakthroughs and had come to some realizations. The psychologist didn't teach me anything, but just observed the growth and stated that he was amazed in my productivity. He said that the realizations and insights were unbelievable and that I was above all the others that he has ever worked with in the prison system. He asked me just the other day if I minded working with others that were willing, and would share those insights. He's even put up some posters of the sayings about impermanence on his wall. **I haven't had to take any medicine for the last year and a half, none at all**[100].

Warmest regards,

Chapter Insights and Highlights

1. Depression is a very common emotional disorder. Currently, it is estimated that at any given time, over 100 million people suffer from it worldwide.

2. Depression strikes people in all walks of life.

3. For our purposes, depression may be subdivided into two types:

    (A) Depression that is caused by erroneous thinking.

    (B) Depression that is caused by factors other than erroneous thinking.

    Most cases of depression belong to type A.

4. Dhamma (Insight Meditation) provides a powerful and effective means to overcome type A depression.

---

[100] Bold-facing is by the author

5. Because of the complex nature of the disorder and its life-threatening potential, a qualified healthcare professional must be consulted before taking any action relating to depression management.

6. The primary cause of depression, as with other forms of mental distress, is belief in views that are not in touch with reality. The view of a *self*, which leads to personalization of happenings, is the dominant cause.

7. The self-blaming view "I did that, but I shouldn't have", is an expression of guilt, and may also contribute to depression. Self-blaming is a groundless and meaningless practice.

8. Physical activity provides appreciable temporary relief from depression and anxiety. So does Calming (breathing) Meditation.

9. The post-1980 era is a good time for people suffering from depression as medical science has provided (a) an understanding of the biology of depression and anxiety and (b) effective drug therapy. Drugs usually produce side effects.

10. Depression and anxiety/stress feed one another in a vicious cycle.

11. When practiced properly, Dhamma provides lasting relief for anxiety, guilt and thinking-caused depression, with no side effects.

33

Sickness and Injury

The diseases which destroy a man are no less natural than the instincts which preserve him.

George Santayana

I f someone suffers a heart attack and reaches the hospital in good time, today's medical teams can, in most cases, provide amazing help to the patient and often he/she can hope to live a heart-healthy life for many more years.

If a person gets cancer and it is detected early, in many cases the patient can hope to realize a full recovery. And so it is for many other conditions, which years ago, meant early death, or suffering until death. So modern medicine can do 'miracles' - sometimes.

Why sometimes? If we go through the pages of any medical encyclopedia, we will be amazed to find the number of medical conditions from which one cannot regain the prior healthy state. For instance, there are incurable illnesses. Some examples are Parkinson's disease, cerebral palsy, muscular dystrophy and hemophilia. Then there are illnesses such as advanced cardiovascular disorders or cancer that have progressed too far to benefit from medical interventions leaving the patient to a remaining life filled with suffering. To these add injuries such as spinal injuries that leave the unfortunate persons disabled for the balance of their lives. In these cases, current medical practice can provide only palliative help.

So what can a person do when he/she has a sickness or injury for which the help available from modern day medicine and science is limited or minimal? Is the person now destined to live without hope for the rest of his/her life in misery or is it possible to continue living with renewed meaning and happiness? Since 'meaning' and 'happiness' are matters of the mind, the answer will become evident in the following analysis. If certain practices are followed, 'meaning' and 'happiness' can be the fortunate outcome. Essentially it requires separating the physical distress from the emotional, learning how best to alleviate and cope with the former and working hard to eventually *overcome* the latter[101]. We will use the Triple-A method to guide us in our analysis.

I.   *Accept all that has happened up to now as the way it is, the reason being x-conditions.*

If it is terminal cancer, we accept what happened. If it is spinal injury we accept. If it is any other we accept. We do not waste our time and energy in thinking that it should not have happened because we know that x-conditions can't be reversed.

Furthermore, the awareness of the operation of x-conditions rules out many common groundless and destructive thoughts. One example is blaming the world ("It's Rhonda's cooking that gave me the heart attack"). Then there is anger and hatred ("I hate him for causing the accident by insisting on taking highway 410", or simply, "I hate being unwell"). Another is the 'poor-me attitude' ("Of all people, what did I do to deserve this sickness?"). And then there is the feeling of guilt or self-blaming ("If only I had exercised when I was healthy, I wouldn't have had the stroke. I can never forgive myself for that.").

The mere act of giving up these meaningless thoughts and totally accepting all that has happened up to now as the way it is, in itself, becomes a great part of our therapy, our healing. The 'happiness neurotransmitters' kick in to produce their results.

II. *Act to improve things from now on, where feasible, with data ("lessons") from past happenings contributing to formulation of this action.*

Given that we are focusing our analysis on situations that lie beyond present capabilities of medical science, some of the actions that can be taken are listed below:

1. Take a new and hard look at our perception of sickness and injury; practice Insight Meditation (chapters 13/14 and 38/40).
2. Deeply contemplate on the truth of no-self – Chapter 5: Me and Mine. ("The sickness is there, but no I that is sick").

---

[101] Perfect mental health (= Sublime Peace) is an achievable target for a practitioner of Dhamma but there is no such possibility with physical health. Even The Buddha had to face physical illness and injury, decay, old age and death.

3. Devote time each day to reflect on the spiritual side of life.
4. Join a self-help group for emotional comfort.
5. Take an active part in preventive health care (for example, through exercise, healthy eating and stress management) to maintain the best possible health in the future.
6. Keep track (one effective means being the Internet) of ongoing medical developments in the area of interest (e.g., spinal surgery).
7. Elicit courage and latent energies to lead a meaningful life in spite of sickness or injury or handicap.

Generate motivation by studying the inspirational efforts of those who have done so. For example, our typical perception of blindness is as one of the worst handicaps. Then comes along Erik Weihenmayer. Erik has been blind since age 13 due to a rare retinal disease. But he has always demonstrated an iron will for conquering adversity. On 24th May 2001, at age 33, he achieved a feat that people with even good eyesight, save for a few courageous ones, would not dream of attempting. He conquered Mount Everest, startling the rest of us, blind and not blind, into profoundly rethinking about our real capabilities[102].

This is not intended to suggest that disabled people (or even those not disabled) should attempt to realize amazing feats such as reaching the summit of the world's tallest mountain, but to show the enormous latent potential available to be utilized if one chooses to put one's mind to it. In passing, it may be appropriate to mention here that *Sublime Peace* is a different type of an Everest that we all have the potential of reaching, with ordinary physical effort but with extraordinary mental endeavor.

It will be noticed that a major part of our action is to change our mindset (attitude) towards the sickness or injury to be in touch with reality. The result is that we alleviate (and with progressive skill, may eventually completely eliminate) the emotional component of our distress.

III. Accept what cannot be done to improve things from now on, also, as the way it is, the reason again being x-conditions.

---

[102] See the TIME Magazine of June 18, 2001 for a full account of Erik Weihenmayer's conquest of Everest.

Some of the things we have to accept in this regard could be:

1. Current limitations in medical science and healthcare that may continue to affect us.

2. In common with all living beings, the vulnerability of human beings to certain physical sickness and injury that are beyond effective prevention.

Chapter Insights and Highlights

1) When sickness and injury have reached a point beyond help from medical science, a person can still lead a meaningful and happy life.

2) Meaning and happiness are matters of the mind. The key is to separate mental distress from the rest, find the means to deal with the mental distress and accept the rest. The Triple-A Method provides a blueprint for achieving this, most effectively when incorporated into Insight Meditation.

34

Aging

People do not quit playing because they grow old.
They grow old because they quit playing.
Oliver Wendell Holmes

Aging is a vast topic. It can cover anything from hair dye to stroke or from skin wrinkles to dementia. Therefore, we need to narrow our discussion of the subject to the context of this book. The following factors will keep us within that boundary.

- ◆ We will keep the mind/brain as the pivotal point of our discussion, since inner peace (our subject) is a phenomenon of the mind. We will deal with the body to the extent that the mind depends on a healthy body in certain aspects for optimum performance to progress to inner peace.
- ◆ Although the aging process starts from birth, for our purposes we will use that term to refer to the time beyond 40 years, the age at which people are usually *perceived* to begin aging.
- ◆ Much progress has been made in Health Science[103] to increase our life expectancy. For example, in 1900 the average life expectancy of a North American was 47 years, while by 2000 it had risen dramatically to about 78 years. However, we will not place emphasis on longevity or athletic prowess or external appearance for their own sake but rather on the *wellbeing* of the individual as the person ages. In essence, a life ending at 42 is as good as a life ending at 105 years, so long as both lives had achieved inner peace before the end.

Aging is a process that virtually all of us are conditioned to look upon with aversion and youthfulness with longing (craving). While youth disregard the topic of aging for the time being, those who are already old worry about all kinds of dreadful things that could happen to them. That

---

[103] In this chapter we will use the term Health Science to comprise of all scientific disciplines directed towards the treatment, cure, prevention and delaying of sickness and injury.

worrying, or anxiety, most often dispirits them further, precipitating additional mental distress. Sometimes the mental distress, if intense and persistent, can also bring about or aggravate physical problems, such as cardiovascular illness.

In view of the forgoing, some important questions arise. Is our aversion of aging in touch with reality? If not, what should one's attitude be towards it? What, if any, are the things one can do to make the aging process one of peace rather than distress?

Aging, as will be established in the analysis below, is not something to be averse to at all. The primary reason behind our aversion to anything, and therefore also to aging, is *ignorance*. When we find out what we are ignorant of, and what is reality with regards to aging, we will be able to *accept* those facts of aging that we can do nothing about. At the same time, this same investigation will also identify *action* we can take to make this phase of life as meaningful as it is meant to be. These two outcomes will alleviate or eliminate not only our aversion to aging but also the anxiety and other emotional problems that always follow aversion.

To make our investigation most meaningful, we will conduct it in two parts, based on the two-pronged statement of the principle of self/no-self discussed in Chapter 28: Anatomy of the Self:

(a) *There is a self*, only as perceived by our truth-distorting sensory mechanisms, and

(b) *There is no self* in Absolute Reality (truth), that is, upon transcending the senses.

The first part, titled *investigation on worldly terms* is based on (a) and the second part titled *investigation on transcendental terms* is based on (b).

(A) INVESTIGATION ON WORLDLY TERMS

First we will list the more common symptoms ('signs') of natural aging, that is, what aging would have entailed, had we not taken into account the beneficial impact of modern Health Science. Next we will try to understand the reasons or causes behind these signs of aging. Finally, we will look at what Health Science can do to alter the course of natural aging within limits, for our benefit.

Symptoms ('Signs') of Natural Aging

Of the many perceptible changes that are characteristic of aging, the common ones are listed below.

- Perhaps the first sign of aging is in our <u>vision</u> in the form of difficulty in reading small print (presbyopia) and this begins at about age 40 for most of us. As we progress in years, we may get glaucoma (loss of vision due to an increase of pressure in the eyeball that damages the optic nerve) and by about age 60 most of us will have cataracts (cloudiness in the lens of the eyes that diminishes vision) to some degree.

- We may experience some <u>hearing</u> loss, in particular, hearing the highest pitched tones. In practice this may appear as inability to hear certain sounds like *s* and *ch* (when someone talks) or certain tones in music we enjoyed fully when younger.

- Many of us will notice our <u>hair</u> graying and most men will have partial baldness.

- The <u>skin</u> becomes wrinkled and thinner. The distribution of fat changes. When younger, the fat was somewhat evenly distributed under the skin. Now, more fat gets deposited in the abdominal area. Also the skin may breakdown due to prolonged pressure caused primarily by immobility.

- People become more prone to developing certain disorders when they are older. These include the following:

  - cardiovascular disorders (including stroke)[104],
  - cancer,
  - bone and joint problems (specially arthritis and osteoporosis),
  - prostate problems in men,
  - urinary incontinence,
  - symptoms of diabetes
  - brain disorders (such as Parkinson's and Alzheimer's), and
  - a certain degree of cognitive impairment including memory loss.

---

[104] Cardiovascular disorders are the #1 cause of death in the general population and cancer is #2.

A number of the above developments collectively, lead to the conclusion that the person "is old" or "looks old". Also, disorders that are latent while a person is young can surface when the person ages and the disease fighting mechanisms weaken.

We must note that, obviously, all the above symptoms do not impact one person. Different disorders affect one person singly or in combination. As we continue to age, more disorders may effect us. On the other hand, some have few of these disorders, or only mild forms of certain disorders, and stay relatively healthy into very old age. Being a 'healthy old person' is dependent on certain conditions, such as genetic factors, lifestyle and the nature of medical care received.

<u>Reasons Behind Signs of Aging</u>

Underlying the perceptible signs of aging which we have discussed above are changes to body systems and organs imperceptible to the direct senses but detectable by scientific means. These are caused by activities at cellular and sub-cellular levels, again detectable by scientific means. Some of these aging-related changes are listed below.

- The maximum heart rate and the maximum volume of blood pumped out by the heart decreases.
- Gradual accumulation of fatty deposits and scar tissue in the blood vessels reduce blood flow to the heart, brain, liver, kidneys and other organs. This may also cause the blood pressure to increase.
- The amount of blood received by the brain, liver and kidneys decreases.
- The lung's pumping capacity decreases while the volume of residual air after exhalation increases.
- The ability of the liver and kidneys to clear toxins decreases. So does their ability to deal with drugs.
- Glucose tolerance drops.
- The ability of cells to fight infection wanes.
- Starting at about age 30, the brain gradually loses weight – about 3 oz (6%) by age 60 and about 5 oz (10%) by age 90.

One of the most important aspects of any healing process is to understand reality and accept it, even if, at the start, we are averse to the reality. This very acceptance dispels the aversion we started with, helping us to move towards inner peace.

Therefore, with regard to aging it is crucially important that we *accept* the above changes as nature's way and the fact that these changes have befallen humans since the inception of the species. Aging is an integral part of nature, because it is a manifestation of the universal law of impermanence. What is born has to die and aging is the bridge that takes one from birth to death.

Once we accept aging as nature's way, we can proceed to take stock of what today's Health Science has to offer us to ameliorate things and consider that help as a bonus.

<u>Impact of Health Science</u>

One of the most important factors that enables one to feel well while aging is one's lifestyle (perhaps in par with hereditary factors). A healthy lifestyle means following guidelines and advice available from Health Science.

It is now known that older adults who keep themselves physically and mentally active and eat a healthy diet can be 10 to 20 years *functionally* younger than older adults who do not follow these lifestyle practices.

Even identical twins, who have greater commonality than other siblings, have been shown to display stark differences in their physical conditions and appearances when their lifestyles have been very different, thus establishing the major role played by nurture (especially lifestyle) on how we age.

For our inspiration, here are a few cases of seniors who chose to be active. Ella Peckham was 86 when she took part in a competition swimming event at the Masters Games in Toronto. Great-grandmother Ida Birdie Berk was 91 when she enrolled in a criminal psychology degree program at the University of Toronto. Lucille Jeffrey Thompson was 88 when she enrolled in a karate program and 90 when she got her black belt. Frank Kennedy was 72 when he climbed all the stairs of CN tower and reached the top. Astronaut John Glenn was 77 when he relived his glory days (of being the first American to orbit the earth) by making his second trip to space, aboard the shuttle Discovery. Konrad Adenauer was Chancellor of West Germany at age 87.

Our purpose in listing the achievements of these seniors is not to suggest that we strive for the kind of goals reached by these people, but to bring out the message that aging should not be a barrier to maintaining an active and fruitful life. If we use our minds to create active lives utilizing the unique potential each one of us possesses, we too can realize goals that are meaningful to us, as the described accomplishments were to the seniors listed above. In that sense, creating a beautiful garden can be as meaningful as a trip to space.

During the last few decades Health Science has made astonishing progress in the understanding, treatment, prevention and delaying of physical illness. To live at the present juncture in human evolution and not benefit from this progress, at least in so far as it affects mental wellbeing would be unwise. Let's therefore touch briefly on some of the key areas of interest. Detailed discussion of these topics is outside the scope of this book. Therefore for currently available information on Health Sciences topics of interest, the reader may consult from amongst the abundant resources (such as books, TV and the Internet).

For all medically related concerns the reader must consult a physician. In particular, an annual medical examination is highly recommended. Prior to starting an exercise program or re-starting one after a long lapse, a consultation with a physician is a must.

By targeting the underlying causes operating at organ, tissue, cellular and sub-cellular levels discussed earlier, Health Science has been able to provide us proven guidelines from which we can benefit at any age. Some of the most important actions for healthy living are listed below in brief:

- Exercise
    - Swimming, cycling and walking briskly are good exercises, particularly for cardiovascular health.
    - Include some weight-bearing exercises for building bone strength and stretching exercises for toning the muscles.
- Eat a diet rich in vegetables, whole grain and fruits.
- Reduce the intake of foods that are rich in saturated fat and cholesterol.
- Maintain weight at healthy levels.
- Quit smoking. (Quitting even in old age helps).
- Cut down on excessive salt intake.
- Avoid exposure to loud noises as much as possible. If you think you have hearing problems, see your physician. There is plenty of help available.
- Avoid excessive exposure to sunlight.

- Have an annual eye examination. A lot of help is available. For example, presbyopia can be corrected with eyeglasses, glaucoma with medications/surgery and cataracts with surgery.
- Get sufficient sleep
- Do things to keep the mind active (e.g., crossword puzzles, helping younger people with their school work, etc.)

(B) INVESTIGATION ON TRANSCENDENTAL TERMS

Any effective means of overcoming mental distress must transcend the senses and look toward the truth that lies beyond because it is our ignorance of the truth that causes the distress.

At a transcendental level we will look at two views born of ignorance that cause mental distress: (1) the dichotomies created by human beings as reflected in arbitrary labels and (2) the notion of self.

As we grow, we form erroneous views about the world via our truth-distorting senses. Of importance are the views of the dichotomies we make through arbitrary judgements of the world. These can be, for example, that an entity is good or bad, pretty or ugly, and youthful (meant in a glorified sense) and aged (meant in a sense of abhorrence). When we transcend our truth-distorting senses, all these labels are seen to have no existence, therefore no meaning, in reality. Yet, due to the nature of our sensory mechanisms, we crave for the good, the pretty and youthfulness while being averse to the bad, the ugly and the aged, not realizing they are all illusions in reality.

In the eyes of truth, infancy, childhood, youth, adulthood and old age reduce to one indivisible continuum and consequently their separate existences disappear, except in our minds. Therefore, during our brief appearance upon this planet it is meaningless and wasteful of precious mental energy to separate old age from the rest (except for societal convenience, mainly communication purposes) or to worry about a thing called aging.

The other important point relating to the property of truth-distortion of the senses is the core notion of self (Chapter 28: Anatomy of the Self).

Once we erroneously establish, and believe in, a negativity about the aging process as discussed above, the act of personalization by thinking "_I_ am old" or "_My_ ...... is old" (e.g., "My mother is old") becomes a case of adding fuel to the fire. In truth, not only is the label 'old' meaningless as discussed above, but also there is no self (*I* or *My*). This compounded erroneous thinking from negative labeling ('old') and personalization (*I* or *My*) results in aversion, particularly *fear* (anxiety).   Thus deep contemplation of *no-self* will become the ultimate therapy for any mental distress associated with aging. Adapting the famous quotation from the *Path of Purification* referred to earlier in the book on the subject of aging, we can make the transcendental statement "There is aging, but no person (I) that ages."

Miscellaneous points to note:

Before we close this chapter, let's cover some miscellaneous points on the subject of aging.

1. *Physical distress (pain) vs. mental distress.* We can move from any distress (even the 'worst') to inner peace if we separate physical pain from mental distress and view them separately. As stated earlier, the physical distress that exists beyond relief from current Health Science is something we have to live with. However, mental distress can be alleviated, and even eliminated, by altering our thinking patterns to be in touch with reality.

2. *Self-reliance in old age.* While self-reliance is very important during all stages of our adult life, it becomes an essential adjunct in old age if we are to realize inner peace.

    More and more people, in all age groups - youth, middle-aged and elderly - are spending more time alone, or living alone now, than in earlier times. In fact the percentages have been rapidly increasing over the last few decades, most visible in the seniors category. For example, government statistics show that in 1971, in Canada, 39% of widowed seniors over age 65 lived alone. Thirty years later, in 2001, that rose to 72%, almost doubling the 1971 figure. Thus, living alone is a hard fact of modern times, particularly as we grow older. Whether life lived alone will be a happy period or a miserable one will be primarily determined by one factor – our degree of self-reliance. For a detailed discussion of self-reliance see chapter 10.

3. *Maximum lifespan.* Even with the best lifestyle and best help from Health Science, we cannot live more than about 120 years, because that is what the dictates of nature/nurture (genes/environment) allow us. When we compare that with cosmic time frames, any life on this

planet is like the 'blink of an eye'. For that reason alone, it is prudent for us to live meaningfully whatever is left of our lives.

4. *Aging is a fact of existence.* The fact that one ages is known even as a being is born. So why be averse toward something that was known as an immutable fact of existence ever since intelligent human life began?

5. *We all age.* Except for those who die prematurely due to illness or accident, we all will age – that is billions of us. So, it would be prudent on our part not to 'make a big issue' of our individual aging.

6. *Can it be too late for action?* We have discussed things that can be done (exercise, healthy diet, transcendental thinking etc.) to make our aging process as peaceful as possible. However, what if I am a very old person, frail in health, who missed the window of knowing when able and young and who does not now have the energy or motivation to carry out all these wholesome practices? There is still hope, as discussed in Chapter 36: Unfinished Business, coming up.

Chapter Insights and Highlights

1. The youth view aging with aversion and the elderly look at age with fear and anxiety. This is all due to *ignorance*.

2. We can replace this ignorance with wisdom, that is, understanding the facts of aging in touch with reality. Then we will be able to separate what's changeable from what must be *accepted* for peaceful aging.

3. Worldly view. Specific signs (e.g., cataracts) accompany aging. Health Science has revealed to us the underlying reasons for these changes (e.g., cloudiness in the lens of the eye) and furthermore, what can be done to treat, prevent or delay illness (e.g., surgery for cataract).

4. We can help the body age healthily by exercising, eating a healthy diet and using other help available from Health Science.

5. Transcendental View

a) Any mental distress we undergo on account of aging is due to personalization of the aging process and arbitrarily assigning labels of aversion to it, which are meaningless in reality. Therefore meditating on no-self is the lasting cure for mental distress associated with aging (or for any mental distress).

b) Infancy, childhood, youth, adulthood and old age reduce to one indivisible continuum in the eyes of nature and consequently their separate existences disappear, except in our minds.

35

Dying and Death

Neither in the sky, nor deep in the ocean, nor in a mountain cave, nor anywhere, can a man be free from the power of death.

The Dhammapada (verse 128)

Better than a hundred years lived in vice, without contemplation, is one single day lived in virtue and in deep contemplation.

Better than a hundred years lived in ignorance, without contemplation, is one single day lived in wisdom and deep contemplation.

Better than a hundred years lived in idleness and in weakness is a single day lived with courage and powerful striving.

Better than a hundred years not considering how all things arise and pass away is one single day of life if one considers how all things arise and pass away.

Better than a hundred years not seeing one's own immortality is one single day of life if one sees one's own immortality.

Better than a hundred years not seeing the Path supreme is one single day of life if one sees the Path supreme.

The Dhammapada (verses 110-115)

Imagine a guest at a party who, for some reason, becomes inordinately *attached* to the property and the residents and decides to overstay the kindness of the host to the surprise of the latter. The guest begins to believe that these entities are his. The man refuses to leave and eventually, in struggling to continue to stay hurts himself and others and damages the property.

What would be the consequences of such outlandish action? He would be forced out (at the owner's initiative, or perhaps by the police), most likely be locked up in jail and face further dire consequences for damage to property etc. The common fallout from all of these is intense mental distress. Had he not developed attachment to what was not his, there would have been no struggle, he would have left the party peacefully and most importantly, there would be no resulting distress.

Our life on this planet is somewhat analogous to this hypothetical story. In cosmic terms, this life is an incredibly short guest appearance. Our host is Mother Nature and all the property belongs to her. However, although we come with nothing and leave with nothing, during this short stay we get *attached* to a lot of things thinking we are the owners. We think so because of our strongly held but false beliefs, in other words, our ignorance of reality. Our attachment to things is second nature because our ignorance has burrowed deep into our minds over time. Because of our attachment, brought about by our ignorance that we own things (i.e., our illusion), we foolishly struggle right through life and finally, often with the greatest intensity, when the time comes to let go of the attachments and depart for good (die).

This vain struggle results in mental distress. It is in vain because, in spite of the struggle, Mother Nature ensures that we leave (die) when the time comes, i.e., when the appropriate x-conditions cone in. We are 'evicted', whether we struggle or not. Therefore, isn't it only sensible and sane that we eliminate this struggle and make the final phase of this guest appearance, the departure, one of peace rather than distress? Of course! It is obvious that the way to move from distress to peace when dying and at death (and before, while living) is to let go of our attachment to what is not ours (which is every worldly thing).

In practice, it is the erroneous clinging to such entities as parent, spouse, child, friend, home, property, business and views and the refusal to (mentally) let go of these that cause our mental distress while living and at dying and death. If we want to live a distress-free life, the sooner we learn the golden lesson about ownership, the better: *in reality, none of us own another and none of us own a thing. There's only one owner - Mother Nature.*

Now we examine some facts and ideas that will help us deal with death in a meaningful way. Following the same approach as in the last chapter (34: Aging), we will discuss the subject is two parts (a) Investigation on Worldly Terms and (b) Investigation on Transcendental Terms. The crucial investigation will be in (b) where the focus will be the means to let go of our attachments.

(A) INVESTIGATION ON WORLDLY TERMS

Benjamin Franklin identified what's certain for us humans in his famous statement: "In this world nothing can be said to be certain, except death and taxes". However, one can choose not to pay taxes and face the consequences (perhaps go to prison). That leaves us with just *one* certainty – death. Sorry, Mr. Franklin!

Given that death is our certainty, do we live with awareness of that fact? Hardly. The reason is our fear of death, which is due to our attachments, which in turn are due to our ignorance. So we live hiding the subject of death. The result is mental distress.

We start our investigation with two insightful stories from Buddhist scriptures about the inevitable reality of death, the essence of which is captured here[105].

1) Kisa Gotami believed that there had to be a medicine somewhere that would bring her dead infant back to life. With that intention, she searched, failed, and finally ended up in front of the Buddha. Since no ordinary explanation would penetrate her mind with the reality, the Buddha resorted to a clever means by which he would convince her.

    He told Kisa Gotami that it would be possible to make the medicine that would bring her child back to life but only if she would bring some mustard seeds from a house that had not known death. She went from house to house, combing the whole village, but could not find a single house that had not known death.

    Kisa Gotami was insightfully convinced of the reality of death for all beings and her suffering abated. Eventually she was able to realize Sublime Peace.

2) Within a very short period of time, Patacara lost her two sons, husband, brother, mother and father to tragedy. The resulting agony was so overpowering that she became insane. Soon she met the Buddha. Upon seeing the All Enlightened One, she came out of her insanity, related to him her plight of agony and was able to understand a sermon given by him in response. The sermon, which was based on the Buddhist doctrine of (countless) rebirths, i.e., *Samsara,* essentially was as follows:

---

[105] For detailed accounts of the two stories, see The Wheel Publication No. 354/356 BUDDHIST STORIES From The Dhammapada Commentary Part IV, published by the Buddhist Publication Society, PO Box 61, 54 Sri Sangharaja Mawatha, Kandy, Sri Lanka. Alternative reference: Therigatha, part of Sutta Pitaka of the Pali Canon.

" Patacara, you have shed many tears in this life of yours due to the loss of dear ones. So have you, in each one of your previous births, which are countless. If all those tears are collected, they would exceed the total water mass of the great oceans. And all that suffering, all that crying is to no avail, because death is a natural certainty for all that is born." Hearing the Buddha's words so far, Patacara's grief became less intense. Then the Buddha continued:

"Your attachment to loved ones cannot provide the refuge you are seeking when death takes them away. Instead the wise will work on the (Dhamma) Path as their refuge and be on their way to Sublime Peace."

With grief overcome, she worked on the Path and eventually attained Sublime Peace.

We grow up thinking 'Death shouldn't be' and specifically 'Death should not happen to me and mine (those near and dear to me)', because our growth environment teaches us to think so. Through ignorance everyone around us shunned the subject of death as we were growing; so we, students of ignorance, followed suit and we pass on the tradition to our descendents.

Death is such a normal a phenomenon of nature – as natural as the fall of a ripe apple as it separates from the stem – that we have no choice but to calmly accept it. Ideally we should not even be concerned about it, just as we are not concerned about the ripe apple falling to the ground.

Dhamma practice includes a number of methods to correct our foolish and erroneous approach to death. The most important of these methods is a daily reminder to oneself in the chanting *"It is of the nature to die"* (usually following the similar utterance about aging *"It is of the nature to decay"*). This is an element of Insight Meditation, because acceptance of the fact and repeating it makes it our new and retrained awareness. In other words, the intent behind the practice is to gradually erase the conditioned and erroneous thought "Death shouldn't be" to "Death should be" because that's nature, the way things are. With that practice we move from evasion to acceptance, from anxiety to calm and from fear to fearlessness. In short, from mental distress to inner peace.

Other perspectives on death further emphasize the need to calmly accept our inevitable end. For example consider evolution. Evolution implies natural selection of survival-hardy characteristics of ancestors and rejection of their weaker characteristics to form descendents with hardier characteristics. That means, giving way to future generations, as all generations in the past have done. Thus we are here only because our ancestors existed, lived, and perished for the benefit of future generations and our species. Each generation, in dying, provides a support for the next generation. Thus there is no reason for any one of us to wish not to die or 'die later', or our generation to not perish. It is foolhardy and ignorant to think so. And it is wisdom to accept calmly our death as a matter of fact.

All other living organisms go through the life process as it is meant to be – in virtual acceptance of reality and in harmony with it. We humans are the only species that makes an issue of death and that is because we have the faculty of thinking. We can learn wonderful lessons about birth, life and death from other living organisms. Take coral for example. If we were to view coral in a glass-bottomed boat, we will see the new (living) coral being supported by the old (dead) coral, generation after generation – a perfect enactment of acceptance and harmony. Why can't we? Why shouldn't we?

Death is the great equalizer of our human-made (worldly) differences. After death, atoms and molecules of the richest man and the poorest, the king and the commoner, the doctor and the hospital laborer, the boss and the worker, are all cast back into the common pool called the universe. From there, they are used again by Mother Nature to make anything she wishes in any combination as her plans dictate. Amongst them, we can imagine atoms and molecules of the king *and* the commoner 'sitting' side by side inside a new king, in "royal blood" or inside a new commoner in "common blood"! Inevitable equality from what was once man-made status differences. Then, isn't it obvious that, if we are to be in touch with reality, we should shed all our status and class differences and live as equals, before Mother Nature does it for us?

(B) INVESTIGATION ON TRANSCENDENTAL TERMS

We see that our general tendency, particularly when we are young, is to not accept the truth of death. Even if at some point death is accepted as inevitable, the thinking (at a subtle level) would be somewhat like "Yes, I will die, but definitely not today, not this week, or this year. I guess I will accept it on a date far far away from today." The reality is that we don't have the final word on death; instead, when the necessary x-conditions cone in, we will die. Again, as we can clearly see, the culprit behind the anxiety and fear, therefore the evasion, is the erroneous belief in the idea of 'me' and 'mine.' Since attachment is a direct result of the erroneous belief in a self, the practical way to detach from the things we cling to is to totally integrate the notion of no-self into our lives. Then, with the cord of attachment severed, we can meet death anytime, any place, peacefully.

To be attached to something there has to be a self and an object, which is really another self. For example, in the statement of attachment 'My mother' there is me, that is one self and mother, the second self or entity. However, from our earlier discussions we know that both entities exist only as perceived through truth-distorting senses and that they do not exist in reality.

Once again adapting the famous line from the Buddhist scriptural work *The Path of Purification,* we can state the no-self principle as it relates to death as follows: "There is dying but no person that dies."

It is very important that we contemplate deeply on the fact of no-self daily. Once the truth of no-self has taken root firmly in our minds replacing the notion of self, then at death the strings (or shackles) that bind us, causing us to struggle and suffer will no longer exist. We will be free to go in peace. In fact, when we are able to integrate the no-self concept into our lives, this freedom (of not being held in mental shackles) will be felt not only at dying, but also before - while living. Hence, the sooner we start to contemplate no-self and integrate the concept into our lives, the sooner we will realize peace.

In summary, to let go of our worldly attachments and fear of death, the most important action we need to take is to get rid of our notion of self. That is purely mental action requiring only our time and diligence.

Although we, in our worldly living, are used to perceiving birth and death as real and discrete events, how real and discrete are they? This is our next point of investigation. Of all the perceivable important milestones of human life the only two that a person is unaware of (and others are aware) of are his/her Birth and Death. So it seems we accede that these perceptions of birth and death are made with our truth-distorting senses.

In reality (that is, if we were to transcend our senses), we can witness billions of births and deaths occurring in between the 'big' Birth and the 'big' Death. These births and deaths are at cellular and sub-cellular levels, which makes John of this moment different from John of the preceding moment. In other words, John of one moment dies and John of the next moment is born; when John of that moment dies, John of the next moment is born and so on. Therefore, though Birth and Death are the events we perceive with our truth-distorting senses, our life on this planet can be viewed as a seamless and continuous process of birth (arising) and death (ceasing) occurring between what we ordinarily perceive as Birth and Death.

Birth and Death can be considered as mere worldly truths, but that in absolute reality they are illusions. Birth and Death are arbitrary worldly points in a process that is seamless and continuous in Nature's eyes. Then all that remains is "empty phenomena that roll on" *(Path of Purification)*. Empty of what? Of labels such as *birth* and *death* and *I, Me* and *Mine*. What does all this mean in practical and simple terms? The answer: Refrain from making the issue we now make of Death as the most fearsome event, because our worldly perception of Death as a real and discrete event is an illusion created by our truth-distorting senses.

<u>Chapter Insights and Highlights</u>

1. We can overcome our fear of death and therefore all mental distress relating to it by changing two inherent errors in our lives.

2. The first error is evasion of death. The correction, which is at a worldly level, is to accept death as a natural and necessary event.

3. The second error is the belief in a self, which results in cultivating attachment to many things during one's lifetime. The correction, at a transcendental level, is to integrate the notion of no-self into our lives, replacing the belief in a self. This is purely a mental exercise needing only one's time and diligence.

4. When we have realized these two corrections, we will have peace at dying and death instead of distress.

36

Unfinished Business

The life of the average man is an unfinished work,
Full of loose ends of moral problems unresolved,
Of major and minor injustices,
Of wishes not fulfilled,
Of ideals unrealized and,
In not a few cases,
Of crimes unpunished.

Francis Story
(The Buddhist Outlook)

We concluded chapter 34: Aging, with the following:

"Can it be too late for action? We have discussed things that can be done (exercise, healthy diet, transcendental thinking etc.) to make our aging process as peaceful as possible. However, what if I am a very old person, frail in health, who missed the window of knowing when able and young and who does not now have the energy or motivation to carry out all these wholesome practices? ....."

It is the intent of this chapter to provide an answer to the above question and another, both being pivotal on the dual doctrine of *Karma and Rebirth*. To a reader who seriously ponders these questions, the answers will bring some peace.

We dealt with the subject of *Karma* in Chapter 8. Therein it was easy to see the operation of karma as willed action (cause) producing its result (vipaka), *in this present life*. It is when karma is viewed in association with rebirth that we have a powerful basis to answer some otherwise difficult life-related questions.

The doctrine of rebirth is complex and it is outside scope of this book to delve into its details. The reader who is interested in an in-depth analysis of the subject will find sufficient material in the resources listed in the footnote[106]. As advised in the Kalama Sutta, we understand that each individual has to reach his/her own conclusion regarding a belief in rebirth (for that matter, in anything), on the strength of one's unique investigations and realizations. It is hoped that the numerous publications available on the subject, including those listed here, will assist the reader in reaching his/her conclusion. In the meantime, we will proceed to complete this chapter on the basis that rebirth is a fact.

Some key points from the complex doctrine of *Karma and Rebirth*, that are needed for our present discussion are:

a)   Karma is volitional (willed) action, wholesome or unwholesome.

b)   Past karmic activity is a determinant of the present life.

c)   Present karmic activity is a determinant of the future life; i.e., beings have the power to change their destiny by means of present karma.

d)   Karma in one life is the cause (seed) for the continuation of the life-process after death (rebirth); rebirth provides an opportunity to finish 'business' that was not completed in the present life.

e)   As soon as anatta (no-self) has been fully realized (resulting in greed, hate and ignorance being fully extinguished), no more karma is generated and one realizes the goal of Sublime Peace, which means extinction of all rebirth and suffering, the ultimate goal of a Buddhist.

Now we are in a position to answer the 'unanswerable' questions, starting with the question listed at the top of this chapter.

1.   Can it be too late for me for action?

Answer: Given your personal circumstances, it could very well be that you may not be able to complete *The Noble 8-Fold Path* in the balance of your life. However, doing the utmost possible with the balance of your life will lessen the work to be done in the future. Accept that it is OK to die with 'business' unfinished. Future births will provide the opportunity to complete the *Path*.

---

[106] Rebirth as Doctrine and Experience – Essays and Case Studies by Francis Story. Wheel Publication No. 9: Karma and Rebirth by Nyanatiloka Mahathera. The Wheel Publication No. 425/427: The Message in the Teachings of Kamma, Rebirth, Samsara. The Wheel Publication No. 12/13: The Case for Rebirth by Francis Story. All available from Buddhist Publication Society, P.O. Box 61, 54 Sangharaja Mawatha, Kandy, Sri Lanka.

2. Why is there so much injustice in nature?

(For example, why does one person enjoy a long, healthy life when another is snatched by death in youth or infancy? Why is one person bestowed with all the ingredients for happiness whilst all the ingredients that cause distress befall another? Why is one innocent child entrenched in a miserable growth environment during the critical early development years when another is in a loving and enriched environment? Why do law-abiding good citizens suffer when criminals sometimes live the 'good' life with [to re-quote Francis Story], 'crimes unpunished'?)

Answer: Because of the operation of x-conditions (which are comprised of nature, nurture and karma). Since what is involved here is human life, intention is of critical importance and therefore, of the three components, karma is dominant. The unfavorable conditions affecting one person and favorable conditions affecting another are primarily due to the combined effects of (a) residual karmic results from previous births and (b) karmic results in this life from birth to the present. When (a) is predominant, the things we perceive as unjust, such as those listed in the question above, really are due to residual karmic results from previous births. Stated differently, something that we perceive as unjust is no more than the finishing, in this life, of the unfinished (karmic) business of past lives.

Thus Dhamma provides a meaningful answer to perceived injustices through the dual doctrine of *Karma and Rebirth.*

The good thing about distress is that once dispensed, it is paid off forever, like a mortgage. Thus distress experienced in this life, by virtue of prior unwholesome karma, will never have to be re-experienced in future births. This point will also clarify the situation regarding those who, by virtue of their mental condition, abject poverty or other factors do not encounter the Dhamma. When they pay back the unwholesome karma with their present distress, they will have the opportunity in future births to practice Dhamma and realize Sublime Peace.

Our life in this existence is not to be measured in relation to what others have done or achieved. Instead, it has to be a measurement that is self-contained. *Given the x-conditions that prevail in one's life*, if a person has willfully done his/her utmost to change one's destiny for the better, then that person could say that this existence was lived well. It reminds one of Oliver Wendell Holmes' words: "The great thing in the world is not so much where we stand, but in what direction we are moving." We don't have to compare ourselves at all with others. And, if one's x-conditions dictate that Sublime Peace is not within reach in this life, one should calmly accept that fact because it's awaiting one in a future life.

Chapter Insights and Highlights

1) Rebirth provides the opportunity for unfinished (karmic) business of this life to be finished, so one can speedily progress on the Noble Eightfold Path towards the goal of Sublime Peace.

2) Rebirth also provides an explanation for the perceived injustices of nature. These apparent injustices are nothing but the execution of unfinished business from past lives.

37

The Journey of Life:
A Brief History

We go back about 4 billion years in time, to a particular instant where our story begins. **Planet Earth** was still a volcanic cauldron. But what is different about this instant was that the volcanic 'soup' contained all the right conditions needed for the **first life form** to arise. And it did. Smaller than any life form we can imagine, soon this microscopic entity made copies of itself, signifying the earliest, though most rudimentary, form of reproduction for propagation of the species. These life forms commandeered organic material in the environment for their nutrition.

The copies made copies and these in turn made their copies driven by a rudimentary sense of **craving to preserve the species**, thus signifying an equally rudimentary sense of self. Therefore, the rudimentary sense of self arose to fulfill the craving for procreation, not to enable the life form to know reality. Thus, from the beginning of the evolution of life, the sense of self was erroneous from the vantage point of reality. The **root cause of all our distress – the notion of self** – had its origins at the beginning of life itself on planet Earth.

Life forms, from the very first, also lived under hostile conditions. So they developed **survival** mechanisms.

As time passed, the life forms evolved and sometimes branched into different species. As the life forms evolved, the mechanisms for sensing the environment also evolved. Mother Nature equipped each species with **sensory mechanisms** with capabilities just adequate to procreate and survive, but not to perceive reality. **Humans (species: Homo Sapiens)** appeared on Earth 2 to 3 million years ago. For biological sensory mechanisms the human being was equipped with eyes, ears, nose, tongue and touch.

To help survive in the face of hostile elements the human being was also equipped with a **stress-response mechanism** and supplementary mechanisms. These mechanisms evolved as time passed by. **Genes**, with necessary modifications following Darwinian principles of evolution, carried the blueprints of these mechanisms, from one generation to the next. Since genetic transference happens at the time of conception, an individual has no control over his/her genetic make-up.

The **notion of self** matured as it passed from one generation to the next. The **growth environment** at each stage strengthened the notion of self. More generally, the newborn, which is primarily a product of genes, is taken over by the environment, for creation of a complete person during the formative years. Thus, the individual has no control also over his/her 'fine-tuning' during this period of development.

The human being became the most advanced of the species. It was bestowed a sophisticated organ, the **brain**, and its reflective phenomenon, the **mind**, which became the marker of its superiority over other beings.

The human **mind** was equipped with the capability for many superior **functions** including thinking, memory storage and will (volition). All of these functions are supported by **neural mechanisms**, the building block of which is the *neuron* or brain cell. The link between neurons that gives rise to sophisticated networks is the *synapse*. The human mind includes a unique phenomenon that is functionally similar to a sense. This is the mechanism whereby a thought from memory acts as a trigger for the stress-response mechanism. Hence it is referred to as **the sixth sense**.

While the notion of self is the driver that enables human beings to procreate and survive, an inflated notion of self is also the root cause of the distress that befalls them. Since the notion of self is hardwired in the neural network, first genetically and thereafter fine-tuned by the growth environment, achievement of **re-wiring** to reflect the notion of no-self becomes the greatest challenge that a human being faces, if he/she is to realize inner peace. The next chapter shows that this is exactly what The Buddha achieved through **Insight Meditation**, though the Buddha's time predated **neuroscience** and the notion of neural wiring by 2500 years.

38

Re-Wiring for Inner Peace

In the preceding chapters we learned a number of important things, about the various mechanisms behind human unhappiness, happiness and peace, mostly as they happen involuntarily in our daily lives. We also saw, in Chapter 24, how our *will* works. Now it would be an opportune time to review all that information so we can clearly understand how to *willfully* bring inner peace to our lives.

We begin this investigation by reviewing a relevant portion of *Chapter 25: Dhamma at the Synapse*, appearing towards the end of the chapter that reads as follows:

"This one diagram depicts the essence of the biological interaction of a human being with his/her world.

A stimulus from an object or event (the world around us) arrives at the brain/mind through any one of the six senses and is processed by the brain/mind. The processing involves many functions, but of particular interest to us are *perception, thinking, memory, will* and *emotion*. The end results are:
  (c) changes to emotions ...., and
  (d) changes to body organs/systems ....."

In short, the world around us is the starting point, our processing is the mid-point and the resulting changes to our emotions and body, the end point.

The next diagram is essentially a reproduction of the diagram from Chapter 25 referred to above (minus details not relevant to our present discussion).

Observe the two-way arrow between *memory* and *thinking* functions. For now, let's briefly note that memory and thinking always have a two-way interaction. Thinking is fuelled by existing memory and memory is continuously updated, i.e., wired or re-wired, by new thinking. Chapters

25 and 26 addressed the subject of brain wiring and chapter 27 discussed how, specifically, our brains were wired to reflect the notion of self. We will discuss this important two-way interaction in greater detail later in the chapter.

If we study this diagram carefully, we will see that **a human being can intercept the whole process of his/her biological interaction with the world only at two points:**
  1)   the six senses (process point marked as B)
  2)   willed thinking (process points E and F conjointly)

Therefore, these two are the <u>only</u> points at which we have *direct* control to change our lives and destiny. In other words, the effect on our body (process point H) and emotions (process point G), of our interaction with the world, can be influenced (to our advantage) directly and willfully by ourselves at the points of the senses (B) and willed thinking (E-F). Any changes to the other points (particularly memory D, body H and emotions G) will only be as an indirect influence of controls affected at the points of our senses and willed thinking. Therefore, with the knowledge we now possess – that our emotions and body can be influenced to realize wellbeing by thinking thoughts in touch with reality – we are on our way to taking control of our destiny. Of course, the extent of this control will be subject to the natural limits of what we can do with our will, as explained in *Chapter 29: X-Conditions.*

It will be of interest to see how the 2500-year-old Dhamma compares with our scientific deduction of the control (interception) points.

From the Buddhist scriptural work *Sutta Nipata*, we have the following:

> Who is free from **sense perceptions**,
> In him no more bonds exist;
> Who by **insight** freedom gains,
> All delusions cease in him;
> But who clings to sense perceptions,
> And to viewpoints wrong and false,
> He lives wrangling in the world.

It is clear from the above that the Dhamma position and our somewhat scientific deduction concur. To realize inner peace we have to work at two things: (1) inactivating the senses and (2) developing insight (thinking in touch with reality).

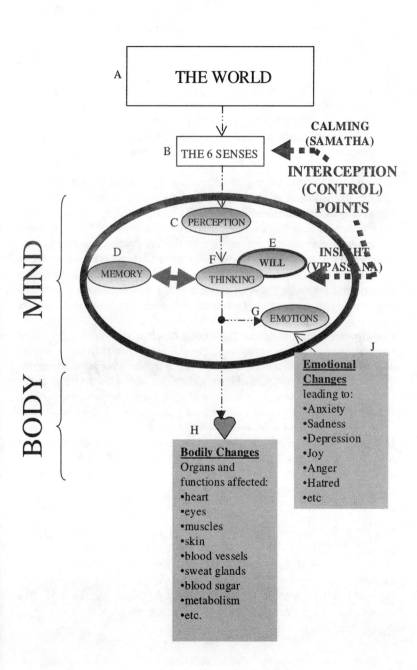

Now, let's examine the two control points in detail.

The Six Senses (Point B of diagram)

We learned earlier that all the six senses constantly send information about the world to our mind. Often the mind receives more information than it can cope with from these senses, the overload resulting in many forms of mental distress (such as anxiety and confusion) and physical problems (e.g., elevated blood pressure and heart rate). On the other hand, if fewer senses input information to the mind, obviously the load that it has to cope with will be lessened and therefore the mind will be calmer. If instead of all six senses being active, one sense faculty – say, the eyes – is temporarily deactivated by closing them, no more visual information is sent to the mind and its load will be lessened by a corresponding amount. Now, if the ears also are plugged, no more sound information reaches the mind, which then will be calmer to a further degree and so on. With this calming, the adverse mental conditions (e.g., anxiety and confusion) and adverse physical problems (e.g., increased blood pressure and heart rate) subside, thus promoting wellbeing.

Recall our analogy of six rambunctious children who are driving their mother crazy. (The six rambunctious children represent the six senses and the mother represents the mind.) As the children are put to sleep one by one, the mother becomes calmer and calmer. So does the mind as the six senses are deactivated one by one. We cannot keep our six senses deactivated all the time because they are needed for the daily businesses of living – that's why Mother Nature equipped us with these senses. However, we can *choose* to deactivate them at selected times when it does not interfere with the essential daily actions of living. This is cleverly achieved by taking advantage of a characteristic of the mind (thought process) we discussed in *Chapter 21: How the Mind Controls the Body*.

To recap, this characteristic of the human thought process is that *only one elemental thought operates in a single thought moment*. This means that when an elemental thought associated with one sense is operative, in that infinitesimal time span, the other five senses are shut off (detached) from the mind. Thus, without having to physically deactivate the other five senses, we can realize the same effect using nature's own design of sensory detachment from all senses but one[107], during this infinitesimal time span.

To illustrate, let's assume that the mind is focused on the breath as it passes through the nostrils. Then the active sense is *touch* - the nostrils *touch*ing the breath. All other five senses will effectively be deactivated during that time, although our eyes may not even be closed and ears not plugged. The mind becomes calm during the period of willed focus, though this time period is miniscule. The more consecutive thought moments in which we can continue maintaining focus on the one event (breathing), the longer the time the other five senses are shut off. The mind remains calm for that sustained period of time. This is the inner mechanism that's operative when we practice Calming Meditation using the breath (*Breathing Meditation*). Disciplined practice of this type – willed sensory restriction – whether the object of focus is the breath, a mantra, a candle or any other, helps build a calmer mind (but, it must be emphasized, not a wiser mind).

The principle of sensory deactivation described above can be also used to our advantage to obtain *temporary* relief to some of our daily problems. For example, let's take the case of Quinn. As of late, he dislikes the company of his roommate Bruno. We know that when Quinn goes for a long walk or visits a compassionate friend his mind feels relatively calm. This is because the walk or the visit effectively creates a temporary deactivation of the senses of sight and hearing as they relate to Bruno – Quinn does not see or hear Bruno. If Quinn is highly skilled in breathing meditation, he can use the technique right in Bruno's company (without Bruno being aware of it). Few people, however, will have perfected the skill to be within sight and hearing (physical phenomena) of someone or something, but *choose* not to see and listen (mental manifestation).

Since we cannot deactivate our senses permanently, sensory control (including breathing meditation) cannot provide a lasting solution to our emotional problems. Then, how can we realize this needed long-range goal? For that, we move to the next section – *Willed Thinking*.

---

[107] To be accurate, we should note that of the single sense selected for focus, only a fraction of the sense 'door' is open, thus the degree of calming achieved is really more than that allowed by closure of the five sense doors. For simplicity we will continue the analysis on the basis of closure of (i.e., detachment from) five senses.

Willed Thinking (Point E-F of previous diagram)

As we saw in Chapter 21, integral to our involuntary (habitual) thinking process is input *('fuel')* from the memory. This is shown clearly in the next diagram.

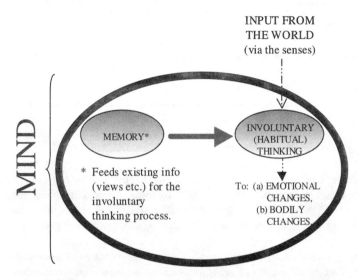

The reverse process is that voluntary (willed) thinking causes memory to be *updated* as shown in the next diagram.

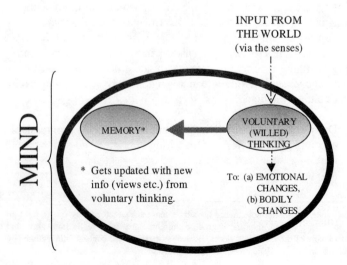

Then, we saw in *Chapter 24: Will* that what places human beings above all other beings (creatures of habit only), is that we are equipped with the mental process called the *will*.

While a review of Chapter 24 is strongly recommended at this point, we reproduce here the paragraph most relevant to our present discussion:

"We need to invoke the process of *will* only when it becomes necessary to think and act differently from involuntary thinking and action. This situation often arises when we realize that some aspect of our present involuntary behavior is unsatisfactory and we desire to change it. When we have carried out the chosen voluntary (*will*ed) thinking and action long enough, it becomes involuntary thinking and action, that is, *habit* or part of one's personality."

The above mechanism is what comes into play in the second (and crucial) stage of meditation - Insight Meditation. We will illustrate the process by considering the important topic of *self/no-self*, taking the case of a person we will call Nimal.

a)   Up to a certain point in time, Nimal's perception of the world and his behavior is based on the belief that there is a self. (Involuntary behavior). As we saw in Chapter 26, a rudimentary notion of self was wired into Nimal's brain by nature while still a fetus and fine-tuned by the environment (nurture) – this view, second nature to Nimal now, is held in Nimal's memory.

b)   In the process of trying to find a way out of his existential stresses, Nimal discovers the doctrine of *no-self*. The doctrine appeals to him, he pursues his inquiry further and becomes convinced of the fact of no-self as a truth. (Voluntary action).

c)   Nimal contemplates no-self, in all his daily activities. (Voluntary action).

d)   During (b) and (c) Nimal's brain (memory) progressively accomplishes the task of re-wiring to reflect no-self as truth replacing the earlier wiring that reflected self as truth. (Voluntary action).

e)   The new view of no-self is completely wired into Nimal's brain (memory). His thinking and actions (behavior) based on no-self is no longer voluntary but becomes involuntary (habitual); the fact of no-self, now second nature to Nimal, becomes an integral part and driver of his personality. (Involuntary action).

Since all input from the world reaching a person has to pass through the point of *thinking*, which always 'consults' *memory*, memory indirectly becomes the judge of all sensory input (the exception being direct sensory-motor action). Therefore, if a person has in current memory the self-view, all relevant input will be judged in relation to this view. Thus, the family physician's announcement of the diagnosis of cancer will be labeled by memory as '*my* cancer'. This labeling and assignment of ownership immediately leads to mental distress.

On the other hand, if the person has in current memory the (totally integrated) view of no-self, the 'consultation' with memory will result in a mental response and feeling that is the polar opposite. That response and feeling will reflect the position: "In reality (upon transcending the senses) there is neither cancer nor 'I' but only no-self (ownerless) phenomena that arise and cease dependent on conditions." In this case, due to the detached awareness, there will be no mental distress and instead, inner peace.

We know from chapters 25 and 26 that underlying any view is a unique (physical) neuro-chemical make-up (which is commonly referred to as 'wiring'). Therefore it is obvious that if we need our memory to have an opposite or a different view, the only way it can be realized is to willfully change the wiring appropriately. In other words, if there is problem wiring, we need to repair (re-wire) the problem wiring. This is what an electrician would do when faced with problem wiring in a building. However we 'do-it-yourself neuron-technicians' face one problem that the electrician doesn't. The electrician has direct physical access to the problem electrical wiring but we do not have such access to our neural wiring (the maze comprising about 100 trillion connections, as we saw earlier, safely concealed by our skull). So, how do we realize the re-wiring (of memory, for views)? The answer: Indirectly, by willfully thinking thoughts in touch with reality, as Nimal in the previous example did, with regard to the self/no-self dichotomy.

By now, we know that the self/no-self dichotomy is the most important issue to be dealt with for emotional peace. However, the above reasoning applies to all other views that have two 'faces' – one face, not in touch with reality, appearing acceptable when viewed through the truth-distorting senses and the other, in touch with reality, appearing acceptable when the truth-distorting senses are transcended. The former results in distress and the latter in inner peace.

It is clear that any therapy or healing that claims to deliver us from mental (emotional) distress must cause the neural wiring underlying that distress – the problem wiring – to be changed to the right wiring, that is, wiring that reflects the way things really are. Such wiring underlies inner peace. The touted therapy may be described under any one of an ever-growing array of labels – religion, psychology, psychiatry, philosophy, esotericism, meditation, mysticism, metaphysics, stress management, cult and so on. *Whatever the label or name used to describe it, if the touted 'therapy' or 'healing' does not result in the right neural re-wiring, specifically to correct the erroneous concept of self, it is not worth spending one minute of our precious life on it.*

The re-wiring (of memory) to achieve the desired goal of eradication of distress, as we have seen, can be achieved only by willful thinking that reflects reality. The essence of Dhamma is Insight Meditation and the essence of Insight Meditation is willful thinking in touch with reality, including thinking based on no-self. In simple and practical terms, Insight Meditation may be thought of as 'the act of spending time alone with reality' - a kind of a tete-a-tete between the meditator and reality. (As desirable, but not mandatory, preparation for Insight Meditation, any form of calming meditation such as breathing meditation may be used). Thus, Insight Meditation achieves the goal of re-wiring memory to reflect reality, including the fundamental reality of no-self, thereby achieving victory over distress.

In the next two chapters, we explore an effective means of using Insight Meditation that is fitting for the modern day.

Chapter Insights and Highlights

1) Memory and thinking have a two-way interaction. Memory fuels (involuntary) thinking. Voluntary (willed) thinking upgrades memory.

2) A human being can intercept (control) the whole process of his/her biological interaction with the world only at two points:

   a) The six senses
   b) Willed thinking

3) The operative point for Calming Meditation (Samatha) is a). The operative point for Insight (Vipassana) Meditation is b).

4) Calming Meditation. By intensely focusing on one sensory contact and curtailing the other five, we achieve calmness of the mind.

5) Insight Meditation. By willfully thinking thoughts in touch with reality we change memory to reflect reality, thus providing fuel for inner peace. Changes to memory manifest as neural re-wiring.

39

To Write
or
To Contemplate?

The Buddha taught the Dhamma, about 2500 years ago, that is, about 500 B.C. The teaching was done verbally in the now defunct Indian language *Pali* and neither the Buddha nor his immediate disciples wrote down his teachings. In fact, it was not the custom in India of the time to record in writing religious or philosophic truths. Instead, teachings of importance were handed down orally from master to disciple. Through continual repetition word for word[108] the disciple committed the teachings to memory. In due course, when the disciple became a master, the process was repeated with his disciple. In this manner, important teachings were propagated through generations.

Dhamma, being a precious teaching involving fundamental truths (of existence) and deliverance from distress, also was subjected to the above technique of oral transmission. During the reign of a famous Indian Buddhist king (Asoka)[109], Dhamma was propagated to Sri Lanka, the island nation south of India. The missionaries who brought the teachings to Sri Lanka were none other than King Asoka's son (Mahinda)[110] and daughter (Sangamitta). About a century and half later[111] the teachings were, for the first time, written down on palm-leaves in Sri Lanka. That was the origin of the first, and most authentic, *written* scriptures of Dhamma, available to us today as the Pali Canon.

The circumstances indicated above show us that during the Buddha's lifetime and for a few centuries thereafter, teachers of Dhamma had <u>no choice</u> but to communicate its message only orally. That changed with

---

[108] It is said that people in those days were so adept at the technique of commitment of teachings to memory, driven by necessity, that it was an art of far superior skill in those people compared to people of today.
[109] King Asoka ruled during the period 259-222 B.C.
[110] In the year 250 B.C. Sangamitta arrived in Sri Lanka later, at the request of Mahinda.
[111] During the reign of king Vattagamini, 104 – 88 B.C.

the creation of the monumental Pali Canon. Since then, and up to this day, the message of Dhamma is communicated not only orally, but also via various writings, including the Pali Canon, to the great benefit of Buddhism and Buddhists worldwide. Thus the means of *communication* of the Dhamma realized a momentous leap with the use of *writing*.

Having discussed the impact of writing on the communication of Dhamma, let's now investigate the method of *practice* of Dhamma, specifically, meditation.

As we know, the essence of Dhamma is Insight Meditation and the core of Insight Meditation is the replacement of wrong views with right views. The technique of Insight Meditation from the time of the Buddha to the present day takes the form of pure mental activity. An inherent characteristic of this type of practice of meditation is that (during a person's initial practice and for some time thereafter until proficiency is acquired), *the wandering and erratic mind is called upon to correct itself with no adjunct to make the practice more effective.*

Now let's look at some of the problems that result from entrusting the wandering and erratic mind to correct itself, in so far as today's practitioner is concerned rather than the practitioner of the Buddha's time.

Using the mind to correct itself is fine if the mind is in a reasonably alert, calm and cognitively sound state for sufficient lengths of time. But most of the time, the mind is under one or more unfortunate conditions of worldly existence – stress, anxiety, depression, worry, confusion and so on. The effect of these conditions is more marked on today's average human being than it was on our ancestors of centuries gone by. Thus the state of mind needed for reflective Insight Meditation is harder to obtain for today's practitioner than it was for practitioners of ancient times.

The natural tendency of the mind is to always try its utmost to return to its *habitual* (most often irrational and disruptive) thinking. But the habitual thinking (e.g., of 'self'), as one starts the practice of meditation, is exactly what we are trying to change to achieve inner peace. So, when called upon to correct itself, this tendency of the mind to return to its habitual thinking becomes a recurrent impediment, instead of a help, to one's practice. Accordingly, the result becomes unfortunate for the vast majority, if not almost all, of the meditators. The result comes out clearly in the comments of meditators, smacking of frustration and failure. "I have practiced for 10 years but do not seem to have made any discernible progress". "My main problem is inability to focus – the mind keeps wandering." "After a few seconds, my mind is back to worldly problems". And so on.

As in the case of *communication* of Dhamma discussed earlier, the practitioners in the time of the Buddha and those of many centuries thereafter, had no choice but to *practice* Insight Meditation as a pure mental activity (and we adhere to the same mode of practice today).

Fortunately for the practitioners of those days, the universal problem of the wandering mind was made somewhat more manageable due to a number of mitigating factors present then. For example, it was easier in those days to find (a) an accomplished master to guide a disciple during the difficult initial periods, (b) a place[112] away from worldly distractions, conducive to mind development and (c) dedicated time for mind control practice. Also, then, the stressful daily issues one had to deal with were lesser in number and intensity. Furthermore, support was available more readily from society to keen practitioners (in the form of provision of essentials such as meals).

The only notable group of practitioners in today's world who have the opportunity to dedicate their time to meditation in that manner is comprised of the monks and nuns. Thus, this form of pure mental practice, quite appropriate for the Buddha's time, poses problems for the typical modern day practitioner.

So, understandably, many people find disappointment in this 'business' called meditation and they conclude it is difficult to practice. Because of the touted benefits, some continue the practice as a purely mechanical exercise hoping one day they will realize inner peace. Some, through frustration, abandon the practice. Achieving the goal of re-wiring the brain (memory) to reflect views in touch with reality, which requires focus and tremendous dedication, becomes impossible or nearly impossible for most people. Hence we often encounter negative perceptions about meditation – such as the practice being very difficult, doable only by a few, suitable only for intellectuals and so on. The good news clearly emerging from the discussion in this book so far is that *the common concept that meditation is a Herculean task need not continue to prevail.*

As we will soon see, we can:

---

[112] Note that the geographical region of the practice in Buddha's time and the immediately following time-period was the year-round-warm South Asia, where Buddhism flourished. So, even sitting under a tree often served the purpose.

(1) override the long-held belief that the goal of meditation is achievable only by a select few, and

(2) make the practice easy to understand so that anybody who is keen to obtain benefits from it can realize that goal with the right understanding, practice and commitment of needed time.

The solution of using an adjunct - writing - was not in vogue amongst the general population in the Buddha's time, but is today. We can make use of *writing* to offset the negative effects of the confused and wandering mind thereby ensuring cumulative progress for the practitioner. Thus, just as *communication* of the Dhamma realized a momentous leap via the art of writing, the other key facet of Dhamma, namely the *practice* (and application to daily life) of meditation can also be most effectively realized with the help of writing. In a sense, we let the technique of writing 'lend the mind a hand'.

The writing is done (1) whenever the cognitive capabilities of the mind are in a reasonable state – not when the mind is confused or otherwise agitated and (2) *not during* an incident, but *after* the incident. While we are writing, if we find that the mind dips into a cognitively unsound state (tired, unable to think properly, sleepy etc.) then we take a break and come back to it when the mind is up to the task. In that manner, we complete the paper work in stages, if we are unable to do it all in one sitting. Thus we arm ourselves with a simple but highly effective technique to successfully overcome the universal problem of the wandering mind. Writing things down is like harnessing a horse. The mind is the horse and the harness is the writing.

While there are many views stored in our mind that are 'wrong' and should be re-wired to be 'right', we have seen clearly, by now, that these many wrong views are all resulting from one *root*-cause wrong view – that of 'self'. It is like a lemon tree that we want to replace with an orange tree. The best way to do it is not to cut the many branches of the lemon tree one by one but to uproot the tree from the roots and plant an orange tree in its place. When the notion of self is removed from the mind, all other beliefs that depended on that notion will automatically be destroyed. Then, just as the orange tree will bear traits (such as leaves and fruits) of orange, the outcome for the 'no-self human being' will be human traits based on no-self, such as compassion, unconditional love for all beings and viewing all things as interconnected.

Let's take a concrete example to illustrate. Recall that when Colin was about 2 years old and his Mom said, "This is Colin", he repeated after

Mom, "This is Colin" pointing the finger towards himself. This became one more of an immense series of affirmations that helped etch the notion of self in Colin's brain through physical (neural) wiring (Chapter 27). And that notion of self, though erroneous, equipped the adult Colin for the purpose of survival and procreation.

Now Colin is 45 years old. He is on the path of self-transformation. What he has to now do is effectively say, "This is Colin as perceived through truth-distorting senses. However, there is no Colin in Absolute Reality." The old wiring will begin to get overwritten with wiring that reflects the new view that is in touch with reality. With *regular repetition* of the new view, it will eventually get securely etched in the brain. Regular repetition means **practice, practice** and more **practice.** The new view will then be behind all relevant involuntary (automatic) responses of Colin. More than the theory behind this change, which by now is easy to understand, abundant evidence from current research in neuroscience confirms that there is actual change to the neural wiring with repeated reinforcement of new views. And that capability exists throughout one's lifetime.

The best way to understand what happens in the process of re-wiring the brain is by way of an analogy.

The young children of the Smith family have been used to taking a certain short-cut route through the woods to get from home to school and back, for no other reason than the fact that for generations this route has been used as the short-cut.

Though it saved a quarter mile on the round trip compared to the street route, the short-cut had problems – it was full of poison ivy and there was a hostile, noisy dog en route. One day, in the process of looking for their lost cat, the eldest of the Smith children discovered another route, free of poison ivy and shorter than the previous route by an additional quarter mile and with no hostile dogs. Plus it was full of sweet edible berries. The only problem with the new route was that the unrestrained growth of weeds over the years resulted in no identifiable track for the children to follow. However, because of the many advantages (sweet berries included!) the children decided to take the new route with the help of landmarks such as rocks and large trees.

As days passed by, weeds began to grow on the old route, eventually leaving no trace of the route. At the same time, due to the children trampling them, the weeds of the new route began to die, eventually leaving an identifiable track. The walk to school and back via the new route became a happy event in the lives of the children.

The 'self route' is like the old route – used as dictated by habit but leads to distress. The 'no-self-route' is like the new route, leads to peace, but needs hard work for some time to establish. Each day, as the new route progresses incrementally, the old route moves towards eradication by a similar degree. Neurologically speaking, the old neural pathways atrophy while the new pathways grow and flourish. Diligence is required until the new path gets established.

The fact that effecting this change is *hard work* is obvious from the above discussion. Hard work? Yes. Results hard to achieve? No. When we are trying to change the wiring in our brains that has been brought about by the genes (through generations) and the environment (from conception, through birth to the present moment), it has got to be hard work. But when one realizes that the hard work changes distress to inner peace, there remains no doubt that it is effort well directed.

We are already accustomed to hard work. We work hard at our studies, to earn a living, to get through the day's chores, to keep fit and so on. So we can work hard here too. In fact, doing this hard work should be the highest priority ever of any man or woman – not being an astronaut or a world famous heart surgeon. After all, humans have traveled in space, even landed on the moon and replaced diseased hearts with artificial hearts, yet the human condition of *mental distress* has not been alleviated by an iota by these technological marvels. So, let's work hard for the sake of inner peace.

We noted earlier that two factors caused the erroneous notion of self to be wired into our brains. The first was the genetic factor, the result of evolution from beginning of life to the present, which guided the wiring of a rudimentary form of self. The second was the environment that refined the rudimentary notion of self to a formidable version that dominates one's existence. Let's note as a matter of interest that the activity of changing the notion of self to no-self results in the removal of the cumulative genetic and environmental effect. That explains why the work involved in affecting that work is certainly hard work.

Now that we know that re-wiring of wrong views in our brain with right views can be done most effectively with the help of the art of writing, let's proceed to discuss practical details of how we "write to re-wire" in the next chapter.

Chapter Insights and Highlights

1) In his time, The Buddha taught the Dhamma orally. Neither The Buddha, nor his immediate disciples, wrote down his teachings. The custom of the day was to pass on all teachings of importance orally. So was it for the Dhamma.

2) About four centuries after The Buddha passed away, the teachings were written down on palm leaves in Sri Lanka. Thus *communication* of the Dhamma took a momentous leap from oral to written format.

3) The *practice* of Insight Meditation (which is the essence of Buddhism) continues to this day as a pure mental exercise.

4) An inherent characteristic of this type of practice of meditation is that (during a person's initial practice and for some time thereafter until proficiency is acquired), *the wandering and erratic mind is called upon to correct itself with no adjunct to make the practice more effective.* This adversely affects the quality and progress of meditation for today's stressed out human being.

5) The solution is to employ the art of writing as an adjunct for meditation, just as the art of writing was used to document the teachings about 2100 years ago. This is a momentous leap in the practice of meditation, and is a definite help, in the important initial stages of practice.

40

Then, Let's Write It Down!

In chapters 11-14 of Part A: Seeker's Digest we used the process of writing down wrong and right views as a therapeutic technique. The manner in which the written work was to be done aptly concluded Part A when it existed as the stand-alone first edition of *The Way to Inner Peace*.

In this book – the second edition – the coverage of subject matter has been significantly expanded in the form of Parts B and C. Seen from a practical aspect, this additional coverage impacts the following two essential 'tools' of the distress resolution technique, used in Part A:

(i) Table 1: Right and Wrong Views (page 83-86) Chapter 11. Table 1 is reprinted at pages 330-333 for ease of reference.

(ii) The Worksheet (page 103) of Chapter 13.

Note, however, that the additional coverage in Parts B and C does not affect the principle and essence of the earlier technique, that is replacement of wrong views with right views and assimilation of totally new right views. The changes are only in refinement and details that bring additional benefit to the practitioner.

The additional coverage has resulted in the following four changes, the first affecting the Table of Right and Wrong Views, and the other three affecting the Worksheet.

1) Table 2, appearing at the end of this chapter (pages 334-340), provides a convenient collection of key listings from 'Chapter Insights and Highlights' of Parts B and C. *Consider these listings (Table 2) as an extension of the second column (Right View) of Table 1* (pages 330-333).

2) As stated in the Preface, the leitmotiv of the Buddha's teaching is the notion of no-self and the replacement of the notion of self with that

of no-self is the crowning achievement on the Path. In daily living we are often unaware that the self-notion underlies every one of our emotional distresses. Once we make a written statement about any distress using the Worksheet, all we need to do to bring the existence of the self-view to our awareness is to simply *underline* all occurrences of the self-notion in our statement of distress. To assist with the integration of this revelation a *new* section "ISOLATION OF ROOT CAUSE (SELF-NOTION)", appearing as Box B, has been added to the Worksheet.

Let's illustrate this new crucial step by revisiting the case of Alicia's lower back pain (Chapter 13), page 106. The section "STATEMENT OF MY DISTRESS" (Box A), with the self statements underlined by Alicia, now appears as follows:

> *I feel worried and hopeless after the news of the medical diagnosis. Why do these things have to always happen to me? Really, I am to blame too because I should have been more careful in the way I used my body in the past; if I had been, this probably would not have happened.*

Next, in the process of completing Box B, ISOLATION OF ROOT CAUSE (SELF-NOTION), Alicia makes the profound discovery that 7 times her mental process was linked to the self-notion. Thus, when she puts down her thought patterns on paper and consciously looks for the self-statements, suddenly the truth of the enormous bearing the notion of self has on her mental processes becomes evident. The pivotal effect the notion has on her distress becomes quantifiable and strikingly clear. She also realizes that, had it not been for the writing, the dominant player of *self* would have been unrecognized this time, as it has been throughout her lifetime, buried under her all-consuming emotions.

(In passing, as a matter of interest, note the following. If this one thought process, which happens at lightning speed, involved 7 iterations of the imposing but concealed self-notion, imagine the thousands of times that the self-notion will dominate the mind of Alicia, and therefore the mind of any person, *in a day*)

So, to integrate the new revelation to her life and help the healing process, Alicia records the following conclusions and contemplates the same:

"My feelings of worry, hopelessness, poor-me attitude and self-blame revolved around my belief in a self, 7 times during this event alone. While self <u>seems</u> real as perceived through my truth-distorting senses, in the absolute sense (in reality) it is an illusion – there is no self. Therefore, my feelings of worry, hopelessness, poor-me attitude and self-blame were ill-founded". (This is Insight at work in real life, solving real problems.)

3) In the new Worksheet, the previous action item has been replaced with TRIPLE-A METHOD SUMMARY, Box D. This change ensures that attention is always paid not only to *action*, but also to the equally important *acceptance* of things not under our control to change.

4) The last modification to the Worksheet is a capsule of three trigger messages, based on impermanence, conditionality and no-self. These messages are in the last section CAPSULE OF HEALING MESSAGES (TRIGGERS), Box E of the Worksheet. These healing messages can be quickly recalled at any time, even when one is pressed for time to look over the complete Worksheet. These brief trigger messages should get the person's mind thinking on the profound realities of existence and help bring tranquility. It is recommended that the messages be committed to memory.

The capsule is:

This too will pass *[Reason: impermanence].*
This is the way it is *[Reason: x-conditions].*
There is no I that owns this *[Reason: truth-distorting senses and hence no-self].*

To reflect the changes outlined in items 2-4 above, a modified Worksheet (template) is provided in the next page. Following that is the new Worksheet completed for Alicia's case, as illustration.

New Worksheet (Template):

(A) <u>STATEMENT OF MY DISTRESS:</u>
(B) <u>ISOLATION OF ROOT CAUSE (SELF-NOTION)</u>
(C) <u>ANALYSIS OF MY VIEWS (THOUGHTS)</u> *Worldly View 1:* *Transcendental Views:* --- *Worldly View 2:* *Transcendental Views:*

(D) <u>TRIPLE-A METHOD SUMMARY</u>

  I.   **Accept** *all that has happened up to now as the way it is, the reason being x-conditions.*

  II. **Act** *to improve things from now on, where feasible, with data ('lessons') from past happenings contributing to formulation of this action.*

  III. **Accept** *what cannot be done to improve things from now on, also, as the way it is, the reason being x-conditions, again.*

(E) <u>CAPSULE OF HEALING MESSAGES (TRIGGERS)</u>

This too will pass *(Reason: impermanence).*
This is the way it is *(Reason: x-conditions).*
There is no I that owns this *(Reason: truth-distorting senses, hence no-self).*

Example (New Worksheet as filled out by Alicia)

(A) STATEMENT OF MY DISTRESS:

I feel worried and hopeless after the news of the medical diagnosis. Why do these things have to always happen to me? Really, I am to blame because I should have been more careful in the way I used my body in the past; if I had been, this probably would not have happened.

(B) ISOLATION OF ROOT CAUSE (SELF-NOTION):

Alicia makes the profound discovery that 7 times her mental process was linked to the self-notion. That is, when she puts down her thought pattern on paper and consciously looks for the self-statements (i.e., underlines them), suddenly the truth of the enormous bearing the notion of self has on her mental process becomes evident. The pivotal effect the notion has on her distress becomes quantifiable and strikingly clear.

So, to integrate the new revelation to her life and help the healing process, Alicia contemplates the following fact:

"My feelings of worry, hopelessness, poor-me attitude and self-blame revolved around my belief in a self, 7 times on this event alone. While self seems real as perceived through my truth-distorting senses, in reality it is an illusion – there is no self and its perception was ill-founded."

(C) ANALYSIS OF MY VIEWS (THOUGHTS)

Worldly View 1:   Bad things always happen to me. But why me, of all people?

Transcendental Views:

Things happen when the right conditions (x-conditions) cone in. Hence, existential distress is universal and has not exclusively chosen me. The law of conditions is impersonal and does not operate on factors such as comparison of one person's state with others or on labels of 'good' and 'bad'.

So, I have to *accept* the fact of the slipped disk and the resulting physical distress (pain) but I need not overburden myself with *mental* distress with irrational thoughts such as labeling a happening (slipped disk) as 'bad', asking "why me?" and comparing my distress with that of others.

Worldly View 2:   I should have been more careful in the way I used my body in the past; if I did, this probably would not have happened.

Transcendental Views:
Things happen exactly the way they are supposed to. The coning in of x-conditions determines any happening. So I cannot blame myself for what I did or didn't do up until now. Neither can I visit the past to change what has happened. And I could only do what I knew to do at each moment in my life dependent on the unique mix of ignorance and wisdom prevailing at each moment.

(D)   TRIPLE-A METHOD SUMMARY

I.   **Accept** *all that has happened up to now as the way it is, the reason being x-conditions.*
What has happened up to now are:
♦   There is a slipped disk
♦   There is physical distress resulting from the slipped disk

II.   **Act** *to improve things from now on, where feasible, with data ('lessons') from past happenings contributing to formulation of this action.*
♦   With continued Insight Meditation, I will facilitate eradication of mental distress by not entertaining such meaningless views as "Why me?"
♦   I will also refrain from labeling any happening (e.g., slipped disk) as 'bad' and self-blaming, which are groundless.
♦   After consulting medical professionals
    Now I have the following possibilities from which to choose an action plan for recovery, subject to discussion with my family and supplementary medical consultation:
    (a)   Bed rest for a number of weeks, and pain relieving drugs when necessary – to be later followed by wearing a corset or supportive collar. This may turn out to be all I need for full recovery.
    (b)   If (a) fails and compression on the nerve root produces muscle weakness (which is not present now), I can consider surgery to relieve the pressure.

III.   **Accept** what cannot be done to improve things from now on, also, as the way it is, the reason being x-conditions, again.
♦   Depending on the future medical outcome, I may have to be on long-term disability. (I will cope, whatever may come.)

(E)   CAPSULE OF HEALING MESSAGES (TRIGGERS)
This too will pass *(Reason: impermanence).*
This is the way it is *(Reason: x-conditions).*
There is no I that owns this *(Reason: truth-distorting senses, hence no-self).*

As Alicia does the paper work, based on insights of reality in place of her prior erroneous thinking, wisdom penetrates her mind. Whenever the emotions relating to this incident interfere with Alicia's daily life, she repeatedly goes over the completed Worksheet until her mind is saturated with wisdom pertaining to this particular problem. Thus she begins to feel emotional relief more often.

With diligent repetition of the process for other problems in her daily life, and with great patience, Alicia's mind wins inner peace over emotional distress. She continues to have physical pain sometimes but she has learned to accept it as the way it is and therefore, to cope.

The principles and technique underlying the above case can be used by all of us in practically **any** real life situation that causes mental distress (e.g., loss, separation, sickness, sense of failure, depression or even the most complex and profound existential issues that sometimes haunt us).

With repeated application, there comes a time when we are so adept at the technique, we can dispense with the adjunct of paper work. Then we can apply the technique any place, any time, *mentally*.

The more one *strives with earnestness*, integrating the new practice to all aspects of daily living, the closer one moves to Sublime Peace. In fact, the mind of the practitioner will move towards its destination of Sublime Peace *effortlessly*, once freed from the pull of worldly distresses. It's like the space vehicle that heads on freely towards its destination once freed from the pull of earth's gravity.

Then one day, when the right x-conditions cone in, the practitioner will suddenly find himself/herself at the destination - sublime, absolutely peaceful and never to turn back from. Then, that person realizes that Nirvana[113] was never an 'entity out there' but was always here waiting to be embraced. In the language of neuroscience, the brain was waiting to be re-wired. In Dhamma terms, the mind was waiting to be purified. Either way, the 'tool' is the same, that is, thinking in touch with reality, for which the truth-distorting senses had to be transcended.

So, what held back the practitioner all this time was the grip of Maya[114]. For the one who completed the task, that grip is now and forever unclasped. Wish you speedy progress on **The Way to Inner Peace**.

---

[113] Sublime Peace
[114] Illusion (of existence, created by our truth-distorting senses)

Table 1: Right and Wrong Views (Reproduced from Chapter 11)

A	B
Wrong View (Worldly)	**Right View** (Transcendental)
View of permanence	All things are impermanent (subject to change). Some change slowly, some rapidly. *(Impermanence).* For perspective, I can reflect on "This too will pass" and ponder on "What will be of this present happening or thing, say, 100 or 1000 years from now?"
View of an abiding self (ego).	There *is* a self only as seen through our senses, which are utterly deficient for perceiving reality. Upon transcending the senses, i.e., in reality, there is no such thing as a 'Self'. "I", "Me", "Mine", "You" etc. are mere conventional terms needed for human communication *(No-self).*
It would be possible to sustain happiness with sensory gratification.	Sensory stimuli sometimes result in transient pleasures but invariably lead to unhappiness when the object (stimuli) or subject (perceiving mechanism - senses) undergoes inevitable change *(Impermanence).*

Table 1: Right and Wrong Views (continued)

A	B
Wrong View (Worldly)	**Right View** (Transcendental)
I should welcome praise and be averse to blame.	I should be unaffected by praise and blame as both are transient[115] (*Impermanence*)
The world is responsible for my distress.	I am responsible for both my inner peace and distress. The root-cause of my distress is my own ignorance of reality (wrong views) (*Karma, Dependent Origination*).
Life is full of problems and they distress me.	Every so-called 'problem' is a teacher in disguise. With that attitude we can gracefully transcend the problems and create inner peace.
I should not have to suffer.	Physical distress (pain) is inherent in change (impermanence) and so I have to accept it. Some pain may be temporarily abated, but many times during my life, I will have to confront pain. Mental distress can be eliminated by replacing ignorance (wrong views) with wisdom (right views) (*Impermanence*).
My mind and my body belong to me. So do my children, spouse and wealth.	In reality they belong to nature, and to me only by convention[116] (*No-self*).

---

[115] "Even as a rock is not shaken by the wind, the wise man is not shaken by praise or blame." – The Dhammapada 81

[116] "'These are my sons. This is my wealth.' In this way the fool troubles himself. He is not even the owner of himself: how much less of his sons and his wealth." – The Dhammapada 62

Table 1: **Right and Wrong Views** (continued)

A	B
Wrong View (Worldly)	**Right View** (Transcendental)
Birth must be celebrated and death mourned.	Birth and death are equal spokes of the same Wheel of Life. Treat them as equals. Develop wisdom to transcend both *(Impermanence)*.
My unpleasant feelings will not go away.	They will. Feelings (in fact all mental activities) are subject to impermanence. They change faster than physical constituents of the body *(Impermanence)*.
The key to inner peace is amassing wealth, being famous and powerful.	The key to inner peace is purification of the mind, that is, to move from ignorance to wisdom *(Link 1 of Dependent Origination)*.
I should develop affection for my dear ones and they in turn should show affection to me. The rest of the world is not really important.	Affection for a select few (dear ones) causes attachment, which in turn brings distress when parting occurs[117]. So develop unconditional love for *all*, including the 'dear ones.' It is a far superior love. *(Impermanence)*

---

[117] "From affection springs grief, from affection springs fear; for him who is wholly free from affection there is no grief, much less fear." – The Dhammapada 213

Table 1: Right and Wrong Views (continued)

A	B
Wrong View (Worldly)	**Right View** (Transcendental)
All I am going through is my fate. There is nothing I can do about it.	My past karma is a determinant of what I have been through and what I am going through now. However I have the power to change the direction of my existence from this point on, in the way I take **action now**, i.e., in the way I generate fresh karma *(Karma)*.
Bad things always happen to me although I don't understand why me, of all people. I have always been a good person. It is not fair.	Things happen dependent on nature's laws of conditionality only – a cause/effect linkage going back endlessly in time. Comparison with others is not a condition for what happens. Neither is 'good' and 'bad'.
Some things (and people) in this world are good, others bad.	Everything in the world just *is* – neither bad nor good. Good and bad are human labels (conventions). Cause and effect chains have brought things (and people) to what and where they are *(Impermanence and karma).*

[Consider the listings contained in Table 2 (following pages) as an extension of Column B (Right View) of Table 1 above]

Table 2: **KEY INSIGHTS AND HIGHLIGHTS OF PARTS B AND C**

PART B

Perception and Reality

1.   That which we perceive is **not** the reality out there.   The human sensory mechanism is equipped to discern less than one-millionth of the reality.   To be accurate we should refer to our senses as **truth-distorting senses.**

2.   The world perceived through our senses is a distortion of reality, i.e., it's an illusion.

3.   Nature provided us with sensory capability for procreation and survival.   To know reality we need to go beyond (transcend) our senses.   Instruments, as adjuncts to our senses, can help.   So can deep meditative contemplation (Insight Meditation).

4.   Measured against reality, judgements made by human beings (particularly about other human beings) are arbitrary and often erroneous.

5.   "Any sufficiently advanced technology is indistinguishable from magic" and the supernatural.

6.   Truth operates independent of human perception.   (Thus, it would be prudent for us not to take our perceptions too seriously).

Stress/Distress Mechanisms; Senses

7.   Unmanaged stress triggers, or contributes to, physiological and mental illness.

8.   Of all our senses, the most active, and the most destructive, is the sixth sense (mental trigger).

9.   We can change our destiny by using the *will* factor wisely.   To change behavior three conditions must be satisfied: (1) *will*ed thinking, (2) related action and (3) adequate repetition.

Neural Underpinnings

10. In every millisecond in the life of a person millions of firing patterns are produced in the brain. Thus the human brain/mind is very much an active entity during every moment of its existence. 2500 years ago the Buddha highlighted this fact.

11. The convergence of Dhamma and modern neuroscience can be aptly summarized in the statement: *Dhamma happens at the synapse.*

12. The incessant synaptic changes explain *why* our thoughts and emotions are subject to continuous change.

13. **The ability to create new neural pathways and synapses (or modify existing ones) in response to experience remains throughout life** thereby making possible personality/behavior modification throughout life. *Any credible technique for overcoming existential stress (mental distress) and maintaining lasting peace <u>must</u> use this ability.*

14. The way we respond to sensory stimuli was wired into our brains at a time when we had no say in our destiny. Depending on the stimulation received in the formative years, the wiring in an adult will be one of two formats: (a) that which responds to sensory stimuli resulting in peace or (b) that which responds to sensory stimuli resulting in stress.

15. In the case of an adult, when the wiring happens to be as in (b) above, (which it is for the vast majority of us), lasting relief can be obtained by re-wiring the problem pathways, and therefore changing to (a), using Insight Meditation. However, this requires diligence and time.

Self Notion

16. **The accurate way to state the principle of self/no-self is:**

   a) *There is a self*, **only as perceived by our truth-distorting sensory mechanisms, and**

   b) *There is no self* **in Absolute Reality (truth), that is, upon transcending the senses.**

17. A rudimentary sense of self is first formed by genetic transference (nature). It is then solidified by the environment (nurture).

18. The notion of *self* is the root cause of our distress. The same, stated differently: *ignorance* of the fact there is no self is the root cause of our distress.

19. When we rid ourselves of the notion of self, all our unwholesome traits such as aversion, desire, craving, attachment and clinging disappear along with it, as when a trunk of a tree falls, all the leaves fall.

Conditionality; x-conditions

20. Every event in this universe is the result of *multiple* conditions.

21. An ever-expanding formation (funnel-like collection) of conditions that extends endlessly back in time precedes any event. For brevity, we will refer to this phenomenon as the principle of *x-conditions*.

22. Every indirect condition, however far removed it is from the present event, is as essential for that event to arise/exist as an immediately preceding condition.

23. With our truth-distorting senses we usually recognize only the immediately preceding apparent condition (or conditions), and mistakenly attribute the existence of the present event only to it (them). This leads to many human fallacies, some of which, such as blame, precipitate dire consequences.

24. X-conditions give us a definitive basis for resolution of problems, particularly those associated with distress, via the following **Triple-A (Accept, Act, Accept) formula:**

I.   *Accept* **all that has happened up to now as the way it is, the reason being x-conditions.**

II.   *Act* **to improve things from now on, where feasible, with data ('lessons') from past happenings contributing to formulation of this action.**

III.   *Accept* **what cannot be done to improve things from now on, also, as the way it is, the reason being x-conditions, again.**

PART C

Blame

25. Human beings are prone to assigning blame, often with disastrous consequences.

26. Seen from truth, blaming is not in touch with reality and is a meaningless and groundless practice.

27. A meaningful alternative to blaming can be realized by application of the Triple-A formula.

Anger, Hatred and Jealousy

28. The important common thread that runs through the emotions of anger, hatred and jealousy is the strong belief (or wish) that a perceived object or event should not be the way it is. The stronger the wish, the stronger the emotion.

29. However, the reality is that objects and events are the way they are because of x-conditions.

30. Anger, hatred and jealousy can be overcome by applying the Triple-A method.

Depression and Anxiety

31. Depression is a very common emotional disorder. It strikes people in all walks of life.

32. For our purposes, depression may be subdivided into two types:

    (A) Depression that is caused by erroneous thinking.

    (B) Depression that is caused by factors other than erroneous thinking.

    Most cases of depression belong to type A.

33. Dhamma (Insight Meditation) provides a powerful and effective means to overcome anxiety and type A depression, with no side effects.

34. A qualified healthcare professional must be consulted before taking any action relating to depression management.

35. The primary cause of depression, as with other forms of mental distress, is belief in views that are not in touch with reality. The view of a *self*, which leads to personalization of happenings, is the dominant cause.

36. The self-blaming view "I did that, but I shouldn't have", is an expression of guilt, and may also contribute to depression. Self-blaming is a groundless and meaningless practice.

37. Physical activity provides appreciable temporary relief from depression and anxiety. So does Calming (breathing) Meditation.

38. The post-1980 era is a good time for people suffering from depression as medical science has provided (a) an understanding of the biology of depression and anxiety and (b) effective drug therapy. Drugs usually produce side effects.

39. Depression and anxiety/stress feed one another in a vicious cycle.

Sickness, Injury and Aging

40. When sickness and injury have reached a point beyond help from medical science, a person can still lead a meaningful and happy life.

41. Meaning and happiness are matters of the mind. The key is to separate mental distress from the rest, find the means to deal with the mental distress and accept the rest. The Triple-A Method provides a blueprint for achieving this.

42. Mental distress can be alleviated and overcome with proper diligence, the specific method being Insight Meditation.

43. Any mental distress we undergo on account of aging is due to personalization of the aging process and arbitrarily assigning labels of aversion to it, which are meaningless in reality. Therefore meditating on no-self is the lasting cure for mental distress associated with aging (or for any mental distress).

44. Infancy, childhood, youth, adulthood and old age reduce to one indivisible continuum in the eyes of nature and consequently their separate existences disappear, except in our minds.

Dying and Death

45. We can overcome our fear of death and therefore all mental distress relating to it by changing two inherent errors in our lives.

46. The first error is evasion of the subject of death. The correction, which is at a worldly level, is to accept death as a natural and necessary event.

47. The second error is the belief in a self, which results in cultivating attachment to many things during one's lifetime. The correction, which is at a transcendental level, is to integrate the notion of no-self into our lives, replacing the belief in a self. This is purely a mental exercise needing only one's time and diligence.

Karma and Rebirth

48. Rebirth provides the opportunity for unfinished (karmic) business of this life to be finished, so one can speedily progress on the Noble Eightfold Path towards the goal of Sublime Peace.

49. Rebirth also provides an explanation for the perceived injustices of nature. These apparent injustices are nothing but the execution of unfinished business from past lives.

Re-wiring for Inner Peace

50. Memory and thinking have a two-way interaction. Memory fuels (involuntary) thinking. Voluntary (willed) thinking upgrades memory.

51. A human being can intercept (control) the whole process of his/her biological interaction with the world only at two points:
    (a) The six senses
    (b) Willed thinking

52. Operative point for Calming Meditation (Samatha) is (a). The operative point for Insight (Vipassana) Meditation is (b).

53. Calming Meditation. By intensely focusing on one sensory contact and curtailing the other five, we achieve calmness of the mind.

54. Insight Meditation. By willfully thinking thoughts in touch with reality we change memory to reflect reality, thus providing fuel for inner peace. Changes to memory manifest as neural re-wiring.

Bibliography

Bodhi, Bhikkhu (Translator). *The Great Discourse on Causation. The Mahanidana Sutta and Its Commentaries.* Buddhist Publication Society (BPS)*, 1983.

Bodhi, Bhikkhu. *Noble Eightfold Path* (Wheel Publication No. 308/311), BPS, 1984.

Burlingame, E.W. (Translator). *Buddhist Stories: From the Dhammapada Commentary, Part IV* (The Wheel Publication No. 354/356). published by the BPS, 1988.

Davids, Mr. & Mrs. Rhys (Translators). *Dialogues of the Buddha* (Digha Nikaya), Pali Text Society (PTS)**, 1899, last reprinted 1995. Note: Sutta #16 *Mahaparinibbana Sutta* is contained in this work.

Gunaratna, Mahathera Henepola. *The Jhanas in Theravada Buddhist Meditation* (Wheel Publication No. 351/353). BPS, 1988.

Ireland, John D., Bhikkhu Nanananda and Walshe, M. O' C (Translators). *Samyutta Nikaya: An Anthology* (in 3 Wheel publications), BPS.

Mascaro, Juan (Translator). The Dhammapada: The Path of Perfection. Penguin Books, 1973.

Nanamoli, Bhikkhu (Translator). *The Path of Purification (Visuddhimagga).* BPS, 1991.

Nanamoli, Bhikkhu and Bodhi, Bhikkhu (Translators). *The Middle Length Discourses of the Buddha: A New Translation of the Majjhima Nikaya.* BPS, 1995.

Norman, K. R (Translator). *Therigatha (Elders' Verses) Volume II; Palms of the Sisters.* PTS, 1971

Nyanaponika Thera (Editor). *Kamma and Its Fruit: Selected Essays* (Wheel Publication No. 221/224). BPS, 1990.

Nyanaponika Thera (Translator). *Anguttara Nikaya: Discourses of the Buddha: An Anthology* (in 4 Wheel publications), BPS.

Nyanatiloka Mahathera. *Karma and Rebirth* (Wheel Publication No. 9). BPS.

Ottama, Ashin. *The Message in the Teachings of Kamma, Rebirth, Samsara: A Gateway to Deeper Understanding* (The Wheel Publication No. 425/427), BPS, 1998.

Sayadaw, Ven Mahasi. *Satipatthana Vipassana: Insight through Mindfulness.* BPS.

Sayadaw, Ven Mahasi. *Practical Insight Meditation: Basic and Progressive Stages.* BPS.

Soma Thera. *Kalama Sutta: The Buddha's Charter of Free Inquiry.* (Wheel Publication No. 8). BPS, 1981

Story, Francis. *The Case for Rebirth* (The Wheel Publication No. 12/13). BPS, 1973.

Story, Francis. *The Four Noble Truths* (The Wheel Publication No. 34/35). BPS, 1961

Story, Francis. *Rebirth as Doctrine and Experience – Essays and Case Studies.* BPS, 1975.

*Address: Buddhist Publication Society, PO Box 61, 54 Sri Sangharaja Mawatha, Kandy, Sri Lanka.

** Address: Pali Text Society, 73 Lime Walk, Headington, Oxford 0X3 7AD, United Kingdom.

INDEX

(Pali and Sanskrit terms are shown in italic)

W

X

Y

ABOUT THE BOOK

For information on how to order the book, excerpts from readers' comments and answers to readers' questions please visit the book's own web site:

www.TheWayToInnerPeace.com

(If you do not have access to the Internet and the book is not available at your local store, you can order the book using the 'ORDER FORM' appearing in the next page.)

Readers' Comments

The author and publisher welcome comments from readers. Please email to:

Info@TheWayToInnerPeace.com
or
SerenaPublications@sympatico.ca

ORDER FORM

If *The Way to Inner Peace* is not available at your local bookstore, copies of the book can be ordered directly from the publisher. Please complete this form and mail, along with the remittance (payable to Serena Publications), to:

> Serena Publications
> Box 5255
> Penetang, ON
> L9M 2G4
> Canada

Remittance Per Book

	Cdn Orders	U.S. Orders	Overseas
Book	Cdn $ 29.95	U.S. $ 19.95	U.S. $ 19.95
Postage and handling	7.00	8.00	10.00
Sub-total	36.95		
Add GST (7%)	2.59		
Total	**Cdn $ 39.54**	**U.S. $ 27.95**	**U.S. $ 29.95**
Mode of Payment	Cheque	Cheque	International Money Order

Please fill out in BLOCK CAPITALS

Your name: ....

Address: ....

....

....

....

Postal or ZIP code: ....

Phone Number: *(Area Code ....)* ....

Email address: ....

READERS' COMMENTS
(continuing from the front)

The following are excerpts from some of the communications received from readers of the first edition of *The Way to Inner Peace:*

NORTH AMERICAN PRISON NETWORK

[From a large donation of books given by the author to the non-profit organization, 'The Buddhist Library' in Fredericton, New Brunswick, Canada, The Way to Inner Peace has been sent to most prison libraries in the USA and Canada (at Federal, State and Provincial levels)

As indicated in the following excerpts from letters from the Secretary of The Buddhist Library and individual prisoners, The Way to Inner Peace made a significant difference in the lives of many prisoners. Excerpts from letters from The Buddhist Library appear first and then those from the prisoners. Names of prisoners are not printed for obvious reasons and only the names of the institutions are given]

Secretary, The Buddhist Library:

... Thank you again for your help. Having your book to send to these men and women is, as my mother would have termed it, a "god-send".

... the material has been the only thing that has made their incarceration bearable, or that it has kept them from going into a downward spiral. ... One prisoner said, "You people may not know it but you save lives." ... Your book means a lot to these men and women.

Estelle Prison, Huntsville, Texas, USA:

The *Way to Inner Peace* was just what I needed to start my spiritual journey. It has made an impact on my life in a way I can't explain.

... I am learning that laws do exist which are unseen, but are real. ... I have read your book 3 times and return often to it. ... I am finding peace every time I read it.

... You have helped change my whole life. ... I do really feel a healing and thank you.

... I use what I learned from the book everyday and share it with my close friends. I doubt very much if, I would have even made it, if it hadn't been for you. *(Excerpts from 4 letters).*

<u>Florence Prison Camp, Florence, Colorado, USA:</u>

I was fortunate enough to find a copy of your book, *The Way to Inner Peace*, in our library. I would like to thank you for writing of this book for it has had a profound effect on my way of thinking. My mind has never been in such a calm state and I know now that this difficult time too shall pass.

<u>Lake Correctional Institution, Clermont, Florida, USA:</u>

I am studying and enjoying your book, *The Way to Inner Peace*, to my great benefit.

... still remains helpful to me after many re-readings. I have shared it with many other inmates who have also enjoyed your practical approach to the everyday ...

<u>Nova (Correctional) Institution, Truro, Nova Scotia, Canada:</u>

I really enjoyed your book *The Way to Inner Peace*, it helped me to look at myself. I have been looking for answers for a long time and when I read your book, I felt very happy and I started taking some responsibility for my life.

... for 7 years I have been going in and out of prison. It is also a blessing in disguise because if I never came here, I wouldn't have come across your book.

<u>Altona Correctional Facility, 555 Devils Den Road, Altona, NY, USA:</u>

I am writing this letter to express my gratitude to you for writing a wonderful book, *The Way to Inner Peace*. ... As a beginner, I found it very easy to understand and it gave me an excellent introduction. ... the book has helped me and had a tremendous effect on me.

... ...